The

FIRST EIGHT

The
FIRST EIGHT

A PERSONAL HISTORY OF THE
PIONEERING BLACK CONGRESSMEN
WHO SHAPED A NATION

JAMES E. CLYBURN

Little, Brown and Company

New York Boston London

Little, Brown and Company
Hachette Book Group
1290 Avenue of the Americas, New York, NY 10104
littlebrown.com

First Edition: November 2025

Little, Brown and Company is a division of Hachette Book Group, Inc. The Little, Brown name and logo are trademarks of Hachette Book Group, Inc.

The publisher is not responsible for websites (or their content) that are not owned by the publisher.

Little, Brown and Company books may be purchased in bulk for business, educational, or promotional use. For information, please contact your local bookseller or the Hachette Book Group Special Markets Department at special.markets@hbgusa.com.

Book interior design by Jeff Stiefel

ISBN 9780316572743
Library of Congress Control Number: 2025943224

Printing 2, 2025

LSC-H

Printed in the United States of America

To my close-knit family and significant number of good friends; parents who nurtured, brothers and sister who encouraged, children and grandchildren, aunts, uncles, nieces, nephews, cousins, in-laws, all of whom have been and are great supporters; and a late wife and current significant other who have been pillars. And lastly, as I stated in the Introduction of my memoir, *Blessed Experiences*, "all my experiences have not been pleasant, but I have considered all of them to be blessings," and throughout my professional experiences I have been blessed with competent and dedicated staffs. To them I owe a great debt of gratitude.

Stony the road we trod, bitter the chast'ning rod
Felt in the days when hope unborn had died
Yet with a steady beat, have not our weary feet
Come to the place for which our people sighed?

—James Weldon Johnson, "Lift Every Voice and Sing"

CONTENTS

The

FIRST EIGHT

FOREWORD

MOST WHO KNOW CONGRESSMAN James E. Clyburn know him as a political leader who has spent decades effecting change in the halls of the U.S. Capitol. But long before his success as a politician, he was Jim Clyburn, a teacher who touched the lives of countless students from underprivileged backgrounds.

We, Ralph and Jaime, are lucky enough to be two such students. And although we are of different generations and met him thirty-one years apart, both of us graduated from Yale University and went on to careers that exceeded societal expectations, thanks, in large measure, to the role Jim Clyburn played in our lives.

After Jim graduated from South Carolina State College, where he had been a student activist and helped found the Student Non-Violent Coordinating Committee, he turned to the task of making a living in the Deep South. Jobs that allowed Black male college graduates to use their educational skills were scarce, so he ended up doing something that he was always drawn to: teaching. One of his early teaching assignments was at C. A. Brown, a new high school that had opened in the poorest part of Charleston in 1962 to relieve pressure to integrate the local public schools, which had remained segregated eight years after the Supreme Court's landmark decision in *Brown v. Board of Education*.

He could have easily gotten along with a lackluster performance from himself and those students; they were not people from whom society was expecting achievement. Instead, he dedicated himself to heightening their goals and strengthening their self-belief. He taught them the importance of seeing the possibilities beyond that confined neighborhood in Charleston.

In particular, he taught us, his students, the importance of knowing our history—Black history—years before it became the subject of organized study in American universities. He taught, indeed he preached, that through proper focus, vision, and hard work, they, the descendants of people who survived the brutal Middle Passage, could reach goals beyond their wildest dreams. He specifically included the history of the Black diaspora, ensuring that those students knew all they could of their past and those unsung who came before.

He was especially effective in his work with the nine students who formed a club called the Corsairs and asked him to be their advisor. While the students had originally focused on the social benefits, Jim Clyburn saw this motley, unsophisticated group as diamonds in the rough that he could help polish into successful young men. He immediately began to shift their attention from parties to position them to reach their potential, going so far as to host their weekly meetings in his home, where he and his beloved wife, Emily, instilled in those students an appreciation of the larger world and its possibilities. He used his vast knowledge, persuasive wit, and personal strength to transform these young men into people hungry for success.

From that group—which included one of us, Ralph—came the first three Black students from Charleston to attend Yale, Harvard, and The Citadel. The other members of the Corsairs were also high-achievers in whatever they elected to pursue, and Jim had a similar effect on many of the students that he encountered even after he left the classroom, and has remained a presence in many of their lives to this day—including in ours, where he has been involved from the start.

Take, for example, Jaime's decision at seventeen to invite Jim to swear him in as the president of his rural Orangeburg-Wilkinson High School's National Honor Society, something they still laugh about now. Jaime was just a curious teenager at the time, enthralled with politics and eager to meet South Carolina's first Black congressman in nearly a century. When Jim received the invitation, he was intrigued. He wanted to meet the kid audacious enough to ask his congressman to come to a high school induction ceremony — so he said yes. Jaime had no idea then that he'd build a lifelong bond with the man he now calls his political father, who taught him life lessons in and out of the classroom. Everything he knows about politics, about service, about fighting for what's right, he learned from Jim Clyburn.

Jaime has also had the privilege of a front-row seat to the work of a truly remarkable public servant. As a staffer in his congressional office, Jaime learned the untold history of South Carolina — the rich legacy and contributions of African Americans that were absent from our textbooks. Through their work together, Jim also taught him that in politics, there are workhorses and there are show horses — and that to truly deliver for the people, you must be a workhorse. And Jim has always delivered — not only for the people of South Carolina, but for the least of those across the nation.

One of the greatest honors of Jaime's life was working alongside Jim to secure the Congressional Gold Medal for the four South Carolina civil rights pioneers behind *Briggs v. Elliott,* the first education desegregation case, which became the foundation of *Brown v. Board of Education.* Later, as floor director in the majority whip's office, Jaime watched Jim's quiet strength and unwavering resolve move mountains. Under his leadership, the party passed landmark legislation — from the Affordable Care Act to the Matthew Shepard and James Byrd Jr. Hate Crimes Prevention Act. And in 2020, it was Jim Clyburn's pragmatic leadership — and his powerful, perfectly timed endorsement of Joe Biden — that helped save American democracy.

On a personal level, Jaime owes everything to the love, support, and unshakable belief of Jim Clyburn. He saw something in Jaime long before Jaime ever saw it in himself. And more than that, he was willing to put his name, his reputation, and his legacy on the line to stand in Jaime's corner. And because of Jim Clyburn's mentorship, a brash seventeen-year-old kid—raised by a teenage mom in rural Orangeburg, South Carolina—defied every odd and rose to chair the oldest political party in the world. That's the power of lifting up. That's the power of Jim Clyburn.

To us, Jim Clyburn is more than a teacher and a political leader. He is a moral compass in uncertain times. A mentor who shaped not only our lives, but our characters. A bridge between generations, movements, and ideals. He is, without question, a national treasure.

So it is only right that in *The First Eight*, Jim Clyburn continues his teaching mission. With a focus on the Black congressmen from South Carolina who served before him, he highlights the historical continuum of which all Black Americans are a part. Through their stories he covers the gamut of Black history and experience during Reconstruction; and, crucially, illuminates the parallels between the challenges then and those Blacks face today, a period that some refer to as a Third Reconstruction. As the ninth Black congressman from South Carolina and a lifelong teacher of history, Jim Clyburn is uniquely positioned to tell this story.

Although this book is dedicated to the First Eight, history will not overlook the ninth. In the decades to come, in lecture halls and libraries alike, students and scholars will turn their eyes to the quiet giant whose voice and acts contributed significantly to the quest to form a more perfect union.

Ralph C. Dawson, Esq.,
and Jaime R. Harrison

INTRODUCTION

I HAVE BEEN TALKING ABOUT the subjects in this book for most of my life. The first eight Black men elected to Congress from South Carolina hold a special significance to me, the ninth. When I became House majority whip in 2007, I requested that their portraits be hung on my conference room wall.

The Library of Congress provided eight elegant black-and-white images, which I still treasure. They are a constant reminder of the shoulders I stand upon. The First Eight's legacies of resistance and resolve, promise and purpose, faith and fortitude, continue to motivate me every day and in every way.

Soon after these portraits were hung, a group came to meet with me, and one of them asked who they were. When I told them, many of them expressed surprise. They had assumed that the first Black person to ever represent South Carolina in Congress was sitting at the table with them. I replied with my playful-with-a-purpose style, "Oh no. Before I was first, there were eight."

Although I have known about these men for most of my life, it doesn't surprise me that many people think I am the first; after all, prior to my election in 1992, it had been nearly one hundred years since the last of the eight, George Washington Murray, had served in Congress. But this conversation solidified my long-held aspiration to tell the stories of the Eight and how they represented the four million Blacks newly emancipated after the Civil War, and who pursued America's promise of equality for all while displaying little malice and much charity in the face of extreme opposition.

I have always maintained that a person can be no more or no less than their life experiences allow them to be. The eight men at the center of this book shared the common experience of being born before the Civil War, when this country was bitterly divided over slavery. Despite this, the differences in their younger, formative years uniquely informed each pioneering man's approach to public service.

Richard Harvey Cain and Robert Brown Elliott were Northerners who did not grow up in slave states. Rather, they arrived in South Carolina as adults, not having experienced the inhumaneness of the nation's original sin.

Meanwhile, Robert Carlos De Large, Alonzo Jacob Ransier, and Thomas Ezekiel Miller had the fortune of growing up in South Carolina with free Black parents. As "mulattos," as they were known—or, in Miller's case, as someone born to white parents and raised by free Black parents—they enjoyed the privileges that their paternity provided.

Finally, Joseph Hayne Rainey, Robert Smalls, and George Washington Murray shared the more common Black experience in antebellum South Carolina; they were born enslaved. However, each secured their freedom through unique means—Rainey through purchase, Smalls through escape, and Murray through emancipation.

Despite their diverse backgrounds and different experiences, each of the First Eight rose to the top of his profession and occupied a unique place in our nation's history during one of its most turbulent periods: the Reconstruction Era. This book tells the history of this era through the perspectives of the First Eight, unfolding chronologically as they contributed to America's reinvention of its political and social structures to reflect the Declaration of Independence's proclamation that "all men are created equal," while incurring the vengeance of former Confederates who wanted to "redeem" South Carolina to its pre-Civil War stance of white supremacy.

Naturally, I define Reconstruction through a South Carolina lens.

Reconstruction came early in parts of my home state with the arrival of the Union troops in late 1861, and ending with the departure of federal troops from its borders in 1877. In this period came African Americans' first opportunity to serve in political office, and over the ensuing decades, the First Eight emerged as leaders among South Carolina's Black majority. While most of them served in Congress during Reconstruction, three— Smalls, Miller, and Murray—were elected in the post-Reconstruction era, although Smalls had been elected earlier, during Reconstruction. Yet, as I will show in the pages that follow, the valiant efforts of the Eight, all Republican lawmakers, could not stop the violence and fraud deployed by the group that often referred to themselves as Conservative Democrats, or Southern Democrats. But I consider both these monikers to be insults to many of my conservative Democratic friends, whom I respect, and my proud Southern family members, whom I love. So throughout this publication I will refer to them, according to their mission of redeeming the antebellum social order of white supremacy, as "Redeemer Democrats."

This history may raise a few questions for today's readers. Why were the First Eight Republicans? And given the history of the Redeemers, why am I, the ninth, a Democrat?

In the nineteenth century, the Republican and Democratic parties espoused very different beliefs than they do today. Founded in 1854 in the lead-up to the Civil War, the Republicans—the anti-slavery party of Abraham Lincoln—were mostly composed of Northern abolitionists, while the Democrats found most of their support in the pro-slavery South. As a result, after the Civil War and well into the beginning of the twentieth century, most Blacks, including my parents, identified as Republicans, remaining loyal to the "party of Lincoln." However, the ideologies of the two parties began to change, a transformation that culminated in the presidency of the Democrat Franklin Delano Roosevelt. During this period, many Black Americans, drawn to Roosevelt's social platform, began to shift toward his party—although his New Deal policies excluded assistance for most Blacks. This shift accelerated under President Harry Truman, a Democrat who became the first president to address the NAACP's

National Convention and whose Fair Deal policies included integration of the armed services; and it continued under subsequent administrations, highlighted by Democratic President Lyndon Baines Johnson's Great Society programs that included Medicare, Medicaid, the 1964 Civil Rights Act, the 1965 Voting Rights Act, the 1968 Fair Housing Act, and other pieces of legislation addressing the effects of past racial discrimination, which the Republican party opposed. Today, the realignment is clear: Civil and political rights for Blacks, among the founding principles of the Republican Party and the fundamental values that I and most African Americans are loyal to, are now championed by Democrats, and consequently, most African Americans today identify with the Democratic Party.

A note about the structure of this book: When comparing any group of political figures, for various reasons, some emerge as more significant than others. By my estimation, Robert Smalls—the only bona fide Civil War hero of the Eight and one of only two Blacks to serve as a delegate to the 1868 and 1895 Constitutional Conventions, which granted, then revoked, Black political and civil rights in the state—lived the most consequential life, not just of the Eight, but of any South Carolinian in memory. Then there is Joseph Hayne Rainey, whose eloquence and status as the first Black man elected to the U.S. House of Representatives made him another man of great significance. Robert Brown Elliott, whose words resonated more deeply than even Rainey's, was a revered orator throughout the country. Smalls, Rainey, and Elliott all rose to national prominence, and their stature naturally results in their receiving more attention in this book, though the lived experiences of the other five also provide lessons to us all.

Finally, a note about language: Throughout this book, words like "Negro," "Colored" (a Black person), and "mulatto" (a person of mixed race) are sparingly used. The majority of the First Eight were "mulattos," a common identifier in the nineteenth and early twentieth centuries that tends to engender uneasiness today. But perhaps the vilest and most frequently used slur directed at the First Eight and their constituents was the N-word. Because of my visceral aversion to that word, I have made an editorial judgment not to spell it out fully in this book. I have also intentionally minimized the use of the term "slave," which dehumanizes the people who were held in bondage against their will. I refer to them as "the enslaved," which recognizes their humanity and speaks to the condition that was forced upon them. Lastly, I have also chosen to follow the new *Chicago Manual of Style* guidelines and capitalize "Black" and lowercase "white." This is a relatively new practice that has evolved, as "Black" is a term now associated more with a culture and race than simply describing skin color. During my fifty-eight years of marriage to a librarian, I became a stickler for grammar and happily adopted this new usage.

Like all of us, the First Eight were not perfect. But they rose to the challenges of their time, determined to demonstrate by example that race does not define one's humanity. They knew that until America lived by its founding principle of "liberty and justice for all," our country could not achieve its democratic ideals.

Like my predecessors, my life has been grounded in faith and fortitude. As I wrote in my memoir, *Blessed Experiences: Genuinely Southern, Proudly Black*, "All my experiences have not been pleasant, but I have considered all of them to be blessings." Indeed, my father, a fundamentalist minister, and my mother, a civic-minded beautician, ensured that I received a foundation grounded in biblical principles, and I have been emboldened by their insistence that I could be successful despite being born under the yoke of Jim Crow. Both of them were adherents to my father's oft-stated philosophy that one should lead by precept and example, and they practiced what Dad preached. Because of their teachings and practices, I became involved with the National Association for the Advancement of Colored People (NAACP) at the age of twelve. As a college student, I naturally resisted laws that stripped civil rights from those who looked like me, becoming a founding member of the Student Non-Violent Coordinating Committee (SNCC) and a student protest leader in the late 1950s and early 1960s. The incarcerations and arrests I accrued during this period only strengthened my dedication to the causes we pursued. Then, in my first professional job as a high school history teacher in Charleston, I found the resolve to tell our history accurately, not through the lens of those whose textbooks sought to diminish and exclude African American achievements.

Through it all, as I looked to the future, the hard-won successes of the movements I had served in—the passage of the 1964 Civil Rights Act, the 1965 Voting Rights Act, and the 1968 Fair Housing Act—provided the faith and promise that I could one day serve in public office. This assurance helped fulfill my political purpose: to do everything in my power to ensure that the greatness of America is accessible and affordable to all.

Just like my eight predecessors, I have encountered opposition and setbacks along my journey. Indeed, South Carolina's history has not always been positive. Some of it has been very unpleasant for me and many others, especially those who look like me. But our history is what it is, and I believe that complete history should be told. And as I tell the history of the First Eight, who have paved the way for me and countless others to come, I have never lost sight of our State's motto: "While I breathe, I hope."

PART I

RECONSTRUCTION

CHAPTER 1

FREEDOM

—— **1861–1865** ——

*"How can I expect to keep my freedom unless I
fight for it?"*

—Robert Smalls

"WHILE I BREATHE, I hope," the most well-known of South Carolina's two mottos, must have resonated deeply in the hearts and minds of enslaved Blacks as the first bombs exploded over Charleston Harbor. It was here, at four thirty a.m. on April 12, 1861, that the Civil War began. Until then, the enslaved, who made up most of Charleston's population, had found little reason for hope. They were held in bondage, forced to labor long hours with no pay, provided inadequate food and shelter, and under threat of physical abuse or even death at the slightest provocation. The blasts that lit up the night sky represented the first real chance for them to realize their collective dream to breathe free.

Among them was Robert Smalls, an intelligent young man who would not be willing to simply wait. If not for this intelligence, none of us may have ever known his name. And, I believe, without his resourcefulness and skillful leadership, the Civil War may have ended very differently.

Smalls had a front-row seat to this unfolding history and a big stake in its outcome, yet as the attack on Fort Sumter commenced, he could

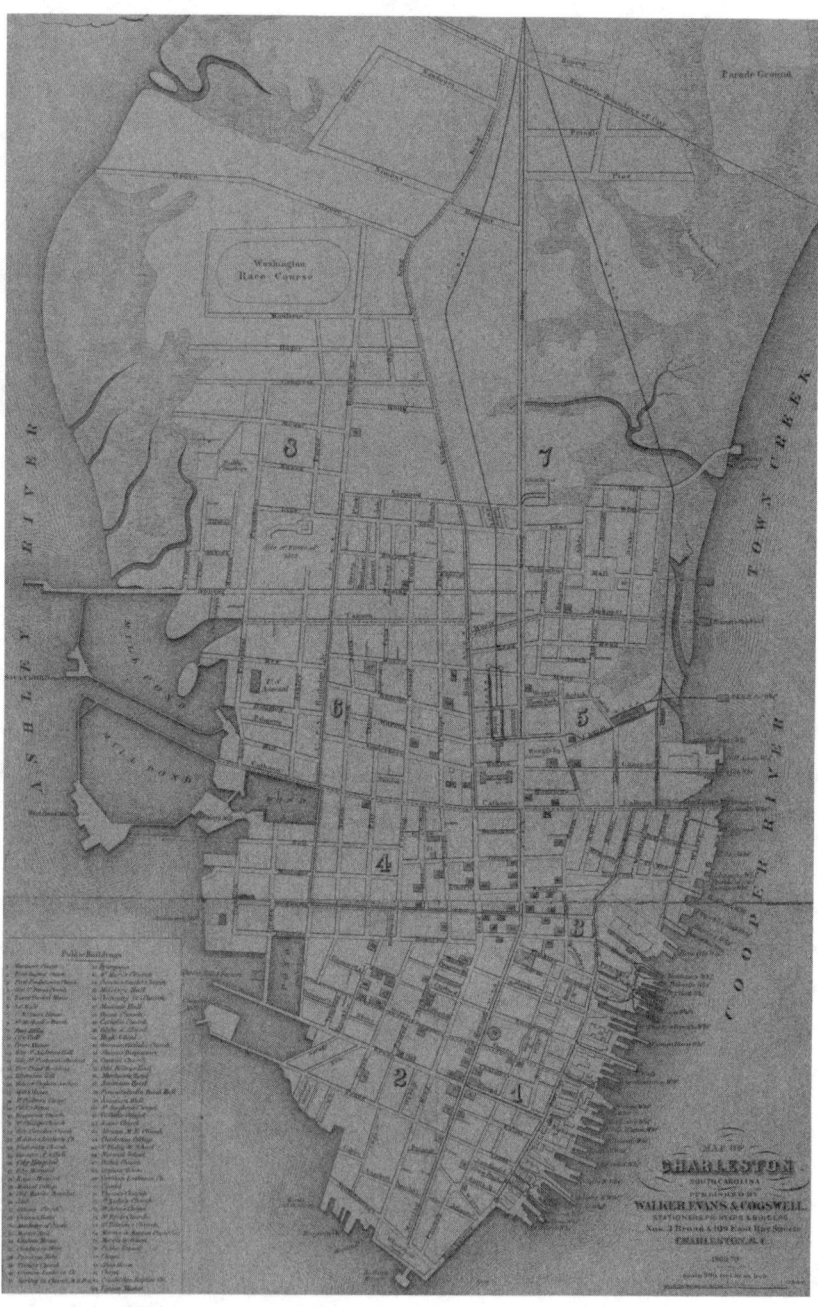

Map of the Charleston peninsula, circa 1869.

not have dreamed of becoming a widely acclaimed war hero and, in my not-so-humble opinion, the most consequential South Carolinian who ever lived. In that moment, though, he and his wife, Hannah, a hotel housekeeper twelve years his senior, likely sat up bleary-eyed with their newborn son, only barely envisioning what their futures might hold.

While Smalls and Hannah listened to the explosions of cannon fire suggesting the dawning of a new day, they may have openly discussed their dreams for freedom. This couple, an exception in the enslaved community, lived together, independent of their owners, in two rooms above a horse stable on East Bay Street.

Although the exact location of their modest home is unknown, I imagine the Smalls family lived near the Charleston City Market, where today's tourists meet at the liveries to catch a historic horse and carriage ride. The market these tourists would visit still looks much as it did back in 1861. The open-air shed buildings that once housed vendors selling vegetables, meat, and fish now contain merchants hawking trinkets, artworks, and food unique to Charleston. In Smalls's day, the stalls began at Market Hall on Meeting Street and ran all the way to the waterfront, where ships brought in much of the inventory harvested, butchered, or caught by enslaved laborers.[1]

Smalls worked on the nearby waterfront. In a show of his ingenuity, he contributed to an entrepreneurial economy among the enslaved by purchasing produce they independently grew on the islands he visited while working on the transport ship the *Planter*; he then sold the produce to sailors as they arrived in port. His earnings from this endeavor allowed him to make money that he kept for himself.

Smalls's experience on the night of April 12, 1861, stood in stark contrast to those of the newly minted South Carolina Confederates holding viewing parties on the stately rooftops along the Battery, celebrating the start of a war they had essentially orchestrated.

Harper's Weekly illustration of Charlestonians watching the first shots of the Civil War fired on Fort Sumter, 1861. (Courtesy of The Charleston Museum, Charleston, South Carolina)

South Carolina had led the Southern secession from the Union just before Christmas 1860. In the lead-up to Abraham Lincoln's election, hysteria had grown among the planter class in the state. One Edisto Island plantation owner published a pamphlet issuing a dramatic warning that a Lincoln victory would lead to "emancipation...then poverty, political equality with their former slaves, insurrection, war of extermination between the two races, and death."[2]

With their worst fears realized after Lincoln's victory, the landed gentry, who controlled the levers of power, voted unanimously to leave the United States to form the Confederate States of America. On Christmas

Day, a Columbia newspaper declared, "Additional zest is given to the enjoyment of this day, in fact, that within a week, South Carolina has declared her independence."[3]

The secessionists sought freedom from the North's increasing abolitionist tendencies and defiance of the Declaration of Independence's proclamation that "all men are created equal." The Confederacy's vice president, Alexander Stephens of Georgia, declared, "Our foundations are laid, its cornerstone rests upon the great truth that the negro is not equal to the white man; that slavery subordination to the superior race is his natural and normal condition. This, our new government, is the first, in the history of the world, based upon this great physical, philosophical, and moral truth."[4]

A UNIQUE CHILDHOOD

Robert Smalls defied Alexander Stephens's characterization of African Americans and the institution of slavery. He would soon prove that he was not only the equal of white men, but a talented leader of all men, who — though he'd yet to have a formal education, and likely had not read the Bible — lived up to Matthew 25:14–30 and always used the many talents he possessed, none of which would go buried.

Smalls was born on April 5, 1839, in Beaufort, a coastal town seventy miles south of Charleston that shares much with its more visited neighbor: moss-draped live oak trees, historic buildings with distinct southern character, and a legacy of slavery. Beaufort also shares Charleston's proximity to water. The home where Smalls spent his childhood still stands a few blocks from the Beaufort River, which feeds into Port Royal Sound.

Smalls lived in a tiny two-room shack with his mother, Lydia, just behind their owner Henry McKee's white wood framed home at 511 Prince Street. Despite his enslavement, Smalls enjoyed many of the benefits of family life during his childhood. His mother's presence throughout his youth ensured their strong bond, and he shared a familial closeness with the McKee children.[5] Smalls likely had a white father, whose identity Lydia never disclosed; some have speculated that it may have been Henry McKee himself.

The McKee home on Prince Street in Beaufort, where Smalls spent his early years enslaved. He would later purchase the home and live there until his death in 1933. (Library of Congress, Prints & Photographs Division, HABS SC,7-BEAUF,32–1)

Smalls's mother spent her early years on the Ashdale Plantation, the estate the McKees owned on Lady's Island. Though Lydia was eventually sent to work at their mainland home, at Ashdale she saw the harsh existence and the danger that most enslaved men endured. She worried that her son's life as a house servant who was favored by his owner had given him a false sense of security; she believed he needed to be protected or one day he might be severely injured, maimed, or even killed for his rebelliousness. After a twelve-year-old Smalls began to get into trouble for defying laws that required Blacks to be off Beaufort's streets by sundown, she asked McKee to send him to Charleston.

Smalls thrived in Charleston, a city that built its economy on its port

and slavery. Founded in 1670 as Charles Town, the peninsula and its surrounding sea islands became the destination for wealthy plantation owners from the English colony of Barbados who had run out of usable land.
With its similar climate and vast acreage, South Carolina became the only
original American colony that followed the Barbadian model, with an
economy built on commercial agriculture cultivated by enslaved laborers.[6]
The British colonists, with little experience growing rice and living in sub-
tropical conditions, could not have survived without the knowledge and
labor of the Africans, whom they exploited.

And exploit they did. In 1774, Gadsden's Wharf, a popular entry point
for the burgeoning slave trade, opened on Charleston's waterfront. By 1775,
South Carolina's reliance on slavery had made it the wealthiest of the original thirteen colonies, and established Charleston, as one historical account
dubs it, as "a hub of human trafficking."[7] In fact, at least forty percent of all
enslaved Africans entered America through Charleston Harbor before Congress legally ended the transatlantic importation of slaves in 1808.[8] As a result,
South Carolina became the only founding American state to have a majority
Black population. During Smalls's time in Charleston, before the Civil War
broke out in 1861, Blacks made up fifty-nine percent of the state's residents.[9]

Smalls enjoyed the cosmopolitan feel of Charleston, and the streets were
filled with throngs of people who looked like him carrying out their required
tasks. Despite being just twelve years old when he arrived, he quickly found
work as a waiter, earning five dollars a month. As he grew older, stronger,
and more knowledgeable about the city, Smalls became a lamplighter and
then a stevedore at the port, loading and unloading cargo. His amiable
personality and willingness to work hard ultimately caught the eye of the
Planter's owner, who taught him how to pilot the 147-foot steamship. Within
a decade of his arrival, and while still enslaved, Smalls had used his resourcefulness to climb to a significant position, earning sixteen dollars a month.[10]

While this was no small accomplishment, Smalls's pay ultimately
belonged to McKee. As a reward for his hard work and increased wages, his
owner allowed him to keep one dollar per month. Smalls, who prioritized
his family over all else, saved the money with a plan to one day purchase

his wife's and children's freedom. He had skillfully negotiated this unusual agreement—an enslaved man "owning" his family—with Hannah's owner, who by the laws of the day also owned their offspring. When agreeing with the arrangement, Smalls paid a good faith one-hundred-dollar deposit, but it would take significant resourcefulness to save enough to pay the seemingly insurmountable price of eight hundred dollars.[11]

Still, Smalls found solace in focusing on his goal of freeing his family. By 1862, Smalls had become, as a biographer would later describe him, "a strong minded, strong-bodied young man...[and] after ten years on the Charleston docks, he had...established a strong commitment and leadership pattern among his peers."[12] One of those peers would inadvertently plant the seed that would become Smalls's fully formed plan to orchestrate his and his family's escape from slavery.

THE GREAT ESCAPE

Smalls found himself in the unique situation of having the opportunity and the skills to escape, but embarking on such a perilous journey could amount to a suicide mission. Yet his desire for freedom remained so strong, he developed the will to take that chance.

By June 1861, the Confederates had pressed the *Planter* and its crew into service because it could easily maneuver shallow intercoastal waterways, delivering supplies to bases along the coast. The Confederates employed three white men to oversee the *Planter* and its enslaved crew. These overseers regularly went into Charleston, leaving the crew unsupervised. Enjoying one of these moments free from scrutiny, the five-foot-five, stocky Smalls playfully picked up the captain's distinctive floppy hat and pranced around the ship, imitating his mannerisms. Laughing at the performance, one of his crewmates remarked that Smalls bore a strong resemblance to the white captain.

Inspired, Smalls hatched a plan to make their escape the next time their supervisors took an unauthorized excursion into Charleston. He prepared

Hannah for the dangers ahead, telling her that if his plan failed, the punishment would be death. Hannah replied without hesitation, "I will go, for where you die, I will die."[13]

The opportunity came on May 12, 1862. The captain and his colleagues departed the ship for their night out. Smalls knew they would not return until the next morning, and he had no intention of being there to greet them. He and the other enslaved crew members sent for their families and waited until three a.m. to set the plan in motion. As the ship's pilot, Smalls took charge and ordered the crew to light the fires that fueled the steamship. Half an hour later, in the pre-dawn darkness, the *Planter* eased its way out into Charleston Harbor on its perilous voyage.

Smalls stood authoritatively behind the ship's wheel, wearing the captain's uniform and his signature floppy hat, focused on the mission ahead. Before the sun rose, the *Planter* had to travel past five Confederate checkpoints to protect their identities under the cover of darkness.

With the *Planter*'s cargo of guns and ammunition loaded for delivery to Fort Ripley, Smalls maneuvered the ship past the first four guard stations with relative ease. But as the ship headed toward Fort Sumter, the Confederates' first line of defense in Charleston Harbor, Smalls steeled himself for closer scrutiny: At the point of passage, he had to steer uncomfortably close to the Confederate watchtower to avoid suspicion.

The *Planter* approached Fort Sumter at 4:15 a.m. After the thirty-six-hour bombardment that had launched the war just thirteen months earlier, Fort Sumter's five-feet-thick and five-feet-high masonry walls stood menacingly, protecting the prized "cradle of the Confederacy." Cool under pressure, Smalls steered the boat as though nothing was unusual, remaining in the pilothouse with his arms crossed as he had watched the captain do many times before. He then gave the correct signal on the horn, one he'd long since memorized: three shrill blasts and one hissing sound. After an agonizingly long pause, the sentry at the fort signaled back for the ship to continue onward, shouting to the "captain," "Blow the damned Yankees to hell!" Smalls responded, "Aye, aye!" and sailed on toward the open waters of the Atlantic Ocean—and straight toward the Union blockade.[14]

Before the Confederates could register the ship's trajectory, the *Planter* picked up speed and was soon out of firing range. Hannah had brought along a white bedsheet, and the crew quickly replaced the Confederate flag that flew above the mast with the white flag of surrender. Smalls later acknowledged this moment worried him the most. He knew Confederate protocol, but he couldn't anticipate how the Union would react to an enemy ship bearing down on their blockade. Smalls and his crew felt great relief when the Union Navy followed the rules of war and withheld fire as the *Planter* drew near.

As Smalls pulled alongside the first Union vessel, the blockade commander boarded the stolen steamship finding, to his great surprise, that enslaved men composed the entire crew. Smalls reportedly told the commander, displaying his wry sense of humor, and, I imagine, a great deal of pride, "I thought this ship might be of some use to Uncle Abe."[15]

Harper's Weekly heralded his successful escape and the delivery of a valuable steamship to the Union as "one of the most daring and heroic adventures since the war commenced."[16]

Harper's Weekly celebrated Robert Smalls's daring escape by featuring illustrations of him and the *Planter* in its June 14, 1862, edition. (Library of Congress, Prints and Photographs Division, LC-USZ62-117998)

To Smalls, his crew, and their families, the events of early May 13, 1862, amounted to much more than an adventure. Smalls led them on a mission that all knew could end in death, and through his cleverness and determination they emerged unscathed and feted. This improbable feat could not have been accomplished by an inferior and unintelligent Black man, as the Confederates considered this hero to be. Rather, Smalls's Great Escape demonstrated that he embodied South Carolina's second motto, *Animis opibusque parati*: "Prepared in mind and resources." As I look back, I agree with the historian who declared Smalls "the most dramatic indication of the capacity of Blacks to fight...for their freedom."[17] My only suggestion would be to add mention, too, of the Union's salvation.

BIRTHPLACE OF RECONSTRUCTION

Smalls surely did not anticipate that freedom would lead to a return to his hometown. And yet Beaufort, South Carolina, was one of the first places to be emancipated by the Union army, and it was there that he found promises of what life could be for the formerly enslaved if the Union won the Civil War.

The Union navy had captured Hilton Head in November 1861 and took over St. Helena and Port Royal Sounds and the surrounding land. There they established the Union's southern headquarters.[18] And it was here that, safely beyond the Confederates' reach, the *Planter* and its "contrabands" — as Union forces described the enslaved people they considered spoils of war — joined the ten thousand Blacks now living free.[19]

Smalls found the islands near his childhood home very different from the way they were when he left. As federal troops moved in, white residents abandoned their stately homes and the nearly two hundred plantations in the area, leaving behind their enslaved laborers. Other "contrabands" had escaped from nearby communities, making their way to safety across Union lines. This mass of humanity presented a significant problem for the Union military, which was not prepared to fight a war and at the same time help transition so many newly freed people to self-sufficiency.

To address this dilemma, the federal government established the Port Royal Experiment, a cooperative endeavor with private philanthropists that one South Carolina historian described as an effort to "prove to a doubting white Northern public that persons of African descent would work for a living and that they would fight for their freedom."[20] As part of this effort, they established Mitchelville, one of the first self-sufficient Black communities near Hilton Head, which at its height reached three thousand residents and had a governing body made up of freedmen.[21]

Today, most people know Hilton Head as a beach resort. But the island first began as the home of indigenous tribes; and after colonizers introduced the plantation system, before liberation, enslaved people made up most of the population. They developed their own culture, known in South Carolina and North Carolina as Gullah. Gullah—also called Geechee in Georgia and Florida—included a distinctive creole language that fused enslaved Africans' diverse dialects with English, enabling them to communicate without their white overseers understanding what they were saying. The planters viewed the Gullah/Geechee language as a sign of ignorance, when in reality it demonstrated the remarkable resourcefulness of the enslaved people. Hilton Head Island remained a thriving Black enclave until 1956, when a bridge was built to connect the isolated island to Beaufort's mainland. This easy access resulted in developers driving many African American families off the land they had owned since the Civil War: a story that has been replicated all along the South Carolina coastline, leading to the loss of wealth and landownership Blacks in Gullah communities accumulated over generations.

But in 1862, Smalls, who had been raised in the Gullah culture, found himself and his family joining a ballooning population of newly freed people participating in the Port Royal Experiment. This transformational program paid laborers for their work and ensured their welfare with food and housing, while planning for a future where Blacks would be self-sufficient by teaching those that had been denied an education to read and write. Reflecting on this denial, I am struck by its intent. Governments don't deny an education to people unless they fear the empowerment that comes with knowledge. Planters denigrated Blacks as inferior "barbarians," yet they employed countless devices to prevent the enslaved from disproving that falsehood. Smalls's courageous escape, outthinking and outmaneuvering a phalanx of white "superiors" and soldiers, proved this point.

ENSLAVEMENT TO EMISSARY

Smalls's trajectory, from enslavement to an emissary for his race, happened quickly. His effectiveness in this role led to a decision that would change the course of the war and ensure freedom for the millions of enslaved Blacks.

Union officers appreciated Smalls's extraordinary abilities and the power of his heroism. Just three months after Smalls gained his freedom by delivering the *Planter* to the Union forces, Brigadier General Rufus Saxton, the military governor of the Department of the South, sent the now twenty-four-year-old to Washington. His mission: meet with President Abraham Lincoln and the secretary of war, Edwin Stanton, and convince them to support the enlistment of Black troops into the Union cause. A difficult mission, even for a war hero.

I can only imagine how overwhelming it was for Smalls when he arrived in the nation's capital for the first time in August 1862. The city perched on the Potomac River had similarities with his home, namely the presence of military regiments mingling with a multitude of free Blacks. Lincoln had signed a proclamation ending slavery in Washington, D.C. in April 1862, eight months before the better-known Emancipation Proclamation took effect in Beaufort and other Confederate states. Boardinghouses had sprung up across the city to accommodate the crushing influx of people seeking to secure their freedom.

Washington looked very different during Smalls's inaugural trip than the imposing and inspiring seat of power that it is today. The Washington Monument stood partially constructed, looking more like the Leaning Tower of Pisa than the modern-day towering obelisk. The U.S. Capitol dome was still under construction, which had continued despite the war; and the White House, minus the familiar West Wing, had just undergone very extensive and expensive renovations thanks to the First Lady. It couldn't have escaped Smalls's attention that the iconic structures symbolizing America's promise of freedom had been built by enslaved laborers who toiled from sunup to sunset six days a week, earning compensation for their owners.

For someone whose life experiences resembled those of the laborers much more than those of the powerful men he had come to meet, this mission to Washington had to be intimidating. But if it was, Smalls didn't show it.

Smalls, accompanied on this trip by Rev. Mansfield French, attended multiple meetings with cabinet members. At each one, Smalls enthralled them, recounting his courageous escape with the confidence of a seasoned storyteller. President Lincoln also met the war hero, for whom he had signed legislation earlier that year granting him a portion of the *Planter*'s value as a reward for its delivery to the Union. No full account exists of what one historian called "perhaps the most consequential meeting Lincoln had with an African American in the first two years of his administration,"[22] but I envision the two raconteurs in Lincoln's second-floor office of the White House, swapping stories and speaking earnestly about the imperative to win the war. We do know that Lincoln asked Smalls why he dared to escape on the *Planter*. The young man simply replied, "Freedom."[23]

But Smalls also had his mission in mind. He carried with him a letter from General Saxton, which read: "I very respectfully but urgently request of you authority to enroll as laborers in the employ of the Quartermaster's Department a force not exceeding 5,000 able-bodied men from among the contrabands in this department...to be furnished with soldiers' rations, for each class. The men to be uniformed, armed, and officered by men detailed from the Army."[24] Smalls offered to recruit troops personally, believing the formerly enslaved would be "better soldiers than the present ones because they will be fighting for their freedom."[25]

The Militia Act of 1792, which in part prohibited African Americans from bearing arms on behalf of the U.S. military, would have been a barrier to this goal. This clause had been included to mitigate white citizens' fears that if armed, Blacks would turn the weapons on their oppressors. However, just a month before Smalls's visit, Lincoln had signed an amended Militia Act that allowed the president to utilize free Blacks in the military for any purpose "he may judge best for the public welfare."[26] Still, the Lincoln administration had, up to that point, resisted enlisting African Americans. A few weeks before Smalls's arrival, Secretary Stanton had even told an Indiana delegation that to enlist Blacks in the Union military "would turn fifty thousand bayonets from loyal Border States against us that were for us."[27] President Lincoln had also raised concerns that Blacks might not make good soldiers since they were untrained and untested on the battlefield.

But Smalls's heroic story and his personal plea to recruit freedmen to the Union cause must have been powerful. Somehow, despite the previous positions taken by the Lincoln administration, Smalls returned to Port Royal with a letter from Secretary of War Stanton authorizing five thousand Black recruits.

Emboldened by his diplomatic success, Smalls offered to join the new Black regiment, the First South Carolina Volunteer Infantry. General Saxton asked, "Why would you enlist?"

Smalls replied, "How can I expect to keep my freedom unless I fight for it?"[28]

Still, the Union navy considered his services as the *Planter's* pilot too valuable to let him fight with the army, so instead, Smalls settled on convincing others to serve. Reportedly, he ended up recruiting five thousand Black soldiers to the Union cause.[29]

But his triumphant mission had greater consequences. According to the National Archives, after Smalls secured permission for their enlistment, 170,000 Black soldiers joined the Union army and an additional 19,000 joined the Union navy, a formidable injection of power. Although they served only a little more than half of the four-year Civil

War, 40,000 Black Union troops lost their lives. They served bravely and defied all expectations.

In 1865, President Lincoln acknowledged their extraordinary contributions, saying, "Without the military help of the Black freedmen, the war against the South could not have been won."[30] Indeed, in my not-so-humble opinion, no Civil War victory or hero can measure up to the consequences that flowed from Smalls's heroic feat with the *Planter* and audience with Abraham Lincoln.

EMANCIPATION DAY

Although General Saxton would not honor Smalls's wish to enlist in the South Carolina First Infantry Regiment, one thousand freedmen joined the first unit of formerly enslaved men. Their service officially began on January 1, 1863, the day the Emancipation Proclamation went into effect. On that auspicious day, the Black troops gathered with many local men, women, and children in a stand of majestic oak trees on a former plantation, known then as Camp Saxton. They came out to hear General Saxton, the camp's namesake, read aloud the document declaring, "All persons held as slaves [within the rebellious states] are, and henceforward shall be free."[31]

Moved by the gravity of the moment, the audience broke into impromptu song. "My country, 'tis of thee, sweet land of liberty" rose from deep within the souls of the freed people, as if they were recognizing for the first time that America was *their* country. The lyrics swelled from this coastal setting, filled with hopes of a people long held in bondage but now free.[32]

Celebrations like this didn't happen all over the South. While emancipation officially came to Black residents of the occupied portions of Beaufort County on that day, most enslaved South Carolinians and those in other slave states didn't learn of their freedom until Union troops moved through their communities. Consequently, today, many states and communities celebrate emancipation on dates other than January 1. Notably, the enslaved in Galveston, Texas, one of the farthest points west in the Confederate states, did not become aware of their freedom until June 19, 1865, two and a half years after the proclamation went into effect. African Americans have celebrated Juneteenth, that day of Jubilee, ever since.

I often refer to this as an example of the atrocities that sometimes flow from the failure to communicate. The Blacks in Galveston, Texas, remained enslaved because nobody communicated to them that they were free. But, as historian Annette Gordon-Reed rightly said, as a holiday, Juneteenth isn't about "commemorating a delayed proclamation, but about celebrating a people's enduring spirit."[33] And while I agree with the sentiment, I take a more unvarnished approach that establishing the Juneteenth holiday was a necessary step toward acknowledging our nation's very spotty history on race. And on June 17, 2021, I took great pride in being among those in Congress to codify Juneteenth as a federal holiday.

When I explain to my white friends the importance of this day in the Black community, I reference how the National Museum of African American History and Culture calls Juneteenth "our country's second Independence Day." This distinction underscores that July 4th marks only white America's independence from British rule in 1776. The enslaved people of this country had to wait nearly a century longer for their independence.[34]

MILITARY SERVICE

Robert Smalls didn't attend the reading of the Emancipation Proclamation on January 1, 1863. Instead, he remained at the helm of his beloved *Planter*, and was very active in the navy during the war, fighting in at least seventeen skirmishes.[35]

One particularly harrowing battle occurred on December 1, 1863, when the *Planter* set off on a mission to take rations from Folly Island to a Union encampment on Morris Island. Confederate troops recognized the stolen steamship and, eager to reclaim it and secure the $4,000 reward offered by the Confederacy for Smalls's capture, they unleashed a barrage of heavy fire on the *Planter* near Secessionville.

The fierceness of the firefight frightened the *Planter*'s white captain. He ordered Smalls to beach the ship and surrender, a move that would have meant certain death for the fugitive slave. Summoning his celebrated bravery and rebellious streak, Smalls responded, "Not by a damn sight will I beach this boat." Fearing the worst, the captain abandoned his post and hid in the coal bunker. Smalls latched the door behind him and took control of the ship, steering the craft to the safety of Morris Island.

Upon hearing what happened, Union commanders immediately dismissed the captain and promoted Smalls to the role. With this elevation, Smalls earned a monthly salary of $150, a far cry from the $16 he earned a few years earlier.[36] It also marked the first time he could be called Captain Smalls, a title that had never been granted a Black man—enslaved or free.

TRIUMPHANT RETURN TO CHARLESTON

As Smalls's status continued to rise across the country, the tide of the war turned in the Union's favor, and President Lincoln easily won his reelection in November 1864. Smalls lived among the free Blacks who thrived in the Union-controlled areas of Beaufort County; all the while the war continued to rage in Charleston, the city he'd left behind.

In a twist of fate, Smalls, in the meantime, purchased the former McKee home on Prince Street at an auction for properties forfeited due to unpaid taxes. During the war, Smalls's mother had continued to live in the house as a free woman employed to look after the Union troops garrisoned there. After Smalls acquired the property, Lydia lived there with her son and his family for the rest of her life. And, in an act of kindness and generosity, the Smalls-McKee family connection came full circle.

Smalls invited Henry McKee's widow, Jane, to live in her former house after her husband's death in 1875, and he cared for her until she passed away in 1904. Smalls and his descendants owned the home for ninety years. Today, thanks to Congress's favorable response to legislation I introduced, the house is now under the auspices of the National Trust of Historic Preservation. The National Park Service also conducts limited tours of the home so that visitors may experience its rich history and learn more about the remarkable life of Robert Smalls firsthand.

While the fate of Beaufort and its occupants rose with the Union's fortunes, the Confederate crown jewel of Charleston lost its luster. The city was under constant bombardment by the Union. One prisoner of war referred to it as "the burnt district." The formerly enslaved were the only Charlestonians who remained. They took great joy in occupying the abandoned mansions that they could once enter only through the back door.[37]

After a 545-day siege — longer than any other in American history — February 18, 1865, became Charleston's Emancipation Day. (Today, the city celebrates on January 1.) Victorious Union soldiers led by the Twenty-First U.S. Colored Troops marched into the conquered "cradle of the Confederacy."[38] Troops extinguished the more than two dozen fires that still burned from the Confederate soldiers igniting cotton and ammunition stores as they fled the city. The smoke-filled air cleared and, despite the rubble-filled streets lined with blackened shells of buildings, the city transformed into a scene of new possibilities rising from the ashes. The transcendent spirit that emerged celebrated the most significant casualty of the war — slavery.

In the days that followed, Black Charlestonians joined the arriving Fifty-Fourth, an all-Black regiment made famous in the movie *Glory* that chronicled its courageous but ill-fated assault on Fort Wagner, and Fifty-Fifth U.S. Colored Infantry, which included some familiar faces of those who once walked these same streets as slaves. Choruses of "John Brown's Body" rang out and shouts of jubilation built as the crowd grew in the streets.

Harper's Weekly illustration of the Fifty-Fifth Colored Infantry marching into Charleston after the Union's victory, 1865. (Courtesy of The Charleston Museum, Charleston, South Carolina)

The city once under the tight grip of the white power structure now erupted with boisterous Blacks filling the streets under the protective watch of their nearly all-Black liberators, who now controlled the city. Colonel Charles Fox of the Massachusetts Fifty-Fifth relayed the feeling of the scene unfolding around him. Fox proclaimed, "The glory and triumph of this hour may be imagined, but it can never be described. It was one of those occasions which happens but once in a lifetime, to be lived over in memory forever."[39]

Two months later, Smalls made his triumphant return to Charleston. On April 14, 1865, he piloted the *Planter* back into the wharf for the first time since it had left under the cover of darkness. This time, returning with three thousand freedmen and -women on board, and everyone in the city knew his name. Smalls's biographer Andrew Billingsley described him at that time as "courageous and proud, an American hero who wore his heroism well. He was dignified, soft-spoken, and had a ready smile.

He was worshiped by Blacks and highly respected by whites all over the nation."[40]

To me, Smalls's accomplishments are unparalleled in our nation's history. In just two years' time, he escaped enslavement, became an honored war hero and the first Black captain of a naval vessel, and had a consequential meeting with the president of the United States that changed the course of the war and our nation's history. And so, nearly 150 later, it was only fitting to give Smalls some of the recognition by Congress I believe he deserves.

When I was House majority whip, my suite of offices in the U.S. Capitol included the Lincoln Room, where U.S. Capitol historians said Lincoln would sit, in an alcove by the fireplace, telling stories and writing letters home. Today, a large portrait of President Lincoln hangs on a wall for all to see.

When I became the steward of the Lincoln Room, I believed it only fitting to also hang a portrait of Robert Smalls in the space as a tribute to the role he played in persuading Lincoln to allow African Americans to join the Union forces. Alongside Smalls's biographer Dr. Andrew Billingsley, I unveiled the portrait in a ceremony on February 27, 2019 — a tribute to the South Carolinian who met with President Lincoln more than a century ago and changed the course of the Civil War.

April 14, 1865, held all the promise of new beginnings. But while Charleston erupted with joy, that same night, devastation gripped Washington, D.C., when a bullet felled President Lincoln at Ford's Theatre. South Carolina's coast did not hear the news until days later.

I imagine Smalls deeply felt the loss of the president he knew personally, who had the audacity to emancipate the enslaved and the fortitude to allow the freedmen to join the fight to preserve the Union. Upon learning the news, Smalls shared aloud the prayer in every freed person's heart: "Lord have mercy on us all."[41]

CHAPTER 2

"RECONSTRUCTION BEGUN"

—— 1865–1867 ——

"I shall demand for my race an equal share,
everywhere."

—Robert De Large

T HE FAITH AND FORTITUDE of Black soldiers, who joined the Union to fight for their freedom, helped lead to the Confederates' surrender on April 9, 1865. Less than a week later, President Lincoln died at the hand of a Confederate sympathizer. These dramatic events set the stage for the fragility of the freedom Blacks celebrated in the streets of Charleston.

Leaders began to emerge from the state's Black majority to combat former Confederate leaders' efforts to maintain the racial status quo as much as possible. This conflict would play out over the remainder of the century, and the First Eight would be among the leaders shaping how the Black community fought for equality and justice.

The differences in the First Eight's early lives played significant roles in their leadership styles. The first of the Eight to emerge as leaders in Charleston's Black community came from those that were of mixed-race parentage, a status that accorded them the benefit of an education and participation in civic-minded pursuits prior to the war. Among them were Robert Carlos De Large and Alonzo Jacob Ransier, who rose quickly into leadership positions, but took very different approaches to their roles.

PRIVILEGE AND PREFERENCES

As I reflect on the lives of the First Eight, Robert De Large's story gives me the greatest pause.

A "bright mulatto," as newspapers would later describe him, De Large was born on March 15, 1842, to free Black parents in Aiken, South Carolina. He had the great fortune to grow up with both parents at a time when that was uncommon for African American children. Most notably, his family was among the small portion of well-to-do Blacks who owned slaves. Free Blacks in the garment industry were the most common group to own enslaved people; his father, a tailor, and his mother, a cloak maker, likely used these slaves in their business, increasing their personal income and reinforcing the white power structure at the expense of their Black brethren.[1]

Due to his family's wealth, De Large had the opportunity to move to Charleston for an education, despite laws against teaching Blacks to read or write.[2] He exemplified the elite mixed race, or "Brown," population who moved to the city to take advantage of the privileges of their parentage and light skin.[3] The Gullah people would describe De Large as a "cumya," a derogatory term for those not native to Charleston. "Benyas,"

Robert Carlos De Large portrait, circa 1870. (Courtesy of the Schomburg Center for Research in Black Culture, Photographs and Print Division)

referring to those whose roots ran deep in the city's sandy soil, were native Charlestonians and received greater preference.

When I moved to Charleston in January 1962, this hierarchy remained ingrained in the local culture. Evidence of this favoritism confronted me in April 1966, when, at the age of twenty-five, I became director of the Neighborhood Youth Corps, part of the U.S. Labor Department's War on Poverty program. Shortly after I accepted the job, a Charlestonian, with whom I later developed a friendship, visited my new office. She told me that she had applied for the position also, then very comfortably said that traditionally, as a lighter-skinned Charleston native, she would have been hired over me. Although I understood her logic, her forthrightness was a gut punch. Indeed, according to the unwritten but widely understood "rules" of Black culture in Charleston at the time, a "cumya," most especially one with darker skin like mine, would not get a coveted leadership position—something that only fueled my drive to prove this discriminatory assumption wrongheaded.[4] This intraracial bias, of course, is not limited to 1840s or 1960s Charleston; evidence suggests that even today, lighter-skinned Blacks benefit from higher wages and higher levels of education than their darker-skinned counterparts.[5] Today we refer to this as colorism, though it can be traced back to the antebellum era.[6]

During that time, "mulattos" referred to the offspring of white men and the women they enslaved. This sexual exploitation produced a mixed racial class that became the center of a social pyramid, with a small tier of whites above them and a wide base of enslaved Africans below.[7] Many white fathers silently acknowledged paternity by freeing their mixed-race children or providing them an education. Explicit in the charter of some schools was language that they existed for the education of mulattos. If they were kept enslaved, like Robert Smalls, these children often received coveted domestic jobs and better food and shelter.[8]

In 1860, those of mixed race were three-fourths of Charleston's free Black population, and like De Large, they proved to be allies of the white power structure. Always fearful of a violent uprising, whites enlisted them as spies to report any concerning activity within the Black community. For the same reason, they also imposed a prohibition on African Americans gathering in groups larger than six without white supervision. Again, "mulattos" flouted the laws with the permission of their white collaborators.[9]

De Large took advantage of this arrangement and joined the Brown Fellowship Society, an exclusive organization founded in 1790 by a group of free mulattos. The society inducted just fifty members, and its explicit rules "shut the front door [to whites] as well as the back door [to Blacks]." De Large, having grown up in a family that exploited slave labor for their own financial gain, fit in well with a club that described full-blooded Blacks as "the backward race."[10]

The organization continued for two centuries into the 1990s, well after my arrival in Charleston in 1962.[11] However, by then it had dropped the word "Fellowship" from its name, becoming known simply as "the Brown Society"—and had become less exclusionary. I became friends with one of the organization's former presidents, Herbert DeCosta, with whom I shared memberships in several Black organizations, among them the Charleston Business and Professional Men's Association, Sigma Pi Phi fraternity (also known as the Boulé), and a national social club, the Guardsmen. Herbert, a contractor, built our home in Charleston, and he served on the finance committee of my campaign for South Carolina secretary of state in 1978, all signs that some members of the twentieth-century Brown Society had evolved since the organization's more stratified days.

When the Civil War broke out, many members of the Brown Fellowship Society, as it was still called, declared they would "offer up our lives, and all that is dear to us" to serve South Carolina; and so De Large and many of his society members joined the Confederate military. For them, this was a means to preserve their favored relationship with whites.[12] But when Union troops moved through Charleston in 1865 and the war's outcome appeared to be a victory for the Union, De Large and his Brown Fellowship Society brethren knew they had to determine a new path forward. Blacks of all hues were granted freedom, and the former Confederates, filled with resentment, would lash out against any person of color with impunity. Those of mixed race would no longer enjoy a special status.

This change in reception to his racial identity challenged De Large's status in the community and his livelihood as a tailor. Desperate to find his footing, this diminutive man with bushy sideburns and a receding hairline sought to secure a future for himself in this new world order. And on March 30, 1865, just six weeks after Charleston's liberation, De Large organized a public meeting with other Black Confederate veterans. This gathering of once well-to-do mixed-race men approved a resolution written by De Large declaring allegiance to the Union.[13]

De Large moved quickly following this shift in loyalty, serving on a committee of mostly white Union officers to raise money for the proper burial of Union soldiers who had been prisoners of war, many of whom were interred in unmarked graves at the Washington Racecourse in Charleston. Charleston's Black community heeded the call, raising enough money to turn the site into a proper graveyard surrounded by a protective fence. And on May 1, 1865, a crowd of ten thousand Black Union veterans and other members of the African American community turned out to dedicate the Martyrs of the Racecourse cemetery and show their appreciation for the ultimate sacrifice paid by the Union soldiers who had secured their freedom. In 1865, this celebration was called Decoration Day. Today we know it as Memorial Day, a holiday started by emancipated Blacks in Charleston, South Carolina.[14]

Thomas Nast's illustration in *Harper's Weekly* of the Martyr's of the Racecourse Cemetary in Charleston, 1868. (Courtesy of the New York Public Library)

Following this effort, De Large went a step further to rehabilitate his character, donating most of the money he earned while serving in the Confederate navy to the Republican Party, at that time the anti-slavery "party of Lincoln."[15] The Republicans had organized in South Carolina after the war, and most Blacks had gravitated toward them.

As he made amends with the Black community and pledged loyalty to the Union, De Large also sought to straddle the line of claiming his equality with whites and doing his best not to offend them. In September 1865, he signed a petition with other free Black artisans from the antebellum period seeking "an earnest assertion of [their] manhood" in the form of suffrage. But the colorism attitudes remained, and the petitioners offered, "We ask not at this time that the ignorant shall be admitted to the exercises [sic] of a privilege which they might use to the injury of the State." They were seeking the vote for themselves but not for illiterate Black Americans, an attempt to distinguish themselves from those they saw as lesser. They also tried to appease the powers that be, stating, "Notwithstanding the bitterness of the past, and of the present, we cherish feelings of respect and affection" toward former white Confederates.[16]

THE REDEEMERS

The former Confederates did not share De Large's eagerness to give educated Blacks the right to vote—or to give African Americans any rights at all. Instead they did their best to recreate the social and political structure of the antebellum age in the postwar era, intentionally ignoring the consequences of their defeat.

President Lincoln's death in 1865 bolstered their efforts, presenting a barrier to the "righteous and speedy peace" that his administration had envisioned.[17] When Vice President Andrew Johnson, a Tennessee native and states' rights supporter, assumed the presidency, he didn't share the vision of his predecessor. In fact, Lincoln had selected Johnson as his vice president only as a capitulation to the former slave states. Johnson, who himself owned slaves (whom he freed eight months after the Emancipation Proclamation went into effect), offered blanket pardons to most Confederates that allowed them to hold elective office, which would have enabled De Large to pursue a political career. At the same time, the unexpected president provided little guidance for the path forward to reunify the country.

As president, Johnson left the insurgent Southern states to make their own way toward recovery from the war. He also attempted, without Senate approval, to fire the secretary of war, Edwin Stanton, for his support for freedmen's rights. This raised the ire of Republicans in Congress, resulting in Johnson's impeachment—which marked a first for the House of Representatives. The Senate failed to convict him by one vote. [18]

In South Carolina, most whites held contempt and intolerance for the now free Black majority, as well as "mulattos" like De Large, whom they'd once tolerated. The former Confederate captain Thomas Lowndes Pinckney captured the prevailing sentiment in the state regarding the Blacks and white men who aligned themselves with the Republican Party, declaring, "For us the war was not ended." He continued, "We had met the enemy in the field and lost our fight, but now we were threatened with a servile war, a war in which the negro savage backed by the U.S. and the intelligent white scoundrel as his leader was our enemy." Animosity grew between the races, and Blacks saw their former owners, who held fast to their Confederate sympathies, as rebels against the now-reunified states.[19] Politically, these disaffected whites made up the Southern wing of the Democratic Party, who sought to "redeem" the prewar society, limiting the rights and privileges of the formerly enslaved.[20]

BLACK CODES

South Carolina's Redeemer Democrats took advantage of President Johnson's lack of oversight and sought to curtail the rights of Blacks. And when a federal directive ordered former Confederate states to rewrite their

Thomas Nast's illustration of Redeemers declaring "this is a white man's government," 1868. (Library of Congress, Prints and Photographs Divsion, LC-DIG-ppmsca-71958)

constitutions in order to be readmitted to the Union, they were more than happy to try to reap the benefits.

In September 1865, these Redeemers held an all-white constitutional convention. This gathering bore more resemblance to the secessionists' convention than to a representation of the inhabitants of the defeated insurgent state. They adopted a new constitution acknowledging the freedom of the formerly enslaved, but ignored the request of De Large and his Brown elite colleagues for the right to vote. Instead, their new constitution allowed the election of only white men to the General Assembly and refused Blacks any citizenship rights, including the right to bear arms, to serve on juries, and to protect their lives and property. Just one month later, an all-white Redeemer Democratic legislature convened under this constitution, while President Johnson continued his hands-off approach, and they reestablished a power structure that reflected their belief in white superiority.

President Johnson had handpicked Benjamin Franklin Perry to be South Carolina's provisional governor after the war, and under him, the codification of anti-Black legislation continued. Perry ordered law-yers to draft codes for "the regulation of labor and the protection and government of the Colored Population of the State." These lawyers con-sulted Edmund Rhett, a contributing editor to his family's newspaper, *The Charleston Mercury*, the leading purveyor of secessionist propaganda before the war. Rhett declared, "The general interest of both the white man and the negro requires that he should be kept as near to the condition of slav-ery as possible, as far from the condition of the white man as practicable."[21] Paternalistic whites argued that this was a means of protecting African Americans from the dangers of their own ignorance.[22] At Rhett's direc-tion, under this guise—the vague directive to "protect" the newly freed people—the legislature proposed Black Codes that backed a social and political order that kept Blacks subjugated.

The Codes also established rules restricting the movement of Blacks after sunset, eerily echoing antebellum laws like the one that the rebel-lious young Robert Smalls had broken while enslaved in Beaufort. They also criminalized being homeless or unemployed, with penalties includ-ing prison, forced public labor, or being auctioned to a needy employer. Simultaneously, in a provision that greatly limited the prospects of De Large and the Brown Society, they restricted Black employment to farm laborers or house servants.[23]

De Large, who had worked in the family business as a tailor before the war, wanted to continue his lucrative profession. Yet under the pro-posed Black Codes, he would have to purchase a special waiver from a district judge, who had the power to deny his request even if he could pay the high price.[24]

COLORED PEOPLE'S CONVENTION

The proposal to suppress the new "citizens" of South Carolina with Black Codes drew significant resistance from the majority population of the state. On November 20, 1865, a Colored People's Convention convened in

Charleston, the first such gathering in South Carolina of free Black men seeking to appeal "for justice."[25] De Large served among the forty-five delegates, half of them from Charleston. One of De Large's future congressional colleagues and another one of the First Eight, Alonzo Ransier, also took part in the convention.

Ransier was a light-skinned Black man, a "benya" born in Charleston to Haitian parents, who would have been among the "mulatto elites" in the highly stratified culture of that island nation after its slave rebellion ended in 1804. He enjoyed highly favored status as a native-born Charlestonian among the city's elite Haitian immigrant community. This preferential status helped Ransier obtain a coveted job as an office clerk prior to the war, and his white employer even paid a nominal fine for employing a mixed-race man in a profession forbidden to Blacks.[26]

Portrait of Alonzo Jacob Ransier, date unknown. (Courtesy of the Avery Research Center for African American History and Culture, College of Charleston, Charleston, South Carolina)

Ransier moved in similar circles as De Large and served as president of another Black organization, the Amateur Literary and Fraternal Association. This association focused on "the mutual improvement in elocution, composition, debate and the thorough cultivation of fraternal feelings."[27]

Ransier also helped establish the Columbia Educational Society. These organizations gave Blacks, who had limited political prospects and experiences, opportunities to develop leadership skills and build bases of support. Much of the early Black leadership in the state came from the ranks of these organizations; even today, Black professional and fraternal organizations are at the center of African American leadership.[28] I myself am a thirty-third-degree member of Prince Hall Free and Accepted Masons, which was chartered in the United States in 1775; the Sigma Pi Phi fraternity, also known as the Boulé, an African American professional fraternity co-founded by Columbia native Dr. Henry McKee Minton in 1904; and the Omega Psi Phi fraternity, co-founded at Howard University by Charleston native Dr. Ernest Everett Just in 1911. I can attest to the value of these Black-focused organizations and the subsequent political benefits I derive from them.

The civic training of the first group of emerging Black political leaders in South Carolina, including Ransier and De Large, contributed to their success as delegates to the Colored People's Convention. The gathering convened at Zion Presbyterian Church, the first Black Presbyterian church in the South, established in 1858 at the corner of Meeting and Calhoun Streets in Charleston. The historic African American church could not contain the assembled crowd. Many attendees overflowed into the streets, which still bore the scars of the brutal war.[29]

The newly established Black newspaper the *South Carolina Leader* described the location as "likely to become as identified with the history of the reorganized State of South Carolina as Faneuil Hall is with the history of Massachusetts."[30] However, despite this, like so many African American heritage sites, it was demolished in 1960; only a commemorative marker remains. Today, a Courtyard by Marriott hotel stands on this historic property.

But in 1865, the gravity of the event was undeniable—as was the complexity of the task at hand. Blacks had organized the Colored People's Convention to devise a clear response to the proposed Black Codes, with "plans best calculated to advance the interests of our people."[31] But they also wanted to demonstrate their magnanimity, in part to evade the anger of Redeemer Democrats.

Photograph of the Old Zion Presbyterian Church in Charleston before it was demolished, 1956. (Courtesy of the Avery Research Center for African American History and Culture, College of Charleston, Charleston, South Carolina)

Never one to miss an opportunity for personal gain, De Large made the first motion for a vote during the proceedings. From this day forward, he would become a fixture at every political gathering and, as one biographer noted, he "talked continually at all of them."[32] Intent on drawing attention to himself, De Large sought to set the tone for the convention, declaring, "The simple act of emancipation, if it stops there is not worth much" — though, despite that bold statement on behalf of the Black community, he still continued his proclivity to support efforts to mollify the white community.[33]

One such effort was a resolution stating that those in attendance held no "hatred or malice toward those who have held our brethren as slaves." Another extended "the right hand of fellowship to all."[34]

The original draft of that resolution included the phrase "and thereby cause us to make distinctions among ourselves," a clear reference to the colorism of the era. De Large, who must have felt the accusation that light-skinned Blacks participated in discriminating against their dark-skinned brethren hit too close to home, made a motion to strike the language. Ultimately De Large's position prevailed, most likely because

35

the convention delegates were mostly Brown elites. The amended resolution received a unanimous vote, though it was preceded by what the
convention recorder characterized as a "trying scene," drawing a forceful
challenge by several formerly enslaved delegates.[35]

Ransier, in contrast to De Large's desire for the spotlight, was described
by various biographers as a "mild mannered man." He had a light complexion and "a finely etched profile," and, despite his status as a Brown elite,
Ransier aligned himself at the convention with the formerly enslaved,
whom he defended against accusations that they weren't capable of serving effectively in elective office.[36] He argued that freedmen had served in
the Union military and because of "their strong arms and brave hearts the
American Government stands today." Ransier concluded that this honor-
able service showed "[the Black] man is capable of self-governing."[37] He
proved to be a voice of reason rather than a source of conflict.

As the Colored People's Convention ended on November 25, 1865, the
South Carolina Leader published the headline "Reconstruction Begun."[38]
The paper intended to create an iconic banner like "VE-Day!" and "Nixon
Resigns" that required no explanation, even generations later. However, I
take issue with the paper's characterization of November 1865 as the beginning of Reconstruction. Today, the National Park Service defines Reconstruction as the period when "the United States grappled with the question
of how to integrate millions of newly freed African Americans into social,
political, and labor systems."[39] Per this definition, for the thousands of
"contrabands" living in the Union-controlled territory of Beaufort County,
Reconstruction came in 1861. For me, that marks its true beginning—
it began in South Carolina.

The Leader, however, did correctly acknowledge the historic nature
of the Colored People's Convention. For the first time in South Carolina,
Black men participated in a civic exercise that demonstrated their ability to
lead and demanded that they participate in the political process. This gathering was evidence of their organizational and leadership skills, without
any white participation. The Colored People's Convention demonstrated
that Blacks could articulate the needs of their community and advocate

and agitate for political remedies to address those needs. Observing this significant achievement, the *Leader* proclaimed, "The world will recognize the proceedings as the grandest exhibition of progressive ideas which the State has ever known."[40] Convention delegates also recognized the importance of one of the state's earliest Black newspapers, adopting a resolution to "fully approve the course of the *South Carolina Leader* and pledge ourselves to its support," demonstrating the participants' understanding of the need to tell their own stories.[41] Ransier would soon take his support of the newspaper a step further and join the staff of the *Leader* as an associate editor to further the ideals laid out by the convention, which were stated in its Address to the People of the State of South Carolina:

> "Heretofore we have had no avenues opened to us or our children—we have had no firesides that we could call our own; none of those incentives to work for the development of our minds and the aggrandizement of our race in common with other people...Now that we are freemen, now that we have been lifted up by the providence of God to manhood, we have resolved to come forward, and, like MEN, speak and *act* for ourselves."[42]

At its conclusion, Ransier, who served as one of three convention secretaries, was chosen to be a member of the delegation to deliver the resulting report to Congress. In early 1866, Ransier traveled to Washington, perhaps for the first time. There, he and his colleagues experienced some stark realities of what Blacks could expect, even in the nation's capital, which was still stuck in the mores of the past despite President Lincoln's Proclamation.

Ransier's party, eager to watch the Senate debate the Fourteenth Amendment, which would guarantee Blacks the equal protections granted all American citizens, tried to enter one of the Senate gallery doors. A doorman stopped the group and directed them to a segregated section of the gallery to view the proceedings. Angered by their treatment, the men left and penned a letter on February 1 to the Senate's leading civil rights champion,

Charles Sumner of Massachusetts. They wrote, "The delegation cannot, in self-respect, consent to be colonized and do therefore respectfully pray to you as a friend of justice and impartial liberty to do what in your judgment the case may demand. We are anxious to hear the discussions [of the Fourteenth Amendment], but our self-respect is greater than the desire."[43]

A similar affront occurred when Ransier met with President Johnson during the same visit, on February 7, 1866, as part of a Black delegation advising that the Thirteenth Amendment, which abolished slavery, did not provide enough protection. The group demanded full voting rights, declaring, "Anything less than this will be rendering to us less than our due." President Johnson balked at their demand and lectured the delegation about the dangers facing Blacks if they secured suffrage, a harbinger of what was to come.[44]

During this contentious visit, I doubt that Ransier could have imagined he would be elected as a representative to Congress just eight years later, fulfilling a demand of the Colored People's Convention memorial to Congress. The memorial read in part, "Because 'all free governments derive their just powers from the consent of the governed;' and [Blacks] are largely in the majority in this State . . . we ask for equal suffrage as a protection for the hostility evoked by our known faithfulness to our country's flag under all circumstances."[45]

RISE OF THE "RADICAL" REPUBLICANS

Although President Johnson denied the demands of Ransier and his colleagues, the so-called Radical Republican members of Congress, who were tagged with the moniker for their strong support of equal rights for Blacks, took up their cause. Republicans controlled Congress during this period because Southern states had left the Union and their voting rights had not yet been restored after the war. And although they were in the minority of their party, the Radical Republicans successfully secured passage of a Civil Rights Act in April 1866, which granted citizenship to anyone born in the United States without regard to race, color, or previous condition;

provided equal protection under the law; and prohibited discrimination in employment, housing, and accommodations.[46] While the president tried to thwart this action by vetoing the law, Congress, for the first time in history, overrode a presidential veto.

Emboldened, Congress followed the Civil Rights Act with passage of the Fourteenth Amendment in June 1866, which enshrined those same rights into the Constitution. They took this further action to ensure a future hostile Congress could not overturn these fundamental rights.[47]

In a victory for De Large, Ransier, and their delegation, the Civil Rights Act of 1866 and the Fourteenth Amendment nullified the Black Codes, which the all-white South Carolina legislature had enacted in December 1865. However, South Carolina's power structure remained defiant of the African American community's efforts to secure their rights and the Radical congressional Republicans who supported them. Governor Perry declared, "[The] African has been, in all ages, a savage or a slave . . . God created him inferior to the white man in form, color, and intellect, and no legislation or culture can make him his equal."[48]

Meanwhile, the Redeemer Democrats in South Carolina attempted to skirt these new congressional checks on their power by holding a special session in September 1866 to revise the Black Codes to remove any references to race and to ensure that any challenges would be settled by a state court rather than a federal court.[49]

In December 1866, the all-white Redeemer legislature in South Carolina refused to ratify the Fourteenth Amendment, with the governor asserting that few people in history had "been required to concede more to their conquerors than the people of the South." Again, it would take Congress's might to force the insubordinate South to swallow this pill that the Redeemers considered too bitter.

In retaliation, in March 1867, Congress passed the first and second Reconstruction Acts. These acts removed South Carolina's provisional governor, replacing him with a military commander, ordered all militia to disband, and required a new constitution to be written that would give the franchise to all men regardless of color. They added one last insult to injury in the eyes of the Redeemers: The Republican Congress required South Carolina, and all former Confederate states, to ratify the Fourteenth Amendment in order to be readmitted to the Union.[50]

Given these federal victories, which had occurred under the auspices of the Republicans in Congress, Blacks began to organize the Republican Party in South Carolina. There had been previous Republican political activity in the state in 1864—involving one Robert Smalls, who had been elected as a delegate to the Republican Convention, which met to appeal to Democrats who supported the war. This marked the first time an integrated Southern delegation had been sent to a political convention. However, the convention refused to seat Smalls's group. (There is still debate about whether this was because it came from a state in rebellion, or because it included four Blacks.[51]) Nevertheless, this marked the beginning of Smalls's lifelong devotion to the party; today, he is recognized as one of its principal founders in South Carolina, having paved the way for figures like De Large and Ransier.

And so, in 1867, although members of the First Eight were new to political organizing, they seized the opportunity to build the state's Republican Party to positively impact their community. When Republicans held their first official state convention that May, De Large served as the chairman of the platform committee, and the document his committee produced proved very progressive. It called for popular elections for all elected offices, tax and court reforms, and new policies to end "land monopolies that make the rich richer and the poor poorer and to foster the division and sale of unoccupied land."[52]

For the first time, Blacks in South Carolina had the opportunity to participate in the political arena. De Large, Ransier, and their contemporaries were prepared to lead, although their styles differed, in a common mission to fulfill all the promise this time held for their community. However, the opposition they encountered as they reached this milestone served as a precursor of what was soon to come.

CHAPTER 3

"WHERE THERE IS NO VISION, THE PEOPLE PERISH"

——— 1867–1868 ———

"The sun has lit up the horizon.... The time has come for the Black man to take his place as a free man."

—Richard Cain

As Reconstruction began in earnest, the first generation of Black leaders in South Carolina, all men with no political experience, faced a daunting task—bringing hundreds of thousands of formerly enslaved people into an economic, social, and political system where they were not welcome.

Achieving this would take rewriting the state's constitution to grant Black men suffrage. But their efforts could not end with just the power to vote. This undertaking called for a more comprehensive approach, and the members of the First Eight, who participated in the 1868 South Carolina Constitutional Convention, had ideas about land ownership, education, and democratic reforms to accomplish their important charge—but they faced an uphill battle.

Just as faith had sustained the Black community through the dark centuries of slavery, it also provided guidance for this conundrum. In Proverbs 29:18 we are taught, "Where there is no vision, the people perish." No one understood this more than Richard Harvey Cain, who would become the first Black minister to serve in Congress. Indeed, shortly after this "cumya" arrived in Charleston, Cain felt the promise of a new day, declaring, "The sun has lit up the horizon.... The time has come for the Black man to take his place as a free man."[1]

Richard Harvey Cain, date unknown. (Courtesy of the New York Public Library)

THE POWER OF THE PULPIT

Cain's story began on April 12, 1825, in Greenbriar County, which at the time of his birth was in Virginia. It was an apt birthplace for the man who would grow to be one of the First Eight. In the run-up to the Civil War, the county would become a part of West Virginia, the Union state formed in 1863 after separating from the Confederate Commonwealth of Virginia over the issue of slavery.

Cain was born to a free Black father and a Cherokee mother, and in 1831 the family moved to Ohio, a free state where the young Cain was able to receive an education. There, as a young adult, he felt called to the ministry, became ordained at nineteen years old, and moved to Hannibal, Missouri, to pastor a Methodist Episcopal Church (MEC) congregation. But Cain, a young man with an independent streak and strong convictions, quickly became disillusioned with the controlling nature of the church's all-white leadership and the racial discrimination and separatism in the MEC. He left the church and joined the African Methodist Episcopal Church (AMEC), which had been founded in Philadelphia in 1787 by African Americans who, like Cain, wanted autonomy in how they worshipped. The AMEC sent Cain to Muscatine, Iowa, for his first assignment. By the time the Civil War broke out, he was furthering his ministerial studies at Wilberforce University, the country's first private Black college, which had been founded in 1856 by the AMEC.

At the time, Cain was thirty-six years old. He wrote a letter reflecting on "the coming consequences of that [first] shot" in Charleston, describing "the thrill that ran through my soul" when he heard the news. "Anxious to vindicate the stars and stripes," Cain and 114 classmates tried to enlist in the Union military, but they were turned away from what they were told was the "white man's war."[2]

Wilberforce was shuttered during the war, and Cain returned to the pulpit in 1861, pastoring at Bridge Street AMEC in Brooklyn, New York. Still, his thoughts remained on the destiny of the enslaved in the South. According to one biographer, he didn't want "this historical moment to pass without putting his mark on it."[3]

When the war ended in 1865, Cain got his chance. He left New York for Charleston as part of a mission to help organize Black congregations in the former Confederate state. There, his assignment was to serve as superintendent of AMEC missions in South Carolina, and his greatest achievement was the revitalization of Emanuel Church.[4]

I must take a moment of personal privilege, as we say in Congress, and reflect on the history of Mother Emanuel. This iconic church entered the national consciousness on June 17, 2015, when a white supremacist murdered nine congregants after they had welcomed him into their Bible study, unaware of his intent to start a "race war."[5] I considered many of the victims friends, including the pastor, Rev. Clementa Pinckney. Like Cain, Clementa was a pastor-politician. In fact, he had begun his political work as an intern in my congressional office when he was a student at Allen University, another AMEC-affiliated college. At the time of his murder, Clementa was serving as a beloved member of the South Carolina Senate.

The attack on Emanuel Church was another chapter in the long history of assaults on the Black church, a central pillar in the community. In the case of Mother Emanuel, the murderer had chosen a target, the church that Cain helped build, based on its history and stature in the Black community.

Emanuel, which means "God is with us," was established in 1818 by enslaved Blacks in what one historian called a "rebellious act of revolutionary proportions."[6] Like Cain, these congregants sought freedom in how and where they worshipped. More than four thousand Black parishioners left Charleston's Bethel Church to form Emanuel, which is referred to as Mother Emanuel because it was the city's first African American church, with Morris Brown as their pastor.[7]

This demonstration of Black independence worried whites in the community, and they exerted their dominance by constantly harassing Emanuel's parishioners. Within a year, Charleston authorities had raided Emanuel, arrested 140 congregants, and subjected them to fines and lashings. They raided the church again in 1820 and 1821.[8]

In 1822, an enslaved person of mixed race, Peter Prioleau—later known as Peter Desverney—reported to his owner that Denmark Vesey, a mixed-race Black man who had used lottery winnings to purchase his and his family's freedom, was holding clandestine meetings in Emanuel Church to plan a slave rebellion. The reaction by authorities to the so-called Vesey conspiracy resulted in the hanging of Vesey and over thirty of his alleged co-conspirators, the demolition of the original church, and the curtailing of liberties for both free and enslaved Blacks in Charleston.[9] As a reward for his loyalty to the enslavers, Desverney was granted his freedom and a lifetime pension from the General Assembly. During the 1865 Colored People's Convention, Martin R. Delany, a Union officer who has been called the father of Black nationalism, reflected on this incident and its lasting impact on the African American community, claiming that the betrayal of Vesey by a mulatto caused "the prejudice existing among the different classes of the colored people."[10]

After demolishing Emanuel AMEC, the white authorities built a weapons arsenal just a stone's throw from the site of the church as a warning to Blacks against planning future uprisings. In 1842, the arsenal became home of The Citadel, South Carolina's military college, and is an Embassy Suites Hotel today.[11]

With this history in mind, when the Civil War ended in 1865, Cain was one of the first AMEC ministers to arrive in South Carolina—and he had the task of reestablishing Emanuel. He was forty years old, and according to historians "an extremely charismatic man, short in stature but with a compact physique, a booming voice, and a strong, expressive face." He soon became a leader of the newly emancipated, who dubbed him "Daddy Cain." Meant as an honorific by his congregants, Cain disliked the paternalistic moniker. Whites co-opted the nickname and referred to him as Daddy Cain derisively.[12]

Within a year of his arrival, Cain oversaw work on a new sanctuary for Mother Emanuel, which the son of Denmark Vesey designed. Using his charisma and leadership skills, Cain quickly raised ten thousand dollars and rebuilt Mother Emanuel at a time when most of the postwar damaged buildings in Charleston still needed repairs or reconstruction. His commanding influence among the Charleston Black community, even as a "cumya," was evident: The church could hold two thousand parishioners, and even then the congregation he attracted far exceeded that number when the new structure opened its doors. Under Cain's leadership, this once "invisible institution," as Henry Louis Gates Jr. described the Black church during the antebellum period, emerged from the shadows and established Emanuel Church as a beacon of light in Charleston that could not be dimmed.[13]

Historic Emanuel AME Church building during Richard Cain's time, date unknown. (Courtesy of Emanuel AME Church, Charleston, South Carolina)

Unable to accommodate Emanuel's burgeoning congregation, in 1867 Cain established just blocks away Morris Brown AMEC, in honor of Mother Emanuel's first minister, whom the state had exiled after the Vesey conspiracy.[14] Brown had since moved to Philadelphia, the birthplace of the AMEC, and had become the denomination's second bishop.[15]

I take great pride in my personal connection with Morris Brown AMEC. My late wife and I joined the congregation shortly after we made Charleston our home. We were attracted to its rich history of social activism born of its adherence to the "Gospel of Freedom," popularized after the Civil War when Black Christians believed it was not enough to be free, but that they must use their freedom to pursue justice. Emily and I embraced the activist spirit of the Gospel of Freedom, and thus Morris Brown AMEC became an integral part of our lives. The church served as the site of Emily's homegoing service on September 23, 2019, after she lost a decades-long battle with the debilitating complications of diabetes. I still consider Morris Brown my home church, and it will always be a sacred place for me.

The AMEC also provides an important connection between me and Cain. He served as Morris Brown's first minister, and as one modern-day observer acknowledged, it didn't take long for him to become "the most spectacular personality politically, as well as religiously" in the African American community. A Black contemporary acknowledged Cain's influence, later remarking that he grew the AMEC into "one of the strongest political organizations in the State" during the postbellum period.[16]

Leadership through the faith community is something this "cumya" to Charleston and I share. Politics did not define Cain's commitment to public service, but it provided a practical way to extend his ministry. I often discussed with my father, a pastor in the fundamentalist Church of God, the possibility of following him into the ministry. But unlike Cain, though I listened for it, I never heard the call. When I told my dad of my decision not to become a minister, he responded, "Well, son, I suspect the world would rather see a sermon than hear one." These words, and the Edgar Guest poem from which it was drawn, became guiding principles throughout my public life.

Faith is a through line in American history, particularly in the Black community. In the antebellum period, Emanuel and other Black churches were "invisible institutions" in which Black congregants worshipped secretly in the cabins of the enslaved, in brush arbors, and out in open spaces.[17] It didn't matter where or how they practiced their faith; they had the will to worship, and they found a way. The white community's effort to quash the independent Black church did not achieve its aims. Throughout the centuries, the church provided the Black community the support and strength to shoulder the inequities forced upon them, and leaders that empowered them. In Cain's time, this dynamic enabled "the vigorous and willing orator" to emerge as "one of the most outstanding examples of the preacher-politicians during Reconstruction."[18] I find clergy make good politicians because of their desire and ability to lead their flock, and their flock's allowance of sufficient independence for them to be effective as officeholders.

POLITICAL POWER WITH A PURPOSE

Cain's popularity and effectiveness as South Carolina's superintendent for AMEC missions helped him expand the church outside of Charleston, establishing congregations in Sumter, Columbia, Georgetown, and many of the state's more rural communities. His efforts were such that, a year after his death, Cain was memorialized at an AMEC Board of Bishops as "an untiring worker for his church [and] the chief instrument in building up our work in South Carolina."[19]

In 1865, soon after beginning his work in Charleston, Cain expanded his efforts in the religious community and purchased the fledgling *South Carolina Leader* newspaper, which became an important tool to grow the church's reach. As the editor, Cain changed its name to the *Missionary Record* to reflect its affiliation with the AMEC and created a masthead with the biblical admonition, "Therefore all things whatsoever ye would that men should do to you, do you even so to them," proclaiming his adherence to the Golden Rule as both a religious and political message.[20]

As part of his ministry and mission, Cain believed in empowering the newly free people to be self-sufficient. Toward that end, he employed a staff at the newspaper made up of formerly enslaved men. He believed the paper served as an example of what African Americans could achieve if provided the opportunity, and proved his point by making it the first successful Black-owned newspaper in South Carolina.[21]

The emergence of Black newspapers during the post–Civil War era also provided a voice for a community often misrepresented by the mainstream media of the day. Newspapers in the South were white-owned and reflected the biases of the former Confederates. They helped shape public opinion, instigated secession before the war, and constructed the narrative that Blacks were inept and corrupt in the Reconstruction era: White editors and writers felt they had to use any means necessary to save South Carolina from Black empowerment and to restore white supremacy.

Cain understood the power of the press as a political and public opinion tool. He knew that in order to combat the propaganda disseminated by

Redeemer-controlled newspapers, African Americans would have to create their own ways to tell their truth. Indeed, one historian characterized the *Missionary Record* as "an important voice for Black Carolinians," calling it "another contributor to Cain's ability to establish one of the strongest political organizations in the state."[22]

I share Cain's faith in the power of Black newspapers. For fifteen years, beginning in 1983, I published the *Coastal Times* in Charleston with my daughter Mignon. Like Cain and so many Black publishers who have gone before us, we understood that information and communication are critically important to providing connectivity and clarity within the Black community. Although we no longer publish the *Coastal Times*, I continue to periodically write columns for the National Newspaper Publishers Association's two hundred Black newspapers across the country to make sure our message gets through the fractured and polarized media landscape of today. It is my way of reaching audiences to inform them of issues important to the communities I serve.

As Cain's newspaper grew in popularity, Cain took on associate editors who included Alonzo Ransier, a rising star in Charleston's political circles, and Robert Brown Elliott, a full-blooded Black "cumya" who arrived from Boston.[23] All three men would soon become colleagues in Congress.

With the help of their rising profiles, Cain and Ransier would soon begin stirring up what my good friend and fellow civil rights activist the late John Lewis would call "good trouble." Like Cain and Ransier, John and I met at the beginning of a crucial moment in civil rights history, as nineteen-year-old college students at the second organizing meeting of the Student Nonviolent Coordinating Committee (SNCC), determined to change the world through civil disobedience. Also like Cain and Ransier, John and I drew inspiration through faith-driven politics, with John reflecting Ransier's mild manners and modesty mixed with dogged determination, and me more like Cain.

On March 26, 1867, these two newspapermen, joined by their colleague Elliott, spoke to a mostly Black gathering of nearly two thousand at Citadel Square, now known as Marion Square. Although newspaper accounts do not quote the speakers, they do recount that the assembled, who came to hear about the Republican Party's early organizational meetings, left inspired—much like John and I felt in 1960, at the second meeting of SNCC when we left the meeting with Dr. Martin Luther King Jr.—to continue advocating for civil disobedience. After Cain and Ransier delivered their inspirational remarks, Blacks began to demand that Charleston's streetcars be desegregated. For several weeks, African Americans boarded streetcars to the dismay of white passengers, and put stones on the tracks to prohibit the streetcars' progress.

Two weeks later, on April 12, Mary Bowers, a highly educated Black woman, took a seat on a streetcar and refused to budge, prompting her unceremonious removal. Ms. Bowers filed a complaint with the Freedmen's Bureau. Her activism—eighty-seven years before Sarah Mae Flemming took a similar stance in Columbia and eighty-eight years before the more famous Rosa Parks's stance in Mongomery, Alabama—resulted in an agreement to desegregate Charleston's streetcars.[24]

The defiant actions of Ms. Bowers and Ms. Flemming represent a significant number of South Carolina's forgotten, or intentionally ignored, contributions to America's civil rights struggle. The importance of the Rosa Parks incident cannot be understated; it launched the Montgomery bus boycott and the civil rights career of Dr. King. However, what is often forgotten is that Parks was taught civil disobedience by Septima P. Clark of Charleston, and her sit-down occurred a year after Ms. Flemming's similar action on a Columbia bus, which has been lost to history. Ms. Flemming's case was noted by the United States Supreme Court in its 1956 landmark decision to integrate public transportation.

The streetcar protests inspired by Cain and Ransier took place as the Republican Congress grappled with the South's reluctance to grant African Americans the rights they were owed as citizens. In response, Congress enacted the Reconstruction Acts of 1867, requiring the former Confederate states to hold new constitutional conventions to produce a document with mandatory Black enfranchisement. Members of the First

Eight, who were actively engaged in Republican politics in South Carolina at the time, were ready to join this effort.

1868 CONSTITUTIONAL CONVENTION

Under the auspices of the newly appointed military governor, the election to approve South Carolina's constitutional convention and select its delegates was held on November 19 and 20, 1867. It marked the first opportunity for Black men to vote in the state, and Robert Smalls, who had become a leading figure in the state's Republican party, used the same skills he employed to recruit thousands of Black Union soldiers, to register African Americans to vote for the first time. By the time registration closed in his home county of Beaufort, Black registered voters outnumbered whites nine to one. Statewide, the margin was two to one.[25]

Before the November election, the newly ousted South Carolina governor Benjamin Franklin Perry tapped into the fears of the Redeemer Democrats, warning them of the possibility of "disgracing themselves for ever and ever by adopting a negro government and giving up the rights of their State." Approval of the convention required the affirmative vote of "a majority of those registered," so they encouraged whites to withhold their votes in hopes that turnout would fall short of the established threshold of fifty-percent plus one.[26] Meanwhile, Blacks cast their first ballots in great numbers with pride, and some with tears of joy, at polling places under the protection of the federal military.

Smalls cast his ballot at the Beaufort Hall of Justice, the very same place where the enslaved were brutally punished during his youth.[27] Now, thanks in part to his fortitude, the building had transformed into a polling place filled with the excitement of formerly enslaved men eager to cast their first ballots. Blacks took the franchise seriously, and eighty-five percent of those African Americans registered to vote turned out, exceeding the threshold and approving the convention.[28]

Harper's Weekly cartoon depicting the first African Americans to vote, 1867. (Library of Congress, Prints and Photographs Division, LC-DIG-ppmsca-37947)

The convention delegates met on January 14, 1868, at the Charleston Club House on King Street. The Redeemers considered the choice of the site a slap across the face; their mouthpiece, the Rhett brothers' incendiary *Mercury* tabloid, reminded readers that the Club House had been "erected by a society of Charleston gentlemen for the pleasure of each other's company." The Redeemers seethed at the thought that their high-society hangout would be sullied by the "Black and Tan" attending the "Congo Convention," as other white-owned newspapers described the gathering.

Members of the First Eight were undaunted. Instead, they were exhilarated by the task before them. Elliott summed up the mood, declaring, "Behind us lie two hundred and forty-three years of suffering, anguish, and degradation.... Before us lies our mighty future, with all its hopes and its aspirations.... That future is ours to shape.... Let us realize that upon each of us rest duties commensurate with our rights."

As the delegates took their seats in the center of the floor, masses of Black citizens packed into the gallery. Press from all over the country also came to watch history in the making and sat on either side of the platform from which the president of the convention spoke.[29]

This assembly of mostly political novices faced the enormous challenge of writing a constitution that included Blacks in the state's economic, political, and social systems with the full rights of citizens. What they crafted, as described by a modern-day South Carolina legal scholar, was "a document with a deeper insight into the meaning of freedom, an insight possessed only by the freedmen who had known slavery and the freeborn who knew how precarious freedom could be without constitutional protection."[30] It was a document that responded to the demands and desires of their constituents: access to education, the ability to elect political representatives of their choice, and economic independence and stability for their families.

Knowing the Redeemers' desire to undermine the convention's efforts, Cain sought to ensure that the newly written Constitution would provide no loophole for them to exploit. He implored his fellow delegates, "We do not wish to leave a jot or tittle upon which anything can be built to remind our children of their former state of slavery."[31]

As a leader during the convention discussions, Cain's primary concern was to provide the freedmen with access to landownership. This was of particular importance to him because, just a few months after he arrived in Charleston, he had seen firsthand the anguish that occurred when President Andrew Johnson rescinded General William T. Sherman's Special Field Order 15, in a devastating betrayal for many Black South Carolinians.

General Sherman had issued the order in January 1865, with President Lincoln's blessing, directing the division of 400,000 acres of confiscated land between Charleston and Savannah into forty-acre plots to be distributed to newly freed Black families. About forty thousand Black families had already received homesteads through the program.[32] Some had also received excess Union mules, hence the familiar term "forty acres and a mule." The order to return this land was a crushing blow.

Cain took to heart the agony of Black South Carolinians after the shocking reversal. The aggrieved were directed to appoint a committee to determine the fairest way to return the newly acquired land back to the planters. This committee wrote instead to federal officials imploring, "We want Homesteads, we were promised Homesteads by the government. If it does not carry out promises its agents made to us . . . we are left in a more unpleasant condition than our former. . . . You will see this is not the condition of real free men."[33]

According to one of his biographers, the federal government's refusal to honor its promise spurred Cain to become "South Carolina's most insistent advocate of policies and projects to make land ownership possible for the freed people."[34] As the delegates drafted the state's new constitution, he spoke on the floor, arguing, "The abolition of slavery has thrown these [newly freed] people upon their own resources.... How are they to live?"[35] Cain offered a solution to help Blacks acquire the property necessary to help them achieve self-sufficiency: His proposal entailed the federal government providing a one-million-dollar loan that would allow South Carolina to purchase land and sell it in small parcels to the freedmen, who would pay back the money, with interest. Some Black delegates, including Robert Smalls, feared Cain's idea would not win the support of the federal government and would unnecessarily "raise the hopes of the entire poor people of the country...three-fourths of whom will be compelled to go away with shattered hopes," never realizing their dream of owning land.[36]

I understand Smalls's concerns. More than a century and a half since this debate, the issue of reparations for Black enslavement remains unresolved. To this day, the broken promise of "forty acres and a mule" is the only compensation the formerly enslaved have ever received (and were ordered to return) for their forced bondage and unpaid labor. This has allowed the issue to fester, and the call for reparations has grown louder within some segments of the Black community who now demand cash payments.

The root word of reparations is repair. My long-held position is that for the U.S. government to repair the great harm slavery has done to the Black community, they must sponsor programs addressing the current effects of past discrimination. Admittedly, this would not appease those who insist on monetary compensation. I have spent much time meditating on this issue, and I do not believe that it is possible to fairly and accurately determine the level of remuneration and who should receive it. Should descendants of Robert De Large, who were never enslaved and enjoyed educational opportunities, who accumulated wealth and enjoyed a comfortable life thanks to enslaved labor in the antebellum period, receive the same compensation as the progeny of Robert Smalls, who had to embark on a suicide mission to escape enslavement and spend his youth laboring for his owner? From this, how would one determine the levels of renumeration for each group that reflect the differences in their ancestors' lived experiences? What about those who cannot trace their ancestry? How many descendants of enslaved men and women can prove their lineage when records don't exist for generations of enslaved people? How about those who have been passing as white, or are descendants of some who did, who may also seek reparations?

Like Smalls, I take a practical approach to this issue and seek equitable and attainable solutions that help address the impacts of past discrimination. To me, programs like Affirmative Action, and Diversity, Equity and Inclusion, and funding approaches like my 10-20-30 funding formula—which directs ten percent of federal funding to communities where twenty percent or more of the population have lived below the poverty line for thirty or more years—are more feasible than an unrealistic dream.

During the 1868 constitutional convention, delegates proved that common ground can be found on these very difficult issues. After significant debate, the delegates agreed to a compromise proposed by Cain to create the South Carolina Land Commission. This body had the authority to "purchase at public sale, improved and unimproved real estate" in "suitable tracts" and to sell it in small parcels, on the condition that one-half the land "shall be placed under cultivation."[37]

As part of the compromise, the state retained the titles to the land for up to eight years until the freedmen paid the debt. This addition satisfied a clause offered by the future congressman Joseph Rainey—who will be introduced in more detail in the next chapter—and approved by the convention delegates that land had to be purchased, not given away.[38] The clause was intended to assuage the fears stoked by Redeemer-spread disinformation that former Confederates would have their land confiscated and redistributed to newly freed Blacks without compensation. Governor Perry acknowledged this tactic was used because "most persons are influenced more by their fears than by their honor."[39]

The directive to create the Land Commission made South Carolina's constitution unique in the Reconstructed South: It openly addressed what the historian Steven Hahn has called "the explosive issue of land reform."[40] Despite the program's many challenges and detractors, by the 1890s, the Land Commission had sold nearly forty-five thousand acres to African Americans in the state.[41]

Another issue that emerged during the convention was access to public education, which proved to be another point of controversy. Robert Smalls championed a resolution that became the basis of the free, compulsory public education system we know today. Always conscious of his lack of a formal education, Smalls asserted that having an intelligent government "faithful to the interests and liberties of the people" depended "in great measure on the intelligence of the people themselves." He therefore proposed that children from age seven to fourteen be required to attend school for six months out of the year. This became a point of contention among the Black delegates.[42]

Cain, who grew up outside the South and enjoyed the benefit of a higher education, objected to the term "compulsory," calling it "the obnoxious word." De Large, who received an education as a South Carolinian of mixed race, also opposed making attendance mandatory, believing the idea contradicted "the spirit and principles of republicanism," which in the vernacular of the day meant democratic.

Yet Smalls found allies in Alonzo Ransier and the well-read Robert Elliott, who both believed freedom came with the obligation to be educated. Elliott responded to De Large's dissension with, "It is republicanism to reward virtue. It is republicanism to educate people without discrimination." He continued, "The question is not white or Black united or divided, but whether children shall be sent to school or kept at home."[43]

In the end, the delegates compromised on an education provision that made "compulsory attendance at either public or private schools of all children between the ages of six and sixteen...for a term equivalent to twenty-four months."[44] Despite their differing approaches to regulating public schools, they all agreed that access to education was paramount.

The public education system became one of the lasting contributions of South Carolina's Reconstruction.[45]

But how would they pay for this public education? This was a question that was intertwined with the implementation of Black suffrage. Rainey, a barber who enjoyed significant wealth, proposed funding public education through a one-dollar poll tax. He argued that if one could not afford the tax to support schools, they had "no right to vote."[46]

Elliott led the charge against the poll tax, claiming it created opportunities for corruption. Theoretically, he said, a politician could pay the poll tax for those who could not afford it, in exchange for their vote. Relatedly, Elliott also opposed efforts to prohibit the illiterate from voting, pointing out white suffrage had never been limited by a literacy test. The Reconstruction Act, which led to the convening of this convention, directed states to create a constitution that provided universal suffrage. Elliott chided his fellow delegates for considering a provision that would undermine that directive.

"Here we, who have met together under that very act, under that very authority, propose to say to Congress, you are wrong; you had no right to give any such privileges to the people, and therefore we will restrict the privilege. How could you face your constituents?" he challenged. His words proved persuasive, and the delegates decided against implementing a poll tax and a literacy test and instead extended the vote to all men.[47]

In its final form, the constitution also included election reforms that made the governor's office elected rather than appointed and removed property ownership as a qualification for voting or holding elected office. While active, the latter had left political control during the antebellum period in South Carolina to the oligarchy, who had enriched themselves through the ownership of land and human beings. Today, historians recognize the constitution as a "model document" that dismantled "South Carolina's uniquely undemocratic political culture," and that demanded "public equality, that is, absolute civil and political parity with whites."[48]

After two months of diligent and delicate work, the convention concluded on March 17, 1868. Despite their lack of experience, the Black men who had fulfilled their monumental task led with something greater: a passion to produce a document that would withstand the test of time and bring their communities toward the promise of "a more perfect Union." The *Charleston Daily News* acknowledged their abilities, writing, "The best men in the convention are the colored members. Considering the influences under which they were called together, and their imperfect acquaintance with parliamentary law, they have displayed, for the most part, remarkable moderation and dignity." The paper continued, "They have assembled neither to pull wires like some, nor to make money like others; but to legislate for the welfare of the race to which they belong."[49]

Following the convention, De Large, still trying to straddle the racial lines, appealed to the white community, urging their support on the eve of ratification. "I ask—nay, I plead...that, you, the whites, come forward and bridge over the breach, which should not exist."[50] Despite his pleas, whites soundly rejected the document, with reporting in the *Charleston Mercury* calling it "monstrous," "unjust," and a "subversion of the American republic."[51]

In April 1868, eighty percent of Black voters and less than sixty percent of white voters turned out to cast their ballots for or against this governing document. Ultimately, the constitution was ratified, marking the first and only time in South Carolina's history that a new constitution was ratified by a popular vote.[52]

Yet the celebration among Blacks for this enormous achievement was tempered by comments by the former governor that foretold what was to come. Writing in the *Charleston Courier*, Perry warned that he had thought for some time that "when the negro government went into operation it would be impossible to preserve the peace of the country." He continued, forebodingly, "A war of races must ensue, and it will be the most terrific war of extermination that ever desolated the face of the earth in any age or country."[53]

Whites saw the new constitution as an assault on their way of life. One white Sumter County resident declared he would not follow "a negro constitution, of a negro government, establishing negro equality."[54] Many began to form local Ku Klux Klan groups, a white supremacist organization with roots in the horseback patrols used to terrorize Blacks during the antebellum period.[55]

Despite these protests, it didn't take long for the new constitution to have its desired effect. A new election resulted in Republicans winning all statewide offices and a majority in the state legislature, including seventy-five Black members of the house and ten Black senators.[56] On July 9, 1868, the Republican Robert K. Scott, a white Ohioan who had come to South Carolina to run the Freedmen's Bureau, took the oath of office as the state's first Reconstruction-era governor. He quickly called the historic legislature into session.

I know the feeling of being the first to break a barrier. It is both enthralling and exhausting. Being first means being under a microscope. You must exceed all expectations to ensure that you are not the last. And there is a profound sense of responsibility to represent your community in a way that engenders pride and progress. This must have been the mix of emotions felt by Rainey and Cain as they took their seats in the South Carolina State Senate and De Large, Elliott, Ransier, and Smalls as they joined the first class of Blacks in the South Carolina House of Representatives. These men, who had traveled different paths to public service, now found themselves working together on Reconstruction's rocky road of profound uncertainties—and there were many uncertainties to come.

CHAPTER 4

FIRSTS

—— 1868–1870 ——

"The day of our political deliverance is at hand."

—Alonzo Ransier

O VER THE NEXT THREE years, the adoption of the new South Carolina constitution led to many political firsts for Blacks in the state
legislature and the United States Congress. But these historic moments
enraged Redeemer Democrats, who were unwilling to accept that
the formally enslaved people now had equal and competing political
power.

They employed a two-pronged strategy. First, convince Northerners—
both Democrats and Republicans—that Black Republicans were corrupt
and inept. Second, use this alleged corruption and ineptness to justify the
use of force and violence through the Ku Klux Klan and other paramilitary terrorist organizations to curtail Blacks' newfound power.

All the while, African Americans focused on building a government
that served all the people. Many of the First Eight led the way. Their life
experiences had prepared them to take on this new challenge, but those
who opposed them were hell-bent on redeeming the pre–Civil War South,
doing all they could to stymie the efforts of the newly freed and turn back
the clock.

FIRST BIRACIAL LEGISLATURE

As part of Reconstruction, a federal directive placed South Carolina under military control and disbanded the state's General Assembly in 1867. When the new constitution was adopted, a new legislature was elected and met for the first time in a special session from July 6 to September 26, 1868. Ratifying the Fourteenth Amendment was its first order of business.

This new legislature did not convene for the special session at the capitol building. A new statehouse, the one that stands today, remained under construction after the old wooden capitol burned during General Sherman's march through Columbia at the end of the war. Instead, the eager group of mostly novice politicians gathered at Janney's Hall, an entertainment venue near the capitol grounds.[1] Among the freshmen legislators were Joseph Rainey and Richard Cain in the senate, and Robert Smalls, Robert De Large, Alonzo Ransier, and Robert Brown Elliott in the house.

The Reconstruction-era South Carolina state capitol with a temporary roof that enabled the state's only Black majority legislature to meet in the building in 1869 after starting their session the previous year in Janney's Hall, 1873. (Richard Weam and William Hix, Stereograph of the State House, Historic Columbia collection, HCF 2005.8.2)

These men must have felt a sense of pride and accomplishment that their first significant act as elected officials was ratifying the Fourteenth Amendment, which would grant citizenship and "equal protection under the law" to all people born or naturalized in America, regardless of race. I imagine the members of the First Eight, who took their place in South Carolina's first biracial legislature, experienced exhilaration and trepidation like I felt when I arrived in Columbia 102 years later.

I had hoped to be a member of the first biracial legislature in nearly seventy years when I got to the capital city. However, I didn't have the same success as members of the First Eight, despite our shared background as politicians grounded in civil rights attempting to secure the promise of America for people who were also descendants of the formerly enslaved.

As a student at South Carolina State College (now University) from 1957 to 1961, I, like many of the First Eight, became an active participant in my generation's efforts to freely exercise the rights granted to us via the Thirteenth, Fourteenth, and Fifteenth Amendments. I became a student protest leader and experienced several arrests and spent a few days in South Carolina jails. My fellow protesters and I faced blasts from fire hoses, blows from law enforcement batons, and racist taunts from angry white mobs. And like our predecessors, we remained undaunted because we believed in the righteousness of our cause.

Our efforts led to the enactment of the Civil Rights Act of 1964 and the Voting Rights Act of 1965, which gave African Americans the opportunity to be elected to office for the first time since Jim Crow restrictions imposed by Redeemer Democrats greatly curtailed their voting rights. In South Carolina, much like members of the First Eight did a century earlier, several of us sought legislative seats and, in 1970, four of us secured the Democratic nomination for the South Carolina House of Representatives: Herbert Fielding and I in Charleston County, and Jim Felder and I. S. Leevy Johnson in Richland County. On election night, all four of us were declared winners. But in the wee hours of the next morning, I was informed by an election supervisor that in my race "someone had failed to carry a one" when tallying the votes. Consequently, rather than winning by five hundred votes, as was announced the night before, I had lost by that margin.

Asked by a *Charleston News and Courier* reporter what happened in my race, I simply replied, "I didn't get enough votes." This didn't reflect the disappointment I felt following my loss. But my measured response and acceptance of the situation in that moment did more for my political future than I could have imagined.[2]

In a barrier-breaking moment, the newly elected Democratic governor John West saw my comment and almost immediately offered me a job in his administration. Just as the other three Black Democrats who ran would be the first African Americans in the state legislature since 1901, my new appointment meant I was likely the first Black advisor to a sitting South Carolina governor in the state's history.

I arrived in the state capitol in Columbia at the age of thirty — a young gun full of ideas and enthusiasm. Reality quickly set in. As eager as I was to get to work, others were not so accepting of my new role. In most meetings I attended, no one else looked like me. Most of the issues assigned to me were racially charged, and my efforts to address them met significant resistance. I knew the work would not be easy, but I also knew, just as the First Eight did, that how I conducted myself addressing these issues could determine the future of others hoping to follow in my footsteps.

The First Eight faced similar challenges, but their opposition was more overt, widespread, and coordinated. Local press directed vitriol toward the state's first biracial legislature, such as an *Edgefield Advertiser* editorial that declared: "South Carolina is...*Africanized*."[3] The *Fairfield Herald* wrote that the assembly of the new legislature was proof South Carolina had been "trampled beneath the unholy hoofs of African savages" and was now governed by "gibbering louse-eaten, devil worshiping barbarians."[4] These examples of false depictions of the Reconstruction era would become ingrained in the Redeemer narratives of this period and made it into our history books, to then be perpetuated for generations to come.

THE FIRST BIRACIAL LEGISLATURE

Despite the barbs hurled at them, the 1868 legislative session embodied the spirit of equality as spelled out in the Fourteenth Amendment. And within the overwhelming majority Republican legislature, thanks to the newly enfranchised Blacks remaining loyal to the "party of Lincoln," barriers began to fall away.

South Carolina now had several emerging Black leaders rising to positions of power. Rainey and Cain took their seats in the state senate, and Rainey was selected to chair the Senate Finance Committee. In the South Carolina House of Representatives, De Large, Elliott, Ransier, and Smalls were sworn in; De Large served as chairman of the Ways and Means Committee, Ransier as chair of the Committee on Privileges and Elections, and Elliott as chair of the Railroad Committee.[5] For the twenty-five-year-old Elliott, who had arrived in South Carolina just a year earlier, this marked a quick rise to political power.

Little is certain about Elliott's early life before he arrived in the state, something that may have been intentional on his part due to his political aspirations. Elliott's primary biographer concluded that he was likely born in Liverpool, England, to West Indian parents, making him a British citizen. There, he likely attended High Holborn Academy in London and graduated from Eton College in 1859 at age seventeen, though no existing records currently confirm that. From there, the possibilities diverge: Some reports say that following this education, Elliott served in the British navy and made his way to Boston on a warship. Others claim that after his British education, Elliott studied law in Massachusetts, and in 1863, enlisted in an all-Black Union regiment and fought in South Carolina until the end of the war. (Elliott himself implied he had served with the Union army and attributed his slight limp to a war wound, though it's worth noting that his name isn't found on any known Civil War military roster.)[6]

But another narrative emerged in South Carolina after Elliott's arrival in 1867, one that he may have disseminated himself. This theory held that he was actually born in Boston on August 11, 1842, to West Indian parents, and that following a private school education in the city, he was sent for further schooling in Jamaica. Elliott's biographer believes that he would have encouraged this story due to his aspirations to serve in the U.S. Congress, for which he would have been ineligible as a British citizen. Per the Constitution, an individual must be a naturalized American citizen for at least seven years to be eligible to serve.[7] Having Boston to point to as a birthplace — or at least, having the benefit of the doubt when it came to his potential British origins — would have eased his political path.

Whether he was born in England or Massachusetts, Elliott's life became well documented after he arrived in South Carolina. In 1867, he began working as an assistant editor at the *South Carolina Leader* newspaper with his future congressional colleague Richard Cain. In 1868, as he took his place in the new biracial legislature, Elliott also became one of the first three African Americans admitted to the South Carolina Bar Association, and he co-founded the nation's first known Black law firm in Charleston.[8]

One of Elliott's law partners, William J. Whipper, also became an important Black political leader in South Carolina. Both men married into the prominent mixed-race Rollin family, which put them squarely among the Black elite of the day. The home of the Rollin sisters, who were described by one historian as "the social arbiters of negro and Radical society in the city," served as a gathering spot for the politically connected.[9]

Elliott enjoyed the revelry of Columbia, and his gregarious nature and quick wit helped him gain popularity; but he also had a hot temper. One notable incident occurred on October 25, 1869, when Elliott horsewhipped a white man, who was an assistant private secretary to the governor, in front of the state executive building. The fit of rage was sparked by a letter the secretary had sent to Elliott's wife, suggesting a rendezvous. According to the *Charleston Daily News*, when the secretary's associates made threats on his life, Elliott "stood his ground."[10]

In his work, Elliott's quick temper often manifested itself in verbal assaults on colleagues with whom he disagreed, irrespective of party or race. In September 1868, Elliott's ire targeted Robert De Large, whose "prickly personality" and insatiable need to seek recognition often resulted in conflicts with his peers.[11] De Large had made disparaging remarks on the house floor against Elliott's law partner and fellow representative, William Whipper, over something insignificant. Elliott defended Whipper, calling De Large a "pygmy who is trying to play the part of a giant." He then accused De Large of speaking only to impress the reporters in the chamber, describing him as "elocutionizing himself into a perspiration which stood out upon his skin like warts."[12]

But as Elliott continued to develop a career in public service, he gained a more positive reputation as "one of the most brilliant political organizers in South Carolina during Reconstruction," according to the Reconstruction-era historian Eric Foner. In a sentiment that feels backhanded today, the *Chicago Tribune* wrote of Elliott, "Some think he is the ablest negro, intellectually, in the South."[13] But even that begs the question, what non-Black in the North was more able?

For indeed, Elliott had very quickly become one of South Carolina's most celebrated statesmen, all in spite of early setbacks. One came from Frank Moses, a former Confederate who was once an aide to South Carolina's secessionist governor and later became a "scalawag"—the Redeemer Democrats' derisive term for a native white South Carolinian who aligned with the Republican Party. After they both secured spots in the first biracial legislature, Moses and Elliott ran against each other for speaker of the house. Members of the Brown Fellowship Society in the house supported Moses's candidacy and thwarted the dark-skinned Elliott's opportunity to break the barrier, although he would later succeed.[14]

Perhaps as a consolation prize, Speaker Moses appointed Elliott to serve as assistant adjutant general for the new state militia, which would support existing federal troops.[15] This precursor to today's National Guard was formed to provide protection for Blacks against the growing racial and political violence by paramilitary terrorist groups.

And so it was that despite his volatile personality, Elliott's advantageous marriage, charisma, and political acumen quickly elevated this dark-skinned "carpetbagger"—a derogatory term for a Northern Republican

Robert Brown Elliott portrait, 1874. (The Miriam and Ira D. Wallach Division of Art, Prints and Photographs: Print Collection, The New York Public Library)

who'd moved to South Carolina to take advantage of its changing political landscape—to a place of power and privilege. Elliott also proved to be a consummate politician and a quick study, known for having a photographic memory. One law partner said that Elliott "knew the political condition of every nook and corner throughout the state," as well as "every important person in every county, town or village and the history of the entire state as it related to politics."[16] In the political arena, knowing your constituency and being responsive to their needs is paramount—a lesson that remains relevant and that I carry with me to this day.

Over the years, many in the media have credited my success in politics to what they call "the Clyburn machine," referring to the significant impact my endorsements have had in recent presidential primaries. I consider this a slight to my political acumen and aptitude, which I've developed after a lifetime of public service. My legislative and congressional achievements are enviable, but they are not the stuff of a political machine. Like many of the First Eight, I grew my political base through my memberships and participation in organizations, my lifelong involvement in the Black church, and the efforts I make to understand my constituents and work to help them fulfill their dreams and aspirations.

RISE OF THE KU KLUX KLAN

The Ku Klux Klan (KKK), founded in 1865 in Pulaski, Tennessee, began organizing in South Carolina after ratification of the 1868 Constitution, and targeted Republican voters and elected officials in hopes of ending their political power. On October 16, 1868, three men believed to be members of the KKK shot and killed Benjamin Randolph, the Black Republican Party chair and a member of the South Carolina Senate. The audacious murder occurred at a train station in broad daylight, and no arrests were ever made. Yet Randolph's violent death was not an isolated incident.

The KKK identification of prominent Republicans was facilitated by a composite containing the images and names of the "Radical Members of the South Carolina Legislature" — members of the Republican Party, white and Black. This document was published in various forms and sizes, from posters to pocket cards, created and widely distributed by Redeemer Democrats to scare white citizens. It also placed a target on the backs of the Republican officials depicted. James Martin, a white legislator from Abbeville County included in the composite, met a violent death on his way home from the county courthouse, just eleven days before the murder of his colleague Benjamin Randolph. In June of that same year, Representative Solomon Dill, a white Republican from Kershaw County, was shot and killed in his home before the special session of the General Assembly convened. A Newberry County Union League president, Lee Nance, who was not elected to office, was also among the Republican leaders killed during 1868, allegedly at the hands of the KKK. No one was ever convicted for any of these murders.[17]

After Randolph's assassination, Alonzo Ransier replaced him as the Republican Party chairman. Described by Elliott's biographer as a "typical compromise candidate, a reliable party workhorse, if not a great moving spirit," Ransier had a steady countenance that led him to write a letter to

Redeemer Democrats created this composite, which they labeled "Radical Members of the South Carolina Legislature" as a means of targeting Black and white Republican elected officials for retribution, 1868. (Courtesy of Princeton University Library)

the *Charleston Courier* two days after Randolph's death, urging calm.[18] He cautioned:

> I know there are times when forbearance ceases to be a virtue. I share with you the feeling of indignation, which uncontrolled would lead me to seek vengeance by retaliation. But bear and forbear. The day of our political deliverance is at hand. Let not these outrages intimidate you or lead you to measures of retaliation by which possibly the innocent may suffer along with the guilty.[19]

I hear echoes of my good friend John Lewis in Ransier's call for nonviolence — something my contemporary internalized, but with which I always struggled.

Richard Cain, who had served alongside Randolph in the senate, sent a letter to Governor Scott a week after the murder to report rumors that the KKK planned to assassinate more Charleston Republicans. "We have no confidence in the troops stationed here," he wrote, continuing, "The present police are Democrats and some of them are in the *plot* to murder us."[20] Cain's daughter would later lament, "From the moment he became a candidate for delegate to the [1868] Constitutional Convention, a guard was necessary night and day to watch our homes...We, his family, lived in constant fear at all times."[21]

Meanwhile, as the Klan's political violence rose, another election was taking place. In the run-up to November 1868, Redeemer Democrats struggled to overcome the political might of the newly enfranchised Republican-leaning Black majority. But the KKK, by this point functionally a political arm of the Redeemer Democrats, was not to be deterred; they drew on their Confederate military service to plan what the Board of State Canvassers characterized as "a wholesale system of proscription, terrorism, and assassination." In other words, as the U.S district attorney for South Carolina explained, the Klan intended to defend "the Constitution *as it was*, not as it *now* is."

On the eve of the election, hooded Klansmen "patrolled" the streets of Black neighborhoods, warning Republicans not to go to the polls. For those brave enough to attempt voting, once they arrived, some white election officials claimed they were not registered. In other places, Redeemer Democrats took extraordinary measures, such as carrying ballot boxes to bedridden supporters and allowing underage and out-of-state students at Newberry College to vote.[22]

In Edgefield, historically the epicenter of white domestic terrorism in the state, Redeemers took even more extreme measures, moving the ballot box from its traditional place on the courthouse portico to a room inside. Armed white men filled the interior of the courthouse and surrounded the outside on horseback. They let in only white voters. At the end of Election Day, just thirty-five Blacks had voted at the precinct, and then only because a U.S. Marshall accompanied them.[23]

However, despite the tactics—or "creative devices," as I call them—of the Redeemers and their armed militia, Republicans prevailed in the election, holding the state legislature and all eight statewide positions. And when they took office, they did not allow the chaos of the election to go unaddressed.

The South Carolina House of Representatives established a committee in 1869 to investigate political violence in the state, and Elliott and Smalls were among its members. During the proceedings, Elliott questioned the acting white Constable overseeing the Third Congressional District, an area that included Edgefield and had been the site of four political killings in 1868. Elliott, who would soon represent the district in Congress, asked the Constable about the tactics used by the Klan at polling places. The Constable reported that the Redeemers had threatened Black voters, and had said that "if they voted they would not hire them, and they should not have houses to live in." In response, he had appointed thirteen other constables to stand guard at the polling places, but said, "Not one would serve...they were...afraid of violence from Democrats. That is what they told me."[24]

In the end, the committee traveled to four upstate counties and collected eight hundred pages of testimony. The General Assembly, however, failed to take any action on the report.[25]

LEGISLATING CIVIL RIGHTS

Reelected to a second term in the South Carolina House, Smalls began to find his voice as a legislator, and he used it to seek greater equality for his community. Congress had enacted the Civil Rights Act of 1866, which declared that anyone born in the United States, "without distinction of race or color, or previous condition of slavery or involuntary servitude," was a citizen who possessed equal rights under the law. In the spring of 1870, Smalls introduced supplementary legislation to impose penalties for violating African Americans' right to public accommodations, something establishments in South Carolina did regularly in defiance of federal law.

As he proposed it, this legislation prohibited any business requiring a license or charter from discriminating based on race. Any violator would lose their license or charter, be fined one thousand dollars, and face up to three years in prison. The measure easily passed the Black-majority house. But the predominantly white senate, which included white Republicans, attempted to significantly water down the legislation, a hint at the emerging divide between white and Black members of the governing party.

In a stroke of irony, De Large, a Confederate veteran, charged the senate with trying to deny equal rights to those who fought and bled for the Union cause. Ransier, meanwhile, spoke out against the white senators' attempt to delay the already diluted legislation's implementation until May 1, 1870, at the request of Charleston's new Academy of Music. They wanted to open with segregated seating for its performances.

Ultimately, Black Republicans prevailed, and the legislation passed without any significant differences from the house version. The owner of the Charleston Academy of Music was the only person ever convicted of violating the law, for refusing to allow Black patrons to sit in the theater's floor seats.[26]

The *Charleston Daily News* expressed the outrage felt by many white South Carolinians in both parties, writing that this legislation meant "colored men shall have a legal right to force themselves upon those who do not desire their company, [and] that they shall thrust themselves into the beds which were not made for them, and sit at tables which were not spread for them."[27] As was rapidly becoming clear, the debate over equality would only grow more contentious across racial lines in the years to come — one that was not strictly divided across party lines.

REPRESENTATION MATTERS

Despite increasing tensions between white and Black Republicans, African American leaders continued to exert pressure to move South Carolina closer to racial equality. A Flag Day commemoration at Charleston's Battery on June 14, 1870, turned into an opportunity for political speeches, as Black celebratory events often did. With the recent enactment of South Carolina's Civil Rights law and the ratification of the Fifteenth Amendment, African Americans felt emboldened to demand more political representation within the Republican Party.

At the gathering, speaker after speaker called for greater equity — acknowledging that without Black support, Republican candidates could not win elective office. De Large issued a veiled threat to party officials, proclaiming, "I hold that my race has always been Republican from necessity only."[28]

Ransier, who usually sought to stay above the fray, joined De Large in saying Blacks had been treated unfairly and should be given more representation, especially in political patronage positions. He declared, "Though we dread the issue, it must come." He then expressed concern that if the inequity within the Republican Party remained unaddressed, the racial division could eventually destroy the political alliance.[29]

The following month, De Large, Ransier, and other Black leaders organized a grassroots campaign across the state advocating for more African American representation, causing a rift between most white Republicans and their Black colleagues. De Large formed an important alliance with the powerful white Mackey family of Charleston, whose patriarch had served as president of the 1868 Constitutional Convention. This partnership divided the allegiance of white Republicans, but enough sided with the majority Black wing of the party that at their organizing convention, the De Large–Mackey faction prevailed by a slim margin. As a result, Republicans nominated a number of Black candidates for high office, including Ransier as Lieutenant Governor, and three of the four congressional seats had Black nominees: Rainey, Elliott, and De Large.[30]

Meanwhile, De Large, who was still serving in the South Carolina House, received another political appointment. The state legislature chose De Large to run the South Carolina Land Commission, created at Richard Cain's insistence during the 1868 Constitutional Convention. The first head of the commission, a white man who had in fact spoken out against the commission during the convention, demanded a $45,000 payoff to leave the post after grossly overspending his allocated resources and mismanaging the operation. De Large ran the agency for roughly a year and oversaw the sale of nearly two thousand acres of land to freedmen. However, his political opponents accused him of skimming money from the agency to pay for his congressional campaign, although no charges were filed. Given the real or imagined corruption at the Land Commission, the legislature lost confidence in the agency and disbanded it in 1872.[31] Critics of Reconstruction pointed to this as just one example of the corruption in Republican administrations, especially those with significant Black representation.

Was there any truth to these accusations? Undeniably, many politicians, particularly Black politicians, were leveled by Redeemer-generated controversy, with the aim of kneecapping the civil rights expansions they were fighting for. On the other hand, as one historian noted, this period was "an era when corruption was an ingrained feature of political life," regardless of party. Indeed, many lawmakers of the era, both Black and white, Republicans and Democrats, took bribes for votes on legislation or the appointment of U.S. Senate candidates, who were elected at the time by the state senate. Those who took bribes tried to justify their actions, arguing they would have voted the same way with or without the payoff. As one Black Republican suggested, "The Democrats would buy votes to get into power in order to take away our rights. Republicans, I believe, might buy them if they feared they were getting beat without it."[32] Whether or not this was true, Cain recognized the scope of the issue when he declared, "Get all the money you can, but vote right!"[33]

Corruption charges soon tripped up Cain, but not for his work as a legislator. His advocacy for land ownership as a means for Blacks to build wealth and self-sufficiency led him to purchase two thousand acres of land twenty miles west of Charleston in 1871. There, he founded the town of Lincolnville with a vision to create a Black enclave. To that end, Cain started an African Methodist Episcopal church and began selling plots of land between two and ten acres. However, Cain — whether through disorganization, arrangement, or something in between — failed to make any payments on his initial purchase of the land before he began reselling the property; he was indicted for fraud. Elliott served as Cain's attorney and got the charges dropped in exchange for Cain returning the money. When reporting on the incident, the *New York Times* wrote, "It can very safely be said that South Carolina has more criminals in office than any other state in the Union," to which Cain replied, "I have settled more colored people in comfortable houses than any other man in the State."[34]

The community of Lincolnville still exists today; in fact, a portion of it is in my congressional district. The diverse bedroom community of today may not be what Cain originally envisioned, but despite the "corruption" charges, he and I share the experience of encountering entrenched opposition when we've sought to improve the quality of life in African American communities.

While I have never faced charges of corruption, concocted or otherwise, I often find that my efforts to help Black communities are met with contempt and vitriol. For ten years, I fought to connect two rural Black communities, Rimini and Lone Star, via a bridge. These impoverished majority-Black towns lie along the banks of Lake Marion, a manmade body of water in central South Carolina created when a 1930s New Deal effort to electrify rural areas resulted in the damming of the Santee River. This project displaced Black families, and those that remained at the new lake's water edge were isolated, with no employment opportunities.

In 1968, the state legislature promised to reconnect these communities with the construction of a bridge. In 2003, their promise still unfulfilled, I re-raised the issue, with the support of forty legislators.[35] With ample funding from the government, the area could, I knew, support a commercial corridor that would bring much-needed economic development to the community. To that end, in 2005, I earmarked $25 million in federal transportation funding for a three-mile bridge and six miles of connecting roadways. This earned me a place in the Citizens Against Government Waste's Pig Book, an annual publication that lists purported areas of unnecessary government spending. Over the years, this "nonpartisan" but highly political organization, which was founded by a Ronald Reagan crony, has criticized many projects I've funded to support Black communities in my district, labeling efforts to support low-income neighborhoods and communities of color as a waste of taxpayers' money.

Opponents of the project called it a "bridge from nowhere to nowhere," a dog whistle implying that the African Americans who live there were nobodies.[36] The fight was tinged with racial animus. Some detractors drove by my office and questioned why one of my employees drove a Porsche. Graphic depictions of Black faces with menacing-looking afros filled their online chatrooms, a substitute for banned racial slurs. This area they dismissed as "nowhere" actually served as their weekend retreat for hunting and fishing. The reality was, they didn't want "their" playground disrupted for the betterment of local Black residents. They enlisted the support of local environmental groups and the governor and successfully killed the project.

But I was not deterred. In 1994, I created the Lake Marion Regional Water Agency (LMRWA) to provide safe drinking water and economic opportunities for those communities and surrounding residents. This time, I won. But the big winners are these communities. Because of the LMRWA, residents, schools, and small businesses now have access to safe drinking water. Because of that water system, several large industries have located in the area and are providing highly desirable jobs.

This happens time and again in many rural and Black communities. I, and many others in elective office, try to improve our constituents' quality of life, only to get struck down by the white hegemony that believes they know what is best for the people who live there. These predominantly Black communities never receive the investments or the attention necessary to improve their circumstances. In every election cycle, I get hit with accusations about the worthiness of my efforts—and in my case, and probably in Cain's, these are transparent efforts from the opposition to manipulate and control.

BREAKING THE CONGRESSIONAL COLOR BARRIER

African Americans in South Carolina had already participated in two elections by the time the nation ratified the Fifteenth Amendment in February 1870, and another historic election would take place that same year. Rainey, De Large, and Elliott all won their bids to serve in the Forty-Second Congress, while voters elected Ransier as lieutenant governor, the highest elected state constitutional office a Black person has ever attained in South Carolina, even in my lifetime.

After this historic election, Redeemer Democrats grew more animated in their defiance, which had been festering since secession. Media of the day only fanned the flames of violence. Following the 1870 election, the *Winnsboro News* declared, "This vile, rotten, wicked, corrupt and degrading regime must be reformed or overthrown...We see no practical method of accomplishing it except by some form of revolution."[37]

Undeterred, the Republicans continued the business of governing and breaking barriers. But before the three newly minted Black South Carolinians could take their history-making oath of office in March 1871 for the Forty-Second Congress, a vacancy occurred in the First Congressional District.

In early 1870, the Republican Benjamin F. Whittemore, a "carpetbagger" who was a white Methodist minister from Massachusetts, resigned the

First Congressional seat before the House could censure him for taking bribes for appointments to the U.S. military academies, leaving the position vacant partway through the term. A special election was called to fill the seat; Whittemore entered the contest to fill the position he had just vacated, and he won. But when he arrived in Washington, the House of Representatives refused to seat him, setting in motion a second special election.

As time was short, this special election was held on the same day as the general election for the Forty-Second Congress. Rainey, already the Republican nominee for the seat in that contest, became the nominee for both. He won two victories that day.

As a result, Rainey was sworn into Congress on December 12, 1870, to represent South Carolina's First Congressional District for the remainder of the Forty-First Congress, thereby gaining the distinction of being the first Black person to serve in the U.S. House of Representatives, an unexpected journey for this thirty-eight-year-old formerly enslaved legislator.

This "confident, attractive, outgoing man, with polished manners and regular features," as one historian described him, began life on June 21, 1832, on a plantation in coastal Georgetown, South Carolina.[38] The "owner" of the Rainey family allowed the patriarch to work as a barber on the side and keep some of his earnings. The money he earned enabled the elder Rainey to purchase his family's freedom in the early 1840s, and they moved to Charleston, where there were more opportunities for free mixed-race Blacks.

Rainey trained as a barber under his father and eventually opened his own shop, Rainey's Hair Cutting Salon, at the Mills House at the corner of Queen and Meeting Streets, which still exists as a hotel today. (A restoration of the Mills House took place when I lived in Charleston in the 1960s, and its lounge was one of my and my political associates' favorite watering holes. I may have spent as many hours talking politics at the Mills House as Rainey did.)

In Rainey's day, conversations would have flowed freely in barbershops and beauty salons and often would have drifted to politics. This is a tradition that has persisted. In my childhood, my mother, a beautician, opened her first hair salon in the front room of our home in Sumter, and I learned at an early age that her business was more than a place to get your hair done; it was a gathering place for the Black community, and political discussions were popular. In fact, I often joke that I visit my barber regularly, although I rarely need a haircut. I go there to get the pulse of the community. Underscoring the importance of hair salons in modern-day politics, my barbershop — Toliver's Mane Event — in Columbia has become a go-to spot for presidential candidates as they stump for votes in the hotly contested South Carolina Democratic presidential primary, and photographs of those visits are prominently displayed.

After the first shots of the Civil War were fired within blocks of his barbershop, Rainey had to leave his beloved profession; the Confederate army conscripted Rainey against his will to help build fortifications in the city. He later worked as a steward on a blockade runner taking goods from Charleston to Bermuda. Having no interest in defending slavery, this assignment afforded Rainey and his family the opportunity to escape to the British island territory that had banned slavery in 1834.

In Bermuda, Rainey's wife opened a dress shop, while Rainey renewed his passion for barbering, opening storefronts in the cities of Hamilton and St. George. Bermudans regarded him so highly that the street where his St. George shop was located was later named Barber's Alley in his honor.[39] Being a barber put Rainey in a position to serve a well-to-do clientele, so although he was denied an education while enslaved in South Carolina, he learned the classics from his customers in Bermuda. As a congressman, he would demonstrate his education by peppering his speeches with quotes from the Bible, Plato, and Shakespeare.[40]

Rainey's success in business also contributed to his success in politics. After the Civil War ended, he moved back to Georgetown, and his wealth and experiences made him a prominent player in Republican politics, ultimately leading to his historic election to Congress.

Here I can't help pointing out a similarity between Rainey's early life and my own. My mother, Almeta Dizzley Clyburn, was born on a cotton farm in Lee County, South Carolina. Moms, as I affectionately called her, convinced her father to allow her to attend high school in nearby Camden. Like Rainey's father, she started a beauty salon business. Like Rainey, she received a more robust education later in life — though while his was through business, hers was through a college degree. She hung her diploma on a wall in her beauty shop as a testament to her intellect.

Moms enjoyed the independence of proprietorship and knew she would earn much more financially as an entrepreneur than she ever would utilizing her teaching degree, especially in an era of segregated schools and unequal pay.[41] As I got into politics, I was grateful for her active participation in the South Carolina Cosmetology Association, whose members have been some of my staunchest advocates in every campaign I ever ran.

Portrait of Joseph Hayne Rainey, c. 1870. (Schomburg Center for Research in Black Culture, Photographs and Prints Division, New York Public Library)

Despite Rainey's place in history, when I arrived in Congress, I found no evidence that he had ever been there. As a former history teacher, I recognize how important it is for us to know our past, and I often refer to the hall of the House as America's classroom. So, I led the charge to rectify the slight. In 2005, I proudly assisted in unveiling a portrait of Rainey, which

I helped to secure, in the U.S. Capitol. The portrait was hung above the landing on the grand marble staircase that leads from the first floor of the Capitol to the House chamber.

Then, in 2020, while I was serving as the House majority whip, we commemorated the 150th anniversary of Rainey's arrival in Congress. That year, I introduced and secured passage of legislation to designate a room in the U.S. Capitol in Rainey's honor. We selected H-150 in the Hall of Columns, a prominent corridor near the south entrance that many members of Congress, their staff, and visitors pass through daily. Rainey's portrait was relocated from the staircase landing to a wall adjacent to H-150. Both these commemorations are important ways to recognize Rainey's place in history and ensure future generations will know of his contributions.

When Rainey took office, he caused quite a sensation, positive and negative alike. Newspapers of the day heralded him as "an able man, [who] will do himself and his constituents credit," but also derided him as "snuff-colored contraband" who, they allowed, "dresse[d] unusually well for a Southern member of Congress."[42] Because he was a barber, his appearance received much attention. News reports described Rainey as "a bright mulatto, with straight hair and bushy side whiskers" and said he appeared to be "agreeable and intelligent."[43]

Rainey's historic arrival in the House was met with mixed emotions from the public, but the scene inside was different. When the New York Tribune described Rainey's swearing in, they noted the moment when "the hum and buzz of voices ceased on the floor, and almost every member turned with an air akin to respect, toward the first representative on that floor of the newly enfranchised race."[44] And when the Massachusetts senator Charles Sumner, one of Congress's leading abolitionists and proponents of equal rights, greeted Rainey on his first visit to the Senate, it was with the words, "I welcome you to this Chamber. Come over frequently; you have rights here."[45]

CHAPTER 5

ALARM BELLS

—— 1871–1872 ——

"Tell me nothing of a constitution which fails to shelter beneath its rightful power the people of a country."
—Joseph Hayne Rainey

A s SOUTHERN BLACKS CONTINUED to make political progress during 1871 and 1872, they encountered still more vitriol and violence. Paramount among this was the growing influence of the KKK. Prodded by the newly elected members of the First Eight, a Republican president and a Republican Congress tried to use both appeasement and punishment toward those responsible for the backlash.

The Forty-Second Congress was convened in March 1871, where Joseph Rainey was joined by Robert Elliott and Robert De Large. When the three Black South Carolinians arrived at the U.S. Capitol, it looked much like it does today: The new House and Senate wings had been completed before the Civil War, and the new cast-iron dome had been finished in 1865. Washington then, as it does now, also had a burgeoning Black community; in 1871, its population of 120,000 people included 45,000 African Americans.[1]

Despite this, Congress had been all white until Rainey was sworn in on December 12, 1870. Rainey, Elliott, and De Large, who had previously served together in the South Carolina General Assembly, found a very

The U.S. Capitol as it looked when the first Black Congressmen arrived, 1868. (Library of Congress, Prints and Photographs Divsion, LC-DIG-stereo-1s53396)

different dynamic in their new posts. South Carolina's first biracial legislature had a significant Black membership, and they enjoyed leadership roles and equal treatment. Columbia also provided a lively social scene for Blacks, although many of the gatherings were segregated. Washington, on the other hand, was lonely and isolating, traits that were emphasized as the august body and city adjusted to shifting race relations.

Colorism also presented challenges, especially for one of the new arrivals to the U.S. House. Although Elliott wasn't the only African American to serve in Congress, his colleagues of color were lighter skinned and mixed race. Described as the first "genuine African" in Congress, Elliott fully grasped the gravity of his dark skin when he delivered his first floor speech on March 14. He later recalled:

> I shall never forget that day, when rising in my place to address the House, I found myself the center of attraction.

Everything was still. Those who believed in the natural inferiority of the colored race appeared to feel that the hour had
arrived in which they should exult in triumph over the failure
of the first man of "the despised race" whose voice was about
to be lifted in that chamber. The countenance of those who
sympathized with our cause seemed to indicate their anxiety
for my success, and their heartfelt desire that I might prove
equal to the emergency. I cannot, fellow citizens, picture to
you the emotions that then filled my mind.[2]

My arrival in Washington also happened at a time of great change in
Congress, but my experience differed significantly from that of my eight
predecessors.

In January 1993, the 103rd Congress received much fanfare for being
the largest freshman class in the U.S. House of Representatives since
1948. Eva Clayton of North Carolina was elected to serve as president
of the 110-person class for the first session, and I was elected to serve
for the second. I found this role very helpful, in part because the 103rd
Congress had thirty-nine Black House members, something the House
historian would later describe as "a transformative moment in the history of African American political representation." Seventeen of us
were new, an interesting phenomenon considering the total number
of Blacks that served in Congress during the entire nineteenth century
was also seventeen. Notably, eight of us were the first African Americans to represent our states since that period. I cannot understate how
historic it felt to be a part of a group that the House historian acknowledged "dramatically altered the composition of Black representation in
Congress."[3]

My membership in such a notable class of Black congresspeople differed in obvious ways to Rainey's arrival on Capitol Hill. In the remaining months of the Forty-First Congress, before the arrival of Elliott and
De Large, Rainey stood alone in the House, without the camaraderie and
support I enjoyed when I came to Washington. He had just one Black

colleague—Hiram Revels, a Mississippian who was sworn into the U.S. Senate in February 1870.

When De Large and Elliott joined Rainey in the Forty-Second Congress, they had two other Black colleagues in the freshman class: Benjamin Turner of Alabama and Josiah Walls of Florida. And while six African Americans serving in Congress—five in the U.S. House—was historic, this accomplishment did not lead to celebrations in many segments of the population. Rather, it stoked serious fear and trepidation among white supremacists.

A famous *Currier & Ives* depiction of the Black members of the Forty-First and Forty-Second Congresses. From left to right: Senator Hiram Rhodes Revels of Mississippi, Representatives Benjamin Sterling Turner of Alabama, Robert Carlos De Large of South Carolina, Josiah Thomas Walls of Florida, Jefferson Franklin Long of Georgia, Joseph Hayne Rainey of South Carolina, and Robert Brown Elliott of South Carolina, 1872. (Library of Congress, Prints and Photographs Division, LC-DIG-ppmsca-17564)

CONFEDERATE AMNESTY

One of the first issues presented to the Forty-Second Congress involved the Fourteenth Amendment, which granted citizenship to all born in the United States, regardless of race or previous bondage. Section three of the amendment, the "disqualification clause," prohibited men who "engaged in insurrection or rebellion against" the United States from serving in elective office. But now there was a new proposal—a piece of legislation known as the Amnesty Act that would override the clause and lift these restrictions against most former Confederates.[4]

Just ten days after being sworn into Congress, with all eyes focused on him, Elliott delivered an impassioned plea against the Amnesty Act. He recoiled against the bill, which he characterized as "nothing but an attempt to pay a premium for disloyalty and treason at the expense of loyalty." He accused the former planter class, the oligarchs of his day, of if not participating directly in the KKK's activities, at least orchestrating their efforts to disenfranchise Black voters. The Amnesty Act, Elliott said, would reward this bad behavior; he called for efforts that would instead end the Klan violence and intimidation across the South.

Two days after his floor speech, the *New York Tribune*, a Republican newspaper that in the past would have championed the cause of Black members of Congress, criticized Elliott's accusations against the Southern oligarchs as an "obvious" mistake, insisting there was no proof that Confederate leaders were guiding the Klan's actions.

Elliott and his Black colleagues tried their best to counter the disinformation of the day, but it was a monumental task for such a small group of Black men to capture the nation's attention. Elliott wrote a scathing response that the paper printed on its front page, in which he proclaimed, "Possibly, Mr. Editor, your graciousness to recalcitrant Confederates would be somewhat modified if you lived, as I do, within the theatre of their operations. Men often bear the misfortunes of their neighbors with great equanimity and are ready most graciously to forgive wrongs to which they cannot be personally subjected."[5]

De Large also delivered a floor speech on the Amnesty Act, but, as he often did, took a different approach from that of his Black colleagues. He spoke in favor of the legislation, believing that restoring former Confederates' suffrage and the ability to hold elective office would make them more supportive of the Reconstruction government.[6] The Republican president, Ulysses S. Grant, shared De Large's position and issued pardons to all but five hundred former Confederate leaders, hoping it would help achieve his campaign slogan "Let us have peace."[7] A naïve position for both leaders to take, at best, as the Redeemers had never given any indication that the harassment of Blacks and Republicans would end if their voting rights were restored.

The Blacks in South Carolina's delegation split. Elliott and Rainey voted against the Amnesty Act, while De Large voted for it. The measure passed the House with seventy percent of the vote.[8]

Centuries after the fact, the Amnesty Act received renewed attention following the January 6 insurrection at the U.S. Capitol in 2021, during which armed supporters of President Donald Trump attempted to stop the Electoral College's certification of President-Elect Joe Biden's victory. This violent attack resulted in five deaths, numerous injuries, and the destruction of federal property. I was among the congressional leadership that was evacuated from the House chamber when the violent mob breached the Capitol that day.

Numerous court cases cited the Fourteenth Amendment's disqualification clause, arguing that it meant President Trump and several members of Congress could not hold elective office due to their roles in inciting the mob's actions. However, the U.S. Supreme Court ruled that only Congress, not the states, could use section three to keep a federal candidate off the ballot.[9]

I support the rule of law, and because the United States is a democratic nation, we must abide by the Supreme Court decision. Yet I am reminded that the high court is not immune to partisan and popular influence and has a history of issuing decisions that have had horrific consequences for people who look like me. Indeed, in their years of service to come, members of the First Eight would suffer from the fallibility of the American legal justice system.

CHALLENGING THE KLAN

While the congressional debate over the Amnesty Act was unfolding, South Carolina's Black political leaders were also focused on protecting the promise in the Declaration of Independence of "life, liberty and the pursuit of happiness" to all—rights that were under threat by the Ku Klux Klan in their communities. As Joseph Rainey powerfully argued, "Tell me nothing of a constitution which fails to shelter beneath its rightful power the people of a country."[10]

Republican leaders employed the state militia to combat the growing lawlessness. This militia had grown to twenty thousand strong and was almost exclusively Black, because most whites refused to serve side by side with African Americans. Rather than quelling the KKK's activities, however, the militia only enraged the Redeemers. Blacks with firearms served as a trigger for whites dating back to the antebellum era, when the oppressors feared being violently overthrown by the oppressed. This anxiety resulted in a Klan obsession to disarm Blacks so they could not retaliate, and the mounting tension would soon play a significant role in one of South Carolina's deadliest racial confrontations.[11]

Meanwhile, on the federal level, Republicans in Congress had sought to address the political bloodshed in the South by enacting the Enforcement Act of 1870. This law prohibited the use of violence, intimidation, or bribery to infringe on a person's right to vote, and gave the president the authority to use the military and federal marshals to enforce the law. In February 1871, two months after Rainey took office, Congress passed a second Enforcement Act, which provided federal oversight of congressional elections.

Despite the passage of these important tools, the disenfranchisement continued. In an effort to stop this "bloody war of extermination," South Carolina's lieutenant governor, Alonzo Ransier, traveled to Washington in March 1871, with a biracial state delegation of twenty Republicans to present boxes of evidence to the Grant administration with the clear message: Republicans are under siege and need federal intervention. Indeed, between the November 1870 election and the summer of 1871, the Klan murdered more than six hundred men in South Carolina. All the while, Republican officials were resigning in droves, citing threats upon their lives. Lawlessness and terror controlled the state, and there was little its government could do to defend its citizens.[12]

Ransier's trip to the capital occurred just after the Forty-Second Congress, which included Rainey, Elliott, and De Large, was sworn in. President Grant, who had been reluctant to address the troubling political conditions in the South, heard the pleas of Ransier's delegation and other Southern states and asked the newly seated Congress to act.[13] The House quickly took up a third Enforcement Act, later known as the Ku Klux Klan Act, that enabled the president to suspend habeas corpus and round up suspected Klan members without charging them, and that expanded the authority of federal attorneys to prosecute the Klan.[14]

South Carolina's delegation felt strongly about this legislation, and despite their inexperience in Congress, they took to the floor to urge its passage. Robert Elliott, who had previously served on a South Carolina House committee investigating KKK atrocities, declared the bill was "not only fully warranted, but it [was] imperatively demanded by the present posture of affairs in the southern states." To support his position, Elliott submitted a report to Congress with a record of incidents of Klan violence in his district.[15]

In response to the Black Republicans, who were finally giving voice to the five million African Americans of the day, Redeemer Democrats resurrected the issue of "states' rights." Adherents to this conservative political philosophy, championed in the antebellum period by South Carolina's U.S. senator John C. Calhoun, believed that states could reject any federal law with which they disagreed. (One historian would later dub Calhoun "the man who started the Civil War" for his efforts to fan the flames of secession over Southern states' perceived right to protect slavery from federal intervention.[16]) In the spirit of Calhoun, Redeemer Democrats argued against the KKK Act, saying it would centralize power in the federal government and diminish the power of the states.[17]

Portrait of John C. Calhoun, the father of "states' rights," 1852. (Library of Congress, Prints and Photographs Division, LC-DIG-pga-02499)

Opponents also asserted the bill was unconstitutional because it allowed federal intervention without state request. Just twenty-eight years old and already a very effective lawyer, Elliott took to the floor on Saturday, April 1, 1871, with a "voice clear and penetrating" and delivered a speech that "had a finish and elegance not often heard in Congress oratory," according to press reports. He argued that the federal government's failure to intervene in the face of domestic terrorism would "render the Government of the United States a torpid and paralyzed spectator of the oppression of its citizens."[18]

Elliott's colleague Joseph Rainey spoke on the floor that same evening, also making the case for federal intervention. He argued, "Even now, after the great conflict between slavery and freedom...we can yet see the traces of the disastrous strife and the remains of disease in the body-politic of the South.... The prevailing spirit of the southerner is either to rule or to ruin. Voters must perforce succumb to their wishes or else risk life itself in the attempt to maintain the simple right of common manhood."[19]

When Robert De Large spoke on the KKK Act, he again showed his penchant for equivocating. After conceding that the KKK did pose a threat—though he proclaimed, "Until within the last few months, no one upon the face of God's earth could have convinced me that a secret organization existed in my State for the purpose of committing murder, arson and outrages"—De Large also noted that none of the "outrages" had occurred in his district, despite its sixty-eight percent Black constituency.

In a side note, that overwhelming Black majority didn't translate into political popularity for the mixed-race congressman. In the 1870 election, De Large faced opposition from a white Independent Republican, and he won the seat by less than one thousand votes, just fifty-three percent support.[20] If it is true that De Large's district didn't experience much voter intimidation, his lack of popularity among a Black constituency in want of political representation may have stemmed from his longstanding efforts to appease both sides of the racial divide.

Ultimately, when pressed, De Large fell in with Rainey and Elliott. But, as was his way, he tried to strike a deal with a Missouri Democrat on the Amnesty Act, which at the time was still being debated: If the Democrat would support the legislation to rein in the paramilitary violence and intimidation, De Large would in turn support the Amnesty Act. In a floor speech, De Large declared, "Neither the Republicans of my State nor the Democrats of that State can shake their garments and say that they have had no hand in bringing about this condition of [lawlessness]. Both parties are responsible for it." He explained that he blamed Black Republicans for putting their faith in unscrupulous white Northerners who came to South Carolina to enrich themselves.[21]

De Large's argument didn't sway the Missouri Democrat or any of his Redeemer colleagues, but with Republican majorities in both chambers, it took only six weeks to enact the KKK Act. This new federal law created the U.S. Justice Department to "take on the worst law enforcement crisis in the nation's history," as one historian characterized it.[22] While the country had an individual serving as attorney general since 1789, the sheer volume of legal cases that stemmed from the Klan's rampant domestic terrorism warranted an entire federal agency and its team of lawyers to enforce the protections provided by the Fourteenth and Fifteenth Amendments.

The Klan quickly directed its anger at the new law toward the Black congressmen, whom they held responsible. Less than a month after the law was enacted, Rainey received a threatening letter with a skull and crossbones. Written in red ink, it said, "K.K.K. Beware! Beware! Beware! Your doom is sealed in blood." It continued, "Prepare to meet [your] God. Take heed, stay not. Here the climate is too hot for you. We warn you to flee. You are watched each hour. We warn you to go." Rather than be cowed by this threat, Rainey sent the letter to the *Washington Chronicle*, asking them to publish it and to end speculation that reports of the KKK's violence were untrue.[23] A South Carolina newspaper brushed even this off, proclaiming that Rainey had fallen for "a very poor joke." Rainey knew better but remained resolute in the face of the danger the KKK posed to himself and other Black Republicans. He declared, "[We] have come to the conclusion to remain, and, if needs [sic] be, sell our lives dear as the price of liberty and manhood."[24]

I, too, have been subjected to several threats in my public service career. When I was state human affairs commissioner, I became a vocal proponent of removing the Confederate flag that flew over South Carolina's capitol alongside the U.S. and state flags. In response, in 1987, I received a letter signed by "a larger than you think group" that read: "People have heard you run your mouth about our flag on the state house long enough. Best you shut your mouth before somebody pops a bullet between your eyes."

Since 2004, I have kept a framed picture over my desk that contains four letters I received on the same day, under the heading "All in a Day's Work." Three were letters of thanks from constituents, and the fourth was from a "gentleman" reacting to an interview I did on FOX News. It reads, "F— YOU! N—!! Your family should have been left in Africa or gotten by the sharks!! You . . . are part of what is wrong with America!!" Like Rainey, I know the magnitude of these threats, but rather than allow them to intimidate me as intended, I use them as reminders of the work that is necessary to move our nation toward a "more perfect Union."

In this way, I understand those Black members of Congress who showed enormous courage in their vocal support of the KKK Act. Still, despite his show of bravery, Rainey admitted to his fellow members of Congress, "When myself and colleagues shall leave these halls and turn our footsteps toward our Southern home, we know not but that the assassin may await our coming."[25] Elliott, meanwhile, privately expressed the bearing these threats had on their lives in a letter to his wife dated October 13, 1871, as he began his journey back home from Washington. He laid out the route he would take and instructed her how to access funds from their bank account and his life insurance policy should he not make it home, writing, "I do this, my dear, because life is uncertain."[26]

MAKING AN EXAMPLE OF SOUTH CAROLINA

As Elliott and his fellow members of Congress headed home for recess in October 1871, President Grant decided to use the authority given to him under the newly enacted KKK Act to make an example of South Carolina. He suspended habeas corpus in nine upstate counties and ordered federal troops to arrest Klan members. The roundup resulted in more than twelve hundred KKK cases to be tried.[27]

Because the Klan members had to be tried in federal court, they had to be charged with the limited federal crimes enumerated in the Enforcement Acts. For example, murder is a state crime, so Klan members accused of killing someone faced merely a federal conspiracy count of depriving "a citizen of his right to vote on account of race and color." As a result, five years in prison was the maximum penalty handed down, although most who pled guilty or were convicted ended up receiving even lighter sentences of just six to eighteen months. To add insult to injury, those facing justice were not the masterminds of the violence. Just as Elliott had warned, it was the former-Confederate gentry class, still leaders in their communities during Reconstruction, who had orchestrated the Klan's campaign of terror, and informants reported that as many as two thousand had escaped prosecution by fleeing South Carolina as the federal authorities moved in. Those captured, jailed, and tried were the foot soldiers: those of little means who had been incited to carry out the attacks by leaders who were nowhere to be found when the time came for accountability.[28] The more things change, the more they remain the same.

Even those leading the federal government's offensive against the KKK expressed concerns about the ability to sustain their efforts. Around this time, the U.S. attorney general, Amos Akerman, who oversaw the mass civil rights prosecutions of the Klan in South Carolina, told a colleague that there was a "very strong" feeling in Washington "that the Southern Republicans must cease to look for special support." Akerman also advised a Georgia Republican that the best course of action would be for Southern states to "stand on their own feet. They must not depend always on propping [up] from Washington."[29]

In December 1871, at President Grant's request, Akerman resigned because of growing "public sentiment" against federal intervention in the South. One historian would later point out that, in retrospect, "not for another century would the federal government have a leading law enforcement officer willing to vigorously prosecute civil rights violations in the South."[30]

Another modern-day historian characterized this limited period of federal prosecutions as "largely a matter of sweeping the dirt under the rug." Indeed, for every person who pled guilty, still more were pardoned, or tried then granted clemency. The effort stopped the Klan's efforts only temporarily.[31] By withdrawing its oversight, the federal government demonstrated that it didn't fully comprehend the conditions in the South.

Because of the lack of sustained federal intervention, Redeemer Democrats in South Carolina learned quickly, as one historian put it, that "Republicans...dealt in bluff, while conservatives dealt in blood."[32] In response, they regrouped and formed "rifle clubs" to skirt the prosecution of Klan members. At their peak, there were as many as three hundred rifle clubs in South Carolina with a combined membership of fifteen thousand men.[33]

When asked about the formation of rifle clubs, one white Charlestonian told a *New York Herald* reporter, "We have all around us negro national guards armed and equipped by the Legislature and at our expense.... Regiment after regiment is organized with n— colonels. [Ransier] the Lieutenant Governor of our State is a n—; there are seventy-four n— in the State Legislature who cannot read or write.... We are taxed until we can't draw breath, and...you...ask me what our boys are forming rifle clubs so suddenly for?"[34]

This statement summed up the grievances of the Redeemers. They promoted this narrative of their suffocation under "Black domination" widely, and Northerners saw it reinforced in their publications. Even in the Republican-leaning *New York Tribune* the reporter James S. Pike depicted the African Americans in South Carolina's legislature as lazy, ignorant, and corrupt. "Here, then, is the outcome, the ripe, perfected fruit of the boasted civilization of the South, after two hundred years of experience," Pike bemoaned, following a visit to the state. He continued, "It is the spectacle of a society suddenly turned bottom-side up."[35] Pike would go on to write *The Prostrate State*, a book that fostered Northern sympathies toward white Southerners, whom he described as subjected to "a mass of Black barbarism" during the "tragedy" of Reconstruction.[36]

These attitudes still exist in many places and continue to be expressed by many groups. KKK klaverns still proliferate, and there is today at least one rifle club still active in Charleston. After a highly publicized public spat, they recently admitted their first Black member. I wonder if that gentleman knows the club's history.

Harper's Weekly cartoon lampooning South Carolina's biracial legislature, 1874. (Library of Congress, Prints and Photographs Division, LC-DIG-ds-13145)

COLORED PEOPLE RECONVENED

On October 18, 1871, a Southern States Colored People's Convention gathered in Columbia to fashion a response to the KKK's escalating reign of terror and subsequent campaign to negatively shape public opinion on Black enfranchisement. Alonzo Ransier, the state's sitting lieutenant governor, served as president of the convention. That November, the delegates delivered a report to Congress on the state of the violence, estimating that since Reconstruction began, between fifteen and sixteen hundred "murders and outrages" had been committed against Blacks in the South.[37]

The report also addressed a concern held by many white citizens, emphasizing that the delegates merely sought equality for Blacks, not preference: "We do not ask the Government or people of the United States to treat us with peculiar favor, but that, in the policy of the laws...no invidious distinction be made to our prejudice," they wrote.

The Colored People's Convention reminds us that when they had the chance, Blacks didn't "seek instantaneous relief by imitating their oppressors and taking the law into their own hands."[38] While Redeemer Democrats pursued vigilante violence, they could not provoke their targets to retaliate in kind. I believe this is why Nicole Hannah-Jones, in her seminal work *The 1619 Project*, calls Blacks "the perfectors of this democracy."[39] The three Black members of the Forty-Second Congress from South Carolina, even with De Large's mollifications, set the example for many of their successors in taking the moral high ground. They worked within the law to push and pull our democracy toward its declaration that "all men are created equal."

Hannah-Jones's moniker applies to both past and recent political activists. There are no better examples than Martin Luther King Jr. and John Robert Lewis. Although King limited his activities to traditional civil rights, Lewis transitioned into politics, and why not? The blood he spilled on the Edmund Pettus Bridge in Selma, Alabama, on March 7, 1965, precipitated the passage of the Voting Rights Act, which was signed by President Lyndon Johnson that same year—and which made his and my elections to Congress possible. The dire need for the act, which protected the African American right to vote, cannot be understated: The year before its passage, just six percent of Blacks cast a ballot. By 1969, Black voter turnout increased to nearly sixty percent.[40]

The Voting Rights Act was signed into law on August 6, 1965, and on May 8, 1966, King visited Kingstree, South Carolina, where he delivered his "March on Ballot Boxes" speech. I was among the five thousand hardy souls in attendance in an open field on a rainy day. We were not disappointed. Dr. King's melodic oratory inspired us as he argued that exercising the hard-won franchise would enable Blacks to "have food and material necessities for their bodies, freedom and dignity for their spirits, [and] education and culture for their minds."[41] He knew, as the First Eight did, that the best protection of a democracy is a fair and unfettered vote.

A DISSIMILAR TRIO

Like Dr. King, Rainey, Elliott, and De Large sought access for those same pursuits for their constituents. As elected officials, they tried to work with their opponents without resorting to violence. They each took different approaches. I characterize one as the persuader, another as the appeaser, and the other as the orator; and they had varying degrees of success dealing with the Redeemer Democrats.

Rainey, The Persuader: The senior of the three by ten years, Rainey took an approach that appealed to the "better angels" in his opponents. He exemplified this effort when he said, "We would say to those gentlemen on the other side there is another class of citizens in the country, who have certain rights and immunities which they would like you, sirs, to remember and respect."[42]

Despite the hostility and falsehoods aimed at Blacks' pursuit of equal rights, African American leaders continued to make small steps toward progress. In March 1872, with the number of backlogged Klan cases in South Carolina, Rainey argued for Congress to provide more funds to the federal courts authorized by the KKK Act. During the debate, the New York Democrat Samuel Cox assailed South Carolina as a corrupt state, squarely placing the blame on its Black legislators.[43] It was clear that the disinformation tactics were working.

When De Large got caught up in accusations of fraud related to the State Land Commission, he responded to Cox in his combative way, arguing, "While there may have been extravagance and corruption resulting from the placing of improper men in official positions...these evils have been brought about by the men identified with the race to which the gentleman from New York belongs, and not by our race."[44]

Rainey, however, took a different tack, complimenting Cox as "a gentleman of talent and fine education" and then, with dignity and charm, declaring:

> If the colored people of South Carolina had been accorded the same advantages—if they had had the same wealth and surroundings which the gentleman from New York has had, they would have shown to this nation that their color was no obstacle to their holding positions of trust, political or otherwise.

Not having had these advantages, we cannot at the present time compete with the favored race of this country; but...if the gentleman from New York and other gentlemen on that side of the House will only accord to us right and justice, we shall show to them that we can be useful, intelligent citizens of this country. But...if they will continue to decry the Negro and crush him under foot, then you cannot expect the Negro to rise while the Democrats are trampling upon him and his rights. We ask you, sir, to do by the Negro as you ought to do by him in justice.[45]

The *New York Daily Herald* called Rainey's remarks "the greatest sensation of the season." His talent for persuasion succeeded in securing a one-million-dollar appropriation for the federal court.[46]

De Large, The Appeaser: While Rainey's prominence in Congress was rising, his colleague De Large faced a serious fight to keep his seat. Challenges to congressional seats occurred frequently during a period when dirty political tricks were rampant. In April 1872, De Large took a leave of absence from Congress, also common during that time, to prepare to defend his seat against a challenge from Christopher Bowen, the white Independent Republican who claimed he had won the close 1870 election against De Large.[47]

De Large's proclivity for offending his colleagues on both sides of the aisle, however, hampered his ability to defend his right to the seat before the House Committee on Elections. Democrats opposed him on political grounds, and Republicans withheld their support on very personal grounds; De Large had few allies due to his elitism, volatile temperament, and efforts to appease the oppressors. To add to his woes, De Large's health began to fail in the summer of 1872. Rainey stepped in on De Large's behalf to ask for a delay in the proceedings, but the committee refused.

During their testimony, Bowen accused De Large of stuffing ballot boxes with the help of white Republicans. In response, De Large charged

Bowen with bribing lawyers to withhold evidence that would exonerate him of these allegations. All the while, as De Large battled health issues, Bowen battled bigamy charges alleging he had married three women without divorcing his previous wives.

The *Chicago Tribune* said of the exchange, "It really seems that the only way a South Carolina politician can keep out of the State Prison or in Congress is by proving all the rest to be bigger scoundrels than himself." In the end, the committee determined that corruption was so rampant on both sides they could not issue a ruling. Instead, they declared the seat vacant on January 18, 1873, with fewer than three months remaining in the Forty-Second Congress.

Following his dismissal, De Large returned home to serve as a Charleston magistrate. But his health continued to deteriorate, and he died a year later of tuberculosis, one month shy of his thirty-second birthday.[48]

This proved to be an unceremonious end to the life of the only member of the First Eight toward whom I feel significant discomfort. De Large used colorism to enrich himself politically and personally, sometimes at others' expense. He also enjoyed the advantage of an education, made possible because of his mixed-race status, and had a sharp tongue that he used to tear others down in order to lift himself up. He did not hesitate to articulate the Black cause when it suited him. While he was not the first and certainly not the last to manipulate the colorism issue advantageously, I have little patience for his style of politics.

Elliott, The Orator: While De Large's "star-crossed career," as a modern-day House historian described his brief time in Congress, and life were cut short, Robert Elliott's reputation continued to grow. On April 16, 1872, the District of Columbia invited Elliott, a gifted orator, to keynote the tenth anniversary celebration of the end of slavery in the city, which came eight and a half months before the better-known Emancipation Proclamation ended slavery nationwide. Elliott took the stage to a warm welcome from the crowd, but rather than delivering the expected celebratory speech, he sounded alarm bells. Despite the era's many hard-earned achievements, he said, they must not become complacent. The "trite aphorism that 'revolutions never go backwards'" was a fallacy, he warned, continuing, "By the inscrutable order of Providence, the very dangers that menace our rights are intended to admonish us to be vigilant in guarding them."[49]

In 2016, I was honored to keynote the District of Columbia Emancipation Day celebration, 144 years after Elliott's speech. Although there was a more celebratory theme that year, I see extraordinary parallels between my predecessor's warning and the message I often repeat today: "Anything that has happened before can happen again." I often suggest that politics in America is like a pendulum. It sometimes moves from left to right and at other times from right to left, but in doing so it always passes through the center. At any moment, the overarching political sentiment can shift. Our history bears that out.

The activism of the 1950s and 1960s is often called the Second Reconstruction. I feel blessed to have come of age during that era, during which time I, and my fellow activists, took inspiration from the experiences of the First Eight. In Rainey, De Large, and Elliott's time, following passage of the Civil Rights Acts and other victories for Black Americans, a plethora of groups were formed to suppress the community's civil and voting rights; rifle clubs and the KKK came out of the shadows and undertook violent attempts to deny education and job opportunities to Blacks. Nearly a century later, the Supreme Court's 1954 *Brown v. Board of Education* decision to desegregate public schools generated fierce resistance — and Congress remained silent, but not groups like the John Birch Society, the White Citizens Councils, and, yes, the KKK. For the most part, we activists followed in the footsteps of Ransier's call for nonviolence, but sometimes we were as defiant as Rainey and others of the First Eight, who remained undeterred by the ever-present threats.

Today, some sixty years after the advances of the 1960s, we are again witnessing parallels to the backlash of the "First" Reconstruction, and for similar reasons. Census officials project that white Americans will become a minority of the U.S. population by 2045. Some feel uneasy about these changing demographics and are directing their insecurities at governmental efforts such as affirmative action and other diversity, equity, and inclusion programs, which are rapidly being dismantled. Much of the political rhetoric on the far right seems designed to divide, exclude, and insult, rather than honor America's motto, "E pluribus unum" — out of many, one. The political pendulum is again moving to the right. The question is how far will it go, and for how long?

In these times, I echo the sentiment expressed by Elliott in 1872. He reminded the majority Black crowd that it was their duty to exercise their hard-won rights, declaring, "Let us lift ourselves to the height of our responsibilities... and fear no danger... So living and so acting we shall be worthy of the high privileges we possess, worthy to perform our part in preserving the temple of liberty."[50]

THE 1872 ELECTION

Elliott's words of warning were ominous, but the dangers he foretold didn't immediately come to pass. Despite growing opposition, Republicans in South Carolina expanded their political power and gained an additional congressional seat, thanks to the Fourteenth Amendment, ratified in 1868, which repealed the three-fifths-of-a-person compromise. This infamous compromise held that, when determining a state's population for congressional representation, each of the enslaved would be counted as only three-fifths of a person. Its repeal made the census of 1870 the first to include the actual number of Blacks in America; and when South Carolina redrew its district lines, following the census as per the Constitution, the state gained a congressional seat.

Most of the five new congressional districts favored African American candidates by virtue of the state's nearly sixty percent Black majority. Rainey and Elliott overwhelmingly won reelection to their First and Third Congressional District seats respectively. Alonzo Ransier, the former Republican Party chairman and lieutenant governor, replaced De Large in the Second Congressional District and proved much more popular, winning the seat with seventy-five percent of the vote. Richard Cain, the AMEC minister and *Missionary Record* editor, ran successfully for the newly added at-large district, winning with seventy-one percent against three other candidates in the general election.

Their elections meant Black men held four of South Carolina's five seats during the Forty-Third Congress; a recent House historian described South Carolina at the time as "arguably... the crucible of the Black Congressional experience in the Reconstruction South." During the nineteenth century, seventeen Blacks served in the United States House of Representatives. In addition to South Carolina's eight were four from North Carolina, and one each from Virginia, Georgia, Florida, Alabama, and Mississippi.[51]

Like the election of the historic class of Black South Carolina congressmen in 1872, my historic election in 1992 came after a significant change in the state's congressional districts. As the country prepared to redistrict in accordance with the 1990 decennial, the states covered by the 1965 Voting Rights Act were informed by the United States Justice Department that a 1982 amendment to the act required new congressional districts to be drawn to allow opportunities for minority groups to elect candidates of their choosing. This resulted in many states, including South Carolina, drawing "racially proportional" districts.[52]

South Carolina responded by reapportioning the Sixth Congressional District with a fifty-eight percent Black majority. Four of us ran in the Democratic primary, and I prevailed with over fifty-five percent of the vote, and won the general election by thirty percent. I was sworn into the 103rd Congress in January 1993 at the age of fifty-two, older than any of the First Eight when they were first elected.

I relished this opportunity but felt no sense of certainty about the outcome. I was no stranger to losing. In addition to losing my race for the state house seat in 1970, I'd run for South Carolina secretary of state in 1978 and in 1986, losing both times in the Democratic primary. After that third loss, a friend asked me if, after "three strikes" against me, I should give up on my dream of serving in elective office. I replied, "Life should not be played by baseball rules."

By then, of course, the playing field had changed significantly from the time of my predecessors. Obstacles that had effectively kept those who looked like me from being elected to Congress from South Carolina for ninety-five years had been removed, and the country was beginning to move back to the left.

ALARM BELLS SOUND

While Black Republicans continued to make gains in 1872, on the gubernatorial level, Robert Elliott's warning rang true. Franklin Moses, a former secessionist turned Republican, won the governor's race in a close contest. Trouble began for Moses at the nominating convention when another gubernatorial hopeful, Daniel Chamberlain, and his supporters walked out in protest, accusing Moses of bribing his way to the nomination. Later, this would prove an accurate piece of foreshadowing: Moses would come to be known as "the Robber Governor" for accepting bribes and skimming money from the state's coffers during his administration. When he was eventually indicted for using state funds to pay off personal debts, Moses ordered the state's militia to stand guard around his home to prevent his arrest. His behavior drew the ire of President Ulysses S. Grant and national Republicans.[53]

Meanwhile, on the federal level, Redeemer Democrats were outraged by a string of recent Republican victories. An estimated forty thousand of their party members abstained from voting in the South Carolina election. Their dissatisfaction was not helped by the subsequent 1872 reelection of President Grant, Governor Moses, and four Black members of Congress, which threw gasoline on an already volatile political climate. General Wade Hampton III, the highest-ranking Confederate officer from South Carolina who had since become the Democrats' most revered standard-bearer, declared that the time had come for white Southerners to take up arms and "dedicate themselves to the redemption of the South."

As Redeemer Democrats prepared to follow General Hampton's directive, Black Republicans faced their own internal party outrages. President Grant, a Republican like Lincoln, had won the votes of South Carolina Black Republicans but then rejected their plea for sovereignty, a betrayal that foretold an ominous future.

Grant removed most federal cavalries from the state in 1872, and the remaining three cavalry companies left in March 1873, all of which were redirected to attend to the nation's defense during westward expansion. Although ten infantry companies remained in the state, the General Assembly passed a resolution proclaiming that their removal would be "detrimental to the permanent establishment and maintenance of law and order."[54] Their warning would soon prove prophetic.

PART II

REDEMPTION

CHAPTER 6

POLITICAL TIDES TURNING

—— 1873–1875 ——

"All we seek is equal laws, equal legislation, and equal rights."

—Richard Cain

A s THEY BLAZED TRAILS in Washington, members of the First Eight continued to face discrimination because of their skin color. While the federal government now recognized the rights of African Americans, the U.S. capital city still struggled to integrate them into the government and society at large. All the while, the pressure to push forward was enormous: The Black members represented only two percent of Congress, but they were also the primary advocates for the civil rights of five million African Americans.[1] Yet accusations of corruption, amplified by the Redeemers, threatened to turn the nation against their cause.

Meanwhile, the Forty-Third Congress had officially convened, and with it, the struggle to realize the promise that "all men are created equal" continued. Four of South Carolina's five Congressmen were African Americans, and they fought mightily to codify the citizenship rights granted by the Fourteenth Amendment with a proposed second Civil Rights Act.

The first Civil Rights Act of 1866 declared anyone born in America to be a citizen, regardless of race or previous enslavement. But it was clear that additional legal protections were needed in the face of continuing discrimination. Congress therefore sought to pass a subsequent Civil Rights Act, championed by Joseph Rainey, Robert Elliott, Alonzo Ransier, and Richard Cain, that codified citizens' rights to serve on juries and to have equal access to education, churches, and cemeteries, and to public accommodations and transportation, regardless of race—privileges that Black Americans were still being denied.

Members of the First Eight took to the floor to share their experiences with discrimination, reminding their colleagues that although they too were congressmen, they did not enjoy the same status as their white colleagues. Rainey specifically reported being "charged more for living," relaying his experience ordering a beer in Ralf's, a Washington establishment located near the Capitol. When the waiter there charged him ten times the regular price, Rainey asked, "Is [the upcharge] because I am a colored man?" The waiter responded yes, and Rainey left the restaurant "very much mortified." Members of Congress, he argued, "should not have to go out in fear and trembling when . . . seeking only common necessities of life."

His experience was not unusual. Despite city ordinances prohibiting discrimination in licensed restaurants, many establishments found workarounds, posting menus with exorbitant prices and tiny disclaimers that promised "a liberal reduction for our regular customers," who were, of course, of a lighter hue.[2]

Train travel also proved problematic. Rainey reported riding in first class from Charleston to Savannah but on the return trip being forced to ride in a second-class car. He mused, "Now how can it be that I am all right one way and a social leper on the other?"[3]

Elliott and Cain endured similar treatment. On his way back to Washington one day, Elliott, who had only twenty minutes between trains, wanted to get a quick meal at a North Carolina railway station restaurant. When they denied Elliott service, he flashed his well-known violent temper. He was eventually able to secure his food but later wondered why he had "to fight for it." Cain, meanwhile, told of being refused service in a train dining car. When he acquiesced, instead ordering food to be delivered to his railway car, he was accused of "putting on airs."[4]

Times have changed, of course. Most nights when I am in Washington, I enjoy dinner and social interactions with my friends and colleagues at various restaurants and the National Democratic Club, without issue. (Conversely, during the First Eight's time in the capital city, they were barred from the Republican Club, despite being Republican members of Congress.[5])

But it is not all that unusual for me to occasionally encounter treatment like those experienced by the First Eight. While I haven't been barred from public accommodations or transit during my more than thirty years in Washington, I am not always made to feel welcome in some venues no matter how high I rise in the ranks of Congress, though not all of it is intentional.

On my first plane trip as majority whip, the third ranking member of the U.S. House of Representatives, in 2007, I boarded with my Capitol Hill security detail. The agent stopped to inform the captain that he was accompanying a government official and carrying a service weapon. I proceeded down the aisle of the airplane, and the flight attendant followed me. When I took my assigned aisle seat, in the emergency exit row, I noticed that the flight attendant seemed a bit uncomfortable and retreated to the front of the plane.

As my security escort took his seat behind me, the flight attendant approached him and asked that he follow her to the cockpit. When he returned, I asked, "Was there a problem?" He informed me that the flight attendant thought I was a criminal and had reported to the captain that I had taken a seat in the exit row, where prisoners were not allowed to sit.

This experience took me back to an important lesson I received as a college sophomore from the political scientist Dr. William Howell: "We can be no more or less than that which our experiences allow us to be." That flight attendant happened to be Black, and the only Black men she had seen boarding a plane accompanied by armed protectors were prisoners. Because of the life experiences Jim Crow had visited upon her, it never occurred to her that a Black man could be in the position I occupied at that time.

THE FIGHT OVER LIMITATIONS ON BLACK CIVIL RIGHTS

In 1873, as South Carolina's four Black congressmen continued in their pursuit of civil rights and political acceptance, the U.S. Supreme Court weighed in on the Fourteenth Amendment. Looming large was the infamous *Dred Scott v. Sandford* case of 1857, in which an enslaved man asserted that he had gained his freedom after his owner took him to a free state, where slavery was outlawed, before returning him to a slave state.

In that case, Chief Justice Roger B. Taney wrote a devastating opinion, holding that the U.S. Constitution did not extend American citizenship to people of African descent. "But it is too clear for dispute," he wrote, "that the enslaved African race were not intended to be included, and formed no part of the people who framed and adopted this declaration" [that "all men are created equal"]. In other words, the Court had declared that Blacks could never be American citizens, and therefore could never enjoy the same rights as white men. This decision, which gave cover to the prevailing attitude of the Confederacy, has since been cited by modern legal experts as the worst judicial ruling in American history.[6]

Of course, with the ratification of the Fourteenth Amendment in 1868, the nation nullified Taney's ruling, establishing that Blacks born in America were citizens who should enjoy the same constitutional protections as their white counterparts. But as the high court has swung left and right through history, it has often narrowed, and sometimes broadened, the implementation of that constitutional provision.

In April 1873, South Carolina's Black congressmen were distressed by the Supreme Court's decision in the Slaughterhouse Cases, instigated after Louisiana restricted slaughterhouse operations in New Orleans to a single corporation, essentially granting a monopoly. Louisiana butchers argued that this infringed upon their "immunity and privileges" under section five of the Fourteenth Amendment and would render them unable to earn a livelihood. Ultimately, the high court ruled that the "immunity and privileges" clause applied only to national citizenship rights, not those granted by the states. In other words, the decision limited the federal government's ability to enforce civil rights, putting that power in the hands of the states. Congressional Democrats, by and large Redeemers, seized on this high court ruling and argued that civil rights was a states' rights issue.

Following the decision, Rainey, Elliott, Ransier, and Cain knew that Congress needed to further enshrine their constituents' citizenship rights. The battle heated up in January 1874, when Congress began the new year with a tense debate over the Civil Rights Act, which would codify the right of Blacks to enjoy equal access to public accommodations, transportation, education, and houses of worship, and which the Massachusetts senator Charles Sumner had been trying to enact since 1870.

In one early exchange, the Virginia Democrat John Harris said on the House floor, "I say there is not one gentleman upon this floor who can honestly say he really believes that the colored man is created his equal." According to the *Congressional Record*, acting in contrast to his usual reserved nature, Ransier shot back, "I can."

In response, Harris sneered, "Of course you can, but I am speaking to the white men of the House; and, Mr. Speaker, I do not wish to be interrupted again by *him*." Harris continued, declaring, "Admit that it is prejudice, yet the fact exists, and you, as members of Congress and legislators, are bound to respect that prejudice. It was born in the children of the South; born in our ancestors...that the colored man was inferior to the white."

Ransier snapped, "I deny that!" to which Harris replied, "I do not allow you to interrupt me! Sit down; I am talking to white men; I am talking to gentlemen!"

The gallery snickered at the exchange and Harris's frustration; the Speaker gaveled the House back to order.[7]

Later that day, Ransier felt emboldened to speak on the House floor for the first time, addressing the notion that the states, not the federal government, controlled civil rights. In his speech, he lamented that in most if not all states, there was "no practical freedom" for Blacks, and none at all worth talking about should the matter be left in the hands of their governments. He argued that Congress needed to provide "for a full and complete remedy."[8]

The main event, however, began during the evening session of January 5, 1874. Democrats selected the Georgia congressman Alexander Stephens to make their case against the Civil Rights Act. Stephens, the former vice president of the Confederacy, had gained notoriety for his "Cornerstone" speech, in which he declared the rebel states' new government was built on the idea that a Black man's "subordination to the superior race . . . is his natural and normal condition."[9] The five-foot, ninety-pound sixty-three-year-old, who was infirm and confined to a wheelchair at the time, spoke for two hours in a monotone and halting voice.

Stephens revisited the argument of states' rights and proclaimed, "If there is one truth which stands out prominently above all others, it is that the germinal and seminal principle of American constitutional liberty is the absolute unrestricted right of state self-government in all purely internal municipal affairs."[10]

He argued that per the Slaughterhouse Cases, unless a specific right was conferred in the Constitution, it was not a right protected by the Fourteenth Amendment. For example, he said, access to public education was not a right conferred in the Constitution; therefore, he argued, it should not be covered by the Civil Rights Act.

Because of the late hour, the Republicans' response had to wait until the next morning. They chose the able orator Robert Brown Elliott to speak on their behalf. His performance quickly turned the Democrats' argument on its head. This virile thirty-one-year-old African American, far from being subordinate to the "superior race," stood in stark contrast to Stephens's diminished physical presence. Elliott's "flamboyant and aggressive" legislative style also distinguished him from his older opponent's feeble delivery.[11]

One historian described the scene on the morning of January 6, 1874, a date that would become memorable during my congressional service for far different reasons: "The mood was expectant, the galleries again packed, and the reporters' tables full to see 'the African' challenge 'the Brain of the Confederacy.'" Among the crowd was General William Tecumseh Sherman, who had led the Union to victory over Stephens and his allies' insurgency. Elliott later reflected on the occasion's importance, saying, "With a profound sense of my responsibility to my race, to my immediate constituents, and to my own reputation as a Representative in Congress, I addressed myself to the task."[12]

Elliott spoke from his desk on the floor of the House, an iconic image later captured in a popular lithograph titled *The Shackle Broken — by the Genius of Freedom*. Unlike televised scenes of the House floor today, when members often speak to a near-empty chamber, Elliott stood surrounded by his colleagues; members of Congress had no offices at that time and thus did their congressional work at desks on the House floor. According to the *Chicago Tribune*, as Elliott rose to deliver his address, many of his Democratic colleagues tried to appear busy and uninterested, "but the eloquence of the speaker soon drew them from their preoccupation and compelled them to listen."

The Shackle Broken — by the Genius of Freedom depicts Robert Elliott delivering his defense of the Civil Rights Act on the House floor on January 6, 1874. (Library of Congress, Prints and Photographs Division, LC-DIG-pga-02595)

The man of the hour opened his remarks by addressing Stephens's role in the war, reminding the room that it had been "scarcely twelve years" since he had helped found the Confederacy, "a government which rested on human slavery as its cornerstone." Now, he said, "the race whom he then ruthlessly spurned and trampled on are here to meet him in debate, and to demand that the rights which are enjoyed by their former oppressors...shall be accorded to those who even in the darkness of slavery kept their allegiance true to freedom and the Union."[13]

Elliott, an able attorney as well as orator, then rebutted Stephens's interpretation of the Slaughterhouse Cases as favoring states' rights over federal oversight. Under the Fourteenth Amendment, he said, no state could infringe upon the privileges and immunity accorded to all citizens of the United States. "No matter, therefore, whether his rights are held under the United States or under his particular state," he said, "he is equally protected by this amendment. He is always and everywhere entitled to equal protections of the laws."[14]

Elliott maintained that the Thirteenth, Fourteenth, and Fifteenth Amendments granted Congress the power to protect the rights of all American citizens. "What you give to one class you must give to all; what you deny to one class you shall deny to all," he summarized—except, he said, in circumstances that required "the exercise of the common and universal police power of the state" for "the common good of all."

Elliott then posed a question to Stephens: "Is it pretended anywhere that the evils of which we complain, our exclusion from the public inns, from the saloon and the table of the steamboat, from the sleeping coach on the railway, from the right of sepulcher in the burial ground, are an exercise of the police power of the state?"[15]

After concluding his two-hour rebuttal, Elliott received an extended standing ovation from Blacks in the gallery that took the chairman presiding over the House several minutes to quell.[16] Later that night, a biracial throng of people and a band greeted Elliott at his boardinghouse, giving him a hero's embrace.

He also received glowing accolades from the press. The *National Republican* hailed Elliott, writing, "No more dignified, skillful, exhaustive tearing down of the false theories raised by caste alone has ever been witnessed in legislative halls."[17] The Louisville *Courier Journal* called Elliott's speech "the most extraordinary effort ever made by a Negro in this country."[18] One historian described the rarified recognition Elliott received as "the kind of intellectual prominence only Frederick Douglass and a few other Blacks enjoyed."[19]

Following Elliott's triumph, other Black members of South Carolina's congressional delegation continued the well-crafted assault on conservative Democrats who sought to kill the Civil Rights Act and redeem the South. Ransier delivered a floor speech in which he made it clear that the Civil Rights Act's call for equal educational opportunities was critical to its success. "Let the doors of the public schoolhouse be thrown open to us," he said, "if you mean to give these people equal rights at all, or to protect them in the exercise of the rights and privileges attaching to all free men and citizens of our country."[20] His comments reflected the importance the African American community placed on access to education after the overwhelming majority had been legally prevented from being educated before emancipation.

Cain, meanwhile, took on North Carolina congressman William Robbins, who had declared it a fallacy that Blacks and whites were created equal, and had sarcastically suggested that America adopt a crow rather than an eagle as its national emblem because its "plumage is of the favorite color, so popular with the dominant party." Cain's witty and scathing retort to Robbins became known as the "Nation of Croakers" speech.

"Sir," Cain began, "the crow would, I think, more beautifully represent the condition of the South now — the croaking bird, you know. They have been croaking ever since the rebellion came on, and they have been croaking against emancipation and the Constitution ever since. They are a nation of croakers... like the crow they are cawing, cawing, cawing, eternally cawing."[21]

CHARLES SUMNER'S LEGACY

As the contentious debate continued, the Civil Rights Act's author and most ardent champion, Charles Sumner, passed away. The death of the white senator from Massachusetts and longtime abolitionist on March 11, 1874, gave extra urgency to secure passage of his signature legislation and to honor his legacy.

Sumner, who succumbed to a heart attack at sixty-three years old, had had a previous brush with death. Twenty years earlier, he had survived a nearly fatal caning by Congressman Preston Brooks of South Carolina on the floor of the Senate. Brooks had taken exception to an anti-slavery speech Sumner had given, in which Sumner excoriated Brooks's distant relative, the South Carolina senator Andrew P. Butler. Sumner verbally assailed Butler for choosing "the harlot, slavery," as his "mistress." "For her, his tongue is always profuse in words," Sumner said of his colleague from South Carolina. "Let her be impeached in character, or any proposition made to shut her out from the extension of her wantonness, and no extravagance of manner or hardihood of assertion is then too great for this senator."[22] Brooks responded with physical blows with his cane.

After the brutal attack, Brooks received gifts of walking canes from his supporters and praise from his local newspaper, the *Edgefield Advertiser,* which declared, "Our Representative did exactly right; and we are sure that the people will commend him highly for it."[23]

Elliott, who was serving in the same district Brooks once represented, embodied the ability that African Americans had demonstrated since his predecessor's outrageous assault. In a nod to the progress Sumner made in his fight for civil rights, Elliott, the first congressman of "uninterrupted African descent," was chosen to eulogize him at a memorial service held at Faneuil Hall in Boston.[24] In his remarks on April 14, 1874, Elliott praised his fallen colleague:

> History has been to me the delight and study of my life, but
> I know no figure in history which commands more of my

admiration than that of Charles Sumner in the Senate of the United States...Here was the perfection of moral constancy and daring. Here was sleepless vigilance, unwearying labor, hopefulness born only of deepest faith, buoyant resolution, caring nothing for human odds, but serenely abiding in the perfect peace which the unselfish service of truth alone can bring.[25]

After the moving tribute, Frederick Douglass, the well-known African American who had escaped slavery and become a vaunted orator, newspaper editor, and abolitionist, sent Congressman Elliott a letter of thanks and praise.

"As a colored man as well as an American citizen and a man among men, I am proud that one of my race costumed and scorned for ages, has been able to make a speech at Faneuil Hall, Boston in all respects so worthy of the place and the occasion as you have now delivered," Douglass wrote. "The thought brings satisfaction to my heart and to my gray hair."[26]

The *Boston Evening Transcript* also heralded Elliott's speech, citing "the unity of his topic, the correctness and beauty of his style," declaring that it warranted "high commendation." The *Charleston News and Courier*, however, responded disparagingly, publishing an open letter to Elliott asking who had written the speech for him.[27] The insulting insinuation, to me and surely to those who had worked with Elliott, was laughable considering Elliott's proven history of eloquent oratory and intellect. Then and now, however, it is a common implication that African Americans are incapable of such powerful public speaking without assistance — in particular, without white assistance.

Another South Carolina congressman played an important role in what we in the Black community sometimes call Sumner's "homegoing." Joseph Rainey had the honor of being the only African American in the House delegation to accompany Sumner's body back to Boston. Upon his return to the House, he too eulogized the civil rights champion in a floor speech, in which he remembered the kindness that Sumner had shown him when he first arrived in Congress. "The cause of my race," he said, "was always foremost in his mind."[28]

Two days later, on April 29, 1874, as if propelled by Sumner's vision, Rainey became the first Black representative to preside over the House, taking the gavel during a debate on a bill to improve conditions on Native American reservations. He and the Committee on Indian Affairs met in Room 150, which has since been renamed the Joseph Rainey Room. This barrier-breaking moment in Rainey's career prompted the newspaper headline "Africa in the Chair" and another press recognition that despite this, "the earth continues to rotate on its axis."[29] One might imagine that Sumner enjoyed some heavenly satisfaction in that moment.

CORROSIVE CORRUPTION

As Rainey's presence in Congress grew, so too did the challenges of being a prominent Black official in an era of political violence. To protect his family from the increasing threats in South Carolina, Rainey bought a home in Windsor, Connecticut, in the summer of 1874. He had discovered the town after speaking there the previous summer to mark forty years since the end of slavery in the West Indies. In his speech, Rainey proclaimed that electing more African Americans to Congress would make white representatives recognize that Blacks were their equal.[30]

His hopeful tone didn't reflect the reality in South Carolina politics, which continued to contend with charges of corruption—and the country was taking notice. *Harper's Weekly* wrote that, in the Palmetto State, there were "the [Republican] party of thieves and the [Democratic] party of the murderers."[31] By August 1874, the controversy had reached new heights. The *New York Times* reported that at least thirty local elected officials in the state had been implicated in corruption scandals that flowed from the example of the "Robber Governor" Franklin Moses and members of the legislature.[32] In response, South Carolina's Black congressmen returned home to deliver a message from Washington: Clean up the corruption or face consequences.[33]

Alonzo Ransier helmed the effort to root out corruption in the party.

He asked every voter to act "as if by his individual vote, he could wipe out the odium resting upon our party." He continued, "Let every man feel that society at large will hold him and the party accountable for every misdeed in the administration of government."[34]

Ransier's criticism of his own party proved unpopular among his colleagues, and ultimately cost him the Republican nomination for the Forty-Fourth Congress. And despite sacrificing his political future for the party's greater good, the corruption didn't end. Rather, Ransier alleged that his opponent had spent four thousand dollars to buy the nomination for the Second Congressional District.[35]

Earlier in the year, Elliott had spoken in a similar vein. Addressing a Republican gathering at the Columbia Courthouse, he declared their party's government a disgrace. "To mention South Carolina is to merit the sneers of the commonwealths of the North," he lamented. He warned, "It is not the Democracy that will overthrow us, it is our own party." He continued, "Let us not look abroad for our enemies; they are here, members of our own party, officers elected by our own votes."[36] In fact, Elliott felt the need for reform so urgently that he gave up his seat in Congress before the term ended to return to his home state. He wanted to use his stature within the party to curb the culture of corruption, both real and perceived, that threatened to overshadow Republicans' achievements, especially those on behalf of the Black community.

It is rare to find the level of commitment and sacrifice that both Elliott and Ransier demonstrated in today's politics. But, often in critical moments, it does happen. After the January 6, 2021, insurrection at the U.S. Capitol, two brave Republicans—Liz Cheney and Adam Kinzinger—stood up to their party, which had been overtaken by the Make America Great Again (MAGA) movement.

Cheney, a committed conservative Republican who was serving in House leadership on that day, chastised members of her party for "defending the indefensible." Similarly, Kinzinger, an Air Force veteran and a six-term Republican congressman, broke with members of his party by calling the events of that day an "attempted coup." They were the only members of their party to participate in the special House committee convened to investigate MAGA's threat to our democracy that day. Cheney would later state, "It's hard for me to see how the Republican Party survives, because it's been so corrupted."

Kinzinger declared that he'd taken a stand against his own party to put "our country first," and because of his "allegiance to the rule of law, the Constitution and democracy." Their actions and outspokenness posed a tremendous risk to them personally, and ultimately cost both their seats in Congress.[37] But, like Elliott and Ransier, these "defenders of democracy" made the personal sacrifice for the betterment of the country and its people.

THE 1874 ELECTION

In the lead-up to the 1874 elections, corruption became the focus of both political parties in South Carolina. When the dust settled, Republicans still held the levers of power, but there were signs of trouble. While they held a seventy percent majority in the South Carolina House, this was down from the ninety percent majority they'd enjoyed after the 1868 election. Ultimately, the Republican Daniel Chamberlain, who'd tangled with the "Robber Governor" Moses during the previous primary, easily won the governor's race on a platform of reform. But though he ran as a Republican, once elected, Chamberlain sought to destroy coalitions within his own party and create new alliances with Democrats in the legislature.[38]

Meanwhile, Elliott, who had resigned from Congress to fight corruption in the state, handily won election to the South Carolina House of Representatives and narrowly won his race for speaker of the house. The *Charleston News and Courier* condemned his election as "a very bad beginning" and declared, "Elliott had the reputation of being as big a rascal as can be found anywhere within the ranks of Radicalism and is besides, supremely insolent, arrogant and arbitrary."[39] The indignities were escalating and becoming more widespread — and more trouble was to come.

This 1998 portrait of Speaker Robert Brown Elliott by artist Larry Lebby now hangs in the South Carolina House of Representatives. (Courtesy of the South Carolina House of Representatives)

PASSAGE OF THE CIVIL RIGHTS ACT OF 1875

The change in the political mood impacted not only South Carolina but the entire nation. Issues of Republican corruption in the Grant administration and the pending Civil Rights Act, which many whites feared would force "social equality," emboldened Redeemer Democrats to begin wresting back control. Many of the Southern states were "redeemed" that year, leaving just four former Confederate states under Republican control after the 1874 election. This turn of political fortunes served as a foreboding of what was to come across the region and throughout the nation.

Democrats, backed by a solid wall of Southern Redeemers, seized control of the U.S. House of Representatives, flipping seventy-seven seats in their favor. Rainey became the only Black Republican from South

Carolina reelected to the Forty-Fourth Congress, but he was joined by the war hero Robert Smalls, who had won the new Fifth Congressional District, formerly the at-large seat held by Cain. This marked the first time since before the Civil War that Democrats controlled a chamber of Congress — but they were beholden to a Southern wing that was hell-bent on restoring the social order of the pre–Civil War era.

It was clear that the political pendulum was swinging back to the right. This created a new urgency among the outgoing class of congressmen to pass the Civil Rights Act in the remaining months of the lame duck session. The legislation, they knew, would not stand a chance otherwise.

But the shortened time frame and the unpopularity of the act among the white electorate caused the debate to become fractious. Rainey and Cain found themselves pushing back against accusations that Blacks were causing strife by insisting on passage of the act. Rainey maintained his composure while challenging those critics, saying, "Just as soon as we begin to assert our manhood and demand our rights, we are looked upon as men not worthy to be recognized, we become objectionable, [and] we become obnoxious, and we hear the howl about social equality."[40]

Cain responded to arguments that the legislation would drive wedges between whites and Blacks. He said, "I am at a loss to see how the friendship of our white friends can be lost to us by simply saying we should be permitted to enjoy the rights enjoyed by other citizens...All we ask is equal laws, equal legislation, and equal rights throughout the length and breadth of this land."[41]

Despite this, because of vocal opposition to measures such as integrating public schools, churches, and cemeteries — which were a bridge too far even for many white Republicans — those clauses were struck from the final legislation in order to secure enough votes to bring the bill to a vote. Ransier, who believed fervently that access to education must be a protected right, abstained from voting on the legislation.[42]

Having served for eight years as majority whip, responsible for counting votes when bills came to the floor, I understand the challenge of crafting legislation that will engender enough support to pass. It often requires tough choices, and when that happens, some parties are unhappy with the compromise legislation. Members are expected to determine for themselves and their constituents if the final compromise is worth supporting. And in the case of the Civil Rights Act of 1875, however controversial, Ransier's actions reminded me of my good friend John Lewis, who always took very principled positions on issues of war and peace.

Rainey and Cain reluctantly voted in favor of the limited Civil Rights Act, and Elliott had already vacated his seat in Congress before the vote took place. On February 5, 1875, the House passed the bill by a final vote of 162 to 99. President Grant signed the historic bill into law on March 1, 1875, just two days before the new session of Congress began. Republicans could, for the moment, exhale.

Despite the compromises it had necessitated, Cain, a man of great faith, had high hopes for the legislation's impact. If the new law achieved its purpose, Cain believed the country could proclaim "thank God" because "the last vestige of that old barbarism [of prejudice] will have disappeared, and peace shall spread her wings over a united, prosperous, and happy people."[43]

CHAPTER 7

POLITICAL POLARIZATION

—— 1875–1877 ——

"A carnival of bloodshed and violence."

—Robert Smalls

WHEN THE FORTY-FOURTH CONGRESS convened in 1875, there were two Black members from South Carolina, Joseph Rainey and the newcomer Robert Smalls. With Democrats in control of the U.S. House of Representatives for the first time since the Civil War, the two found themselves a minority within a minority for the first time in their public service careers. The hope of passing sweeping legislation to build on the Civil Rights Act faded as the political pendulum began its swing back to the right, a move that would soon receive a dramatic and dangerous push from a volatile Southern Democrat, Martin Witherspoon Gary.

Having proven his adeptness in military tactics during the Civil War, Smalls also demonstrated his political acumen soon after he arrived for his first term in Congress. He sought to find common ground on issues he thought would appeal to both parties.

As a state senator, Smalls had called on the federal government to establish a permanent naval facility in Beaufort County, where he had served as a Union naval captain. Now, as a member of Congress, he had the power to advocate more forcefully for this project and succeeded in designating Port Royal as a naval station, which today we know as Parris Island, a training base for the Marines.[1] Many future members of South Carolina's congressional delegation followed in Smalls's footsteps, and today South Carolina has eight U.S. military facilities.

Also in his first term, Smalls sought to extend his contributions to the armed services. Since he had secured the opportunity for Blacks to enlist in the military during the Civil War, they had served in segregated regiments. He introduced an amendment to integrate military regiments, which explicitly held that "no distinction whatever shall be made on account of race or color."

Congressman Henry Banning of Ohio, the Democratic chairman of the Committee on Military Affairs and a Union infantry veteran, argued the measure wasn't needed because "the gentleman [from South Carolina] [had] the same right to enlist in the army that he had to run for Congress."

Smalls countered this condescending comment with a patient and prophetic reply. "I know, sir," he said, "that no colored man could have enlisted in the Army if Congress had not passed a special act authorizing such enlistment." Smalls continued, "And I feel if matters go on just as they are going on now, and if we should have one or two more Democratic Houses of Representatives, I shall not be allowed to come here; and no change in the law will be made either."[2] Smalls knew, as the British prime minister William Gladstone had intoned a decade earlier, that justice delayed would be justice denied—a sentiment that echoes throughout the long African American struggle for equality. But ultimately, despite his best efforts, Smalls could not muster the support needed in the Redeemer-controlled House.

This battle, however, would reverberate well into the mid-twentieth century—and would in fact play a role in the Republican Party's evolution from the liberal, abolitionist-founded party of the Civil War to the center- and far-right party it is today. Integration of the armed forces would not happen until July 26, 1948, when the Democratic president Harry Truman signed Executive Orders 9980 and 9981, an act that, over a half-century after Smalls's efforts, was a sidestep of a still-unwilling Congress. The legislation was a response to the racially motivated blinding of Isaac Woodard, a Black army veteran in South Carolina. While in uniform on the way home from service overseas in World War II, Woodard was beaten by a law enforcement officer in the town of Batesburg, South Carolina, for the crime of asking a belligerent bus driver to treat him with the respect he deserved.[3] In the process, his eyes were gouged out and his life forever and brutally altered. An all-white jury acquitted his assailant.

Truman's integration of the armed forces seventy-three years after Smalls's efforts, as well as his support of other civil rights measures—particularly his 1947 address to the NAACP—incensed the then-Democratic governor J. Strom Thurmond of South Carolina, who remained true to the ideals of the Reconstruction-era party. He believed that Truman "stabbed the South in the back."[4] In response, Thurmond abandoned the Democratic Party's ticket and ran for president against Truman as a Dixiecrat, a party made up of "states' rights" Democrats, whose primary purpose was to protect racial segregation.[5]

During his presidential campaign, Thurmond underlined his support for segregation, proclaiming, "All the laws of Washington and all the bayonets of the Army cannot force the Negro into our homes, our schools, our churches and places of recreation." His position was that of the opponents of the Civil Rights Act of 1875, which was championed by members of the First Eight.[6] In hindsight, *The Washington Post* called Thurmond's campaign "a founding stone of the massive white resistance to the [1950s and 60s] civil rights movement," in which I would soon become a student leader.[7]

On September 1, 1954, South Carolina's Democratic senator Burnet Maybank passed. When the party failed to nominate Thurmond in his place, he ran a write-in campaign for the seat and became the only U.S. Senator to be so elected. Three years later, he set a Senate filibuster record arguing against the 1957 Civil Rights Act, still fighting to thwart the issues championed by the First Eight. In 1964, while serving in the Senate, he officially switched from the Democratic to the Republican Party over the former's role in enacting another, more sweeping Civil Rights Act. Thurmond was an early bellwether of conservative whites leaving the Democratic Party to become Republicans.

In my opinion, this evolution, or some might say devolution, of J. Strom Thurmond, as well as Southern states' increasingly negative reactions to various civil rights milestones—including the Democratic Party's 1948 platform, the Supreme Court's 1954 *Brown v. Board of Education* decision to desegregate public schools, and President Lyndon Johnson's Great Society programs, which created Medicare, Medicaid, and the War on Poverty. These accomplishments completed the Republican Party's shift from its progressive positions during the era of the First Eight to its right and far-right positions today.

THE GARY PLAN

Despite their tightening grasp on Congress, the Redeemer Democrats were growing restless. At the Taxpayer Conventions of 1871 and 1874, they complained of "taxation without representation" under South Carolina's Republican government. At the time, Robert Elliott, still critical of his own party's governance, warned his colleagues that the Taxpayer Conventions were not a "sorehead movement," but a calculated effort by the Democrats to use economic issues to their advantage that the Republican Party should be addressing.[8]

The Taxpayer Conventions' loudest voice, the former Confederate brigadier general Martin Witherspoon Gary, defined the problem in racial terms, arguing that white Democrats paid the bulk of the taxes that went to programs and fed corruption that benefitted Blacks. The group voiced their discontent to Congress, accusing the Republicans of "schemes of public plunder," but their complaints received little attention.[9]

Feeling spurned, the Redeemers took action. They knew that white farmers shared their discontent over taxes; these constituents had been raising complaints over their inability to get credit, on affordable terms, for their agricultural pursuits, especially with a decline in the price of cotton. Blacks who made up a majority of the State legislature, including house speaker Elliott, served as easy scapegoats. Now all they needed was a bombastic leader—and they found one in the former Confederate Gary, who according to one historian "some thought genuinely crazy."[10]

Gary hailed from South Carolina's Edgefield County, which is located along the Savannah River just north of Augusta. A longtime epicenter for white supremacy in the state, Edgefield County had also produced Strom Thurmond, whose attitude toward Blacks reflected his community's deep-rooted history.

In the post–Civil War era, Gary was an unrepentant Confederate who had refused to accept Robert E. Lee's surrender at Appomattox, declaring, "South Carolinians never surrender." Staying true to his word, he wrote a campaign plan in 1876 detailing how Redeemer Democrats should form armed militia and laying out a strategy to redeem South Carolina and defeat Black and Republican powers in the upcoming election.[11]

The plan instructed each member of a Democratic club to "control the vote of one Black, either by intimidation, by purchase, or by keeping him from voting." It went so far as to order Democrats to "never threaten a [Republican] individually. If he deserves to be threatened, the necessities of the times require that he should die. A dead Radical is very harmless."

Gary's strategy called for all Democrats to wear red shirts, the color of blood. They must show up to every political gathering and polling place, and must always be armed. At every Republican campaign event, they should harass the speakers and gain the trust of Blacks by demonstrating white superiority and promising them that they would benefit more by electing Democrats than Republicans. They should publicly blame any bloodshed, home burnings, and voting irregularities on "Radical Republicans."[12]

The first Red Shirt militias formed in Edgefield and its neighboring counties of Barnwell and Aiken. They had origins in the rifle clubs that replaced the KKK following the federal ban on Klan activities in 1871.[13] Oftentimes, they armed themselves with weapons meant to protect against violent white supremacists. They would intercept them as they were being transported from the state to the Black militia units that were the precursor to the National Guard. Stealing these weapons not only provided the Red Shirt militia free firearms, but it also helped fulfill their goal of disarming Blacks.[14]

THE HAMBURG MASSACRE

The brutal violence of that election year began that summer, with an encounter between two white Edgefield farmers and the Black militia in the African American enclave of Hamburg—which happened to be represented by Robert Brown Elliott in the statehouse.

On July 4, 1876, the militia paraded down one of the community's deserted streets as they marked the centennial of the country's founding.[15] This display of Black pride and power provided the two white farmers an opportunity to provoke mischief. Riding through in their horse-drawn carriages, the farmers demanded the militia break ranks so they could pass. The militia's commander denied their request, arguing the street was wide enough for the carriages to get around the troops with ease. A standoff ensued, which eventually ended when the Black militia acquiesced.

When the farmers arrived back in Edgefield, they retained an attorney, another former Confederate general, Matthew Butler, who filed a complaint charging the militia with blocking a public highway and demanding they surrender their weapons. Butler showed up to the hearing with a posse of armed Red Shirts.

Aware that trouble lay ahead, rather than appear at the hearing, Hamburg's militia commander sequestered himself in their armory with twenty members of his troop. Butler's armed agitators descended on the brick building and opened fire, calling for reinforcements. A contingent of Red Shirts came across the bridge from Augusta with a six-pound cannon and began firing on the structure. The warlike bombardment forced the militia to run from the building; one of their number was killed as he tried to escape. The remaining militia surrendered, but Butler's forces corralled them, then selected five men for execution on the spot. The others fled, and another man was killed and four others sustained significant injuries during their escape. The Red Shirts then mutilated the bodies of the seven dead militia members.[16]

The *Charleston News and Courier*'s editor published a middling piece on the massacre: "We find little, if any, excuse for the killing of the seven negro prisoners," the piece read, ostensibly condemning the actions of the Red Shirts. This, however, was followed by the equivocal statement, "The presence of armed bodies of negroes is a threat to any community, but we do not understand...demanding the surrender of the arms...laying siege to the house...and killing the negroes who sought to escape."

While there is no definitive evidence that the Red Shirts planned the Hamburg Massacre, Benjamin Tillman, a future governor of South Carolina who would gain notoriety for his fervent racism, bragged that the murders were part of a "policy of terrorizing the negroes at the first opportunity by letting them provoke trouble and then having the whites demonstrate their superiority by killing as many as was justifiable."[17] Meanwhile, as much of the nation expressed outrage over the Hamburg Massacre, some prominent white South Carolinians published a letter to "The People of the United States" claiming, "It is not true that South Carolina is in insurrection, nor is the state disloyal to the United States, nor do the white people intend hostility to the colored people of the state. The rifle clubs are not outlaws. The president has been deceived." The letter then went on to blame Blacks for the violence plaguing the state.[18]

It is hard not to see the parallels to today's politics. In fact, there are tremendous similarities between the Redeemer Democrats and the MAGA Republicans of today. Both employ the logic of blaming the victim for their fate. Both are animated by a desire to return to "the good old days." While those days may have been good for white Americans, they were not for people of color, which is exactly the point.

But most of all, MAGA has a bombastic leader who seems to share traits with the Redeemers' bombastic leader Martin Gary. Most famously, this leader blamed Democrats for the insurrection on January 6, 2021. That morning at the White House, he declared to a crowd of his armed militia, the Proud Boys and Oath Keepers, "All of us here today do not want to see our election victory stolen by emboldened radical-left Democrats, which is what they're doing....You don't concede when there's theft involved.... We will stop the steal."[19] Hours later, his armed supporters attacked the

U.S. Capitol in an attempt to overthrow the election, which ultimately resulted in five deaths.

Those of us in the House chamber that day understood, just as the Hamburg militia holed up in their armory did, that the use of violence to force a political agenda is undemocratic and circumvents the rule of law. There is no justification for it. And just as in 1876, the efforts to upend democracy signify greater danger to come.

BLACK CONGRESSMEN REACT TO HAMBURG MASSACRE

Horrified by the Hamburg Massacre, members of the First Eight warned their colleagues and constituents of the increasing danger. Joseph Rainey called the event a "cold-blooded atrocity." He took to the U.S. House floor and asked his colleagues if Blacks were indeed American citizens or if they were "to be vassals and slaves again."[20]

The week following the massacre, Smalls proposed an amendment to prevent redeploying any of the twenty-eight hundred federal troops that were still in South Carolina.[21] At the time, Congress was poised to send more federal troops to Texas in response to Native American uprisings there. Smalls argued that for the sake of the Black militia who were being "massacred in cold blood by lawless bands of men," the troops still in his home state ought to remain.[22]

The ensuing debate devolved into attacks on South Carolina's Black elected leaders. During the arguments, a Democrat from New York held up a copy of James Pike's *The Prostrate State* and declared that the "crew of robbers called native Africans" should be held responsible for the violence occurring in South Carolina. The Redeemers' narrative that violence was justified to wrest control back from a "corrupt" government had taken hold in Washington.

In South Carolina, Elliott, who was Hamburg's representative, and Rev. Richard Cain responded vociferously to the atrocity. Though Cain was not serving in elective office at the time, he still held sway as a leading moral authority in the Black community. He and Elliott organized a rally in Charleston on July 17, 1876, "to express [their] indignation, and to adopt resolutions setting forth the enormity of General M. C. Butler's outrage in Hamburg." One thousand Blacks and five hundred white onlookers showed up for the event.

Cain asked the whites attending the gathering how they would react if a similar incident happened in their community. He then warned that Blacks must be given "equal protection under this government" or they would be forced to retaliate. Breaking with the Blacks' political tradition of forbearance, Cain proclaimed, "There are eighty thousand Black men in this state who can bear Winchester rifles and know how to use them... and there is a deep determination never, so help their God, to submit to be shot down by lawless regulators."[23]

The *News and Courier,* the paper that had published the lukewarm piece on the events in Hamburg, condemned the rally as an attempt to politicize the tragedy. "We must protest against any move that wears the appearance of taking advantage of a local disturbance to prop up the waning fortunes of South Carolina Republicanism," it declared.

Ignoring the criticism, Elliott continued to raise public awareness about the horrors of the massacre and what they foretold. On July 20, 1876, he assembled the state's Black elected officials in a Convention of Colored People in Columbia.[24] The meeting produced "An Address to the People of the United States" authored by Elliott and signed by the fifty-nine Black participants. The document declared the Hamburg Massacre had its origins in a "settled and well-defined purpose to influence and control the forthcoming political election." It also included a call to action imploring the business and property owners of the state "to bend their energies toward the removal of this deadly nightshade of mob law and violence." Finally, the address demanded more federal protection in South Carolina.

When Governor Daniel Henry Chamberlain wrote to President Grant asking for more federal troops, he enclosed a copy of the address.[25] Grant responded with an expression of hope for the "fair trial and punishment of all offenders, without distinction of 'race, color, or previous condition of servitude,' — and without aid from the federal government.'"[26]

Just as hopes and prayers today are insufficient responses to tragedy, Grant's response failed to deliver the decisive action the besieged Black Republicans in South Carolina required. But his decision to withhold federal troops reflected postwar national sentiment: The North had grown weary of protecting the South from its rebellious tendencies and thought Southern leaders ought to find their own solutions.

TARGETING BLACK CONGRESSMEN

The failure to punish those responsible for the Hamburg Massacre and the federal government's refusal to send additional troops emboldened the Redeemers' mobs, and it didn't take long for South Carolina's Black Congressmen to become targets.

On August 5, 1876, one month after the massacre, Robert Smalls, determined to not let the domestic terrorism threat deter him, went directly into enemy territory, Edgefield County, to speak at a political rally. As fifteen hundred Black and white Republicans gathered for the occasion, Matthew Butler, who had led the Hamburg attack—joined this time by Martin Gary—assembled an army of six hundred Red Shirts, who rode on horseback through the crowd. Rebel yells rang out, and their armed entourage surrounded the stage, as per Gary's playbook. Butler demanded equal time for Democrats to speak. Given the Red Shirts' history of violence, the Republicans, feeling they had no alternative, acquiesced.

As the political rally resumed, the Red Shirts climbed trees and shouted down Republican speakers. When Smalls took the stage, the crowd tore it down, shouting, "No, that God Damn n— shall not speak here today." As the Republicans retreated from the chaotic scene, a band of Red Shirts followed Smalls to the train station, warning him to stay out of Edgefield. They would employ this strategy, later known as the Edgefield Plan, at countless other Republican gatherings during the 1876 election season.[27]

However, Smalls, ever fearless, refused to stay away and returned to Edgefield later in the campaign, bringing with him federal marshals and an election commissioner. Once again, Red Shirts surrounded the defiant congressman on horseback, pistols in view, hurling insults, but this time, no violence occurred.[28]

I remember similar actions being taken against members of Congress in 2010, during the heated debate over the Affordable Care Act (ACA). The conservative populist movement, then known as the Tea Party, took a page from Gary's playbook, storming Democratic town halls and political events that August as we attempted to inform the public of the benefits of the monumental legislation. My colleagues and I experienced firsthand the Tea Party's intimidation tactics as they attempted to disrupt our efforts by shouting us down and overwhelming our town halls.

During the era of the First Eight, white South Carolinians disguised their anger over the progressive gains made under Black Republican leadership by arguing instead about taxation and corruption. Similarly, the tense political battles over the ACA were, for many white Americans, a way to express their anger over the election of Barack Obama, America's first Black president. In 2010, the Tea Party took advantage of this simmering resentment by claiming that the ACA would establish "death panels" that would ration medical care and determine who could receive medical treatment. At protests, Tea Partyers held specious signs that read "Obama lies, grandma dies."[29]

The day before the House voted on the Affordable Care Act, Tea Party adherents swarmed Capitol Hill, much like the Red Shirts did Smalls's political rally. As members of the Democratic Caucus walked from a meeting to the House floor to vote, a Tea Party protester spat on my colleague Emanuel Cleaver, a minister from Missouri, and called John Lewis a "n—." I was walking alongside John and witnessed those assaults and the vitriol of the racial slur, which I had not encountered publicly since my days as a student protest leader. The incident told me and my colleagues all we needed to know about the opposition to the ACA.[30]

The racial animus of the Red Shirts' activities in 1876 was not confined to the incident at Edgefield County. In his own district, Joseph Rainey faced a group of several hundred armed Redeemers as he traveled by horseback between Cheraw and Bennettsville. The political vigilantes surrounded the congressman and his fifty to sixty Republican companions. A bloody confrontation would have occurred but for a company of federal troops that happened upon the scene.

When recounting the incident to the House chamber, Rainey said that if the federal forces had not arrived when they did, he and many members of his group "would have been numbered among the dead." Later, when reflecting on the 1876 campaign, Rainey said, "I felt as though I carried my life in my hands."[31]

As the Red Shirts continued their racially and politically motivated assaults, Ellenton, a town in Aiken County, became the site of an even deadlier, drawn-out incident just two months after the Hamburg Massacre. A white woman claimed she had to brandish a gun to narrowly escape an attack by two Black men as she worked in her field. White rifle clubs rampaged through the area's Black community for a week following, leaving as many as one hundred dead. The woman's accusation was later proven false.

After the Ellenton Massacre, President Grant finally relented, sending eleven hundred new federal troops to South Carolina and ordering the rifle clubs to disband. Instead, the white armed militias merely changed their names: the Allendale Rifle Club became the Allendale Mounted Baseball Club, and the Columbia Flying Artillery rebranded as the Columbia Musical Club with Four Twelve Pounder Flutes, once again thumbing their noses at federal intervention.[32]

REPUBLICAN DIVISIONS

As the election drew closer, Redeemer Democrats defiantly continued their violent campaign to wrest more control of South Carolina state government. For the first time since Reconstruction began, Democrats nominated a slate of candidates. Up until this point, they had been playing the long game—knowing they didn't have the numbers to win at the state level, they abstained from participating in elections by *not* nominating a slate of candidates, in hopes the Republicans would fight amongst themselves without Democratic opponents to coalesce against. Now, though, they were switching tactics. This year, for governor, they nominated the former plantation owner and Confederate general Wade Hampton III, who represented a return to the old days of white supremacy and racial segregation, with *Harper's Weekly* writing that the purpose of his candidacy was "to suppress and destroy the colored vote."[33] Hampton's campaign galvanized the Redeemers, with one Marlboro planter writing to the *Columbia Register,* "The name of General Hampton is electric and will thrill through the nerves of every white man in South Carolina."[34]

Portrait of General Wade Hampton III, 1862. (From the South Carolinian Library, University of South Carolina, Columbia, South Carolina)

The Republicans knew they faced a formidable challenge in the violent Red Shirt militia, who had united behind Hampton's campaign. And, as the Democrats had hoped, they were also contending with growing divisions within the ranks as the issue of public corruption once again reared its head.

Robert Elliott, who had given up his congressional seat to fight corruption back home, was at the time serving as Speaker of the South Carolina House of Representatives. From this position of power, Elliott sought to undermine what he saw as Republican Governor Chamberlain's dalliance with white conservatives and his racial prejudices against Black members of his own party. Elliott had called Chamberlain out publicly for a letter he wrote that said he ran for governor to keep the state from being overrun by "Negroism."[35]

The intraparty tension bubbled over when the governor refused to endorse the popular Black Republican and well-known gambler William Whipper for an important circuit judgeship in Charleston. The governor likewise refused to endorse his own predecessor (and pro–Black Republican head of state), the "Robber Governor" Franklin Moses, for a judgeship in Sumter. In response, while Chamberlain attended an event out of town, Elliott, who despite his protestations was not above dirty tricks of his own, outmaneuvered the governor by holding a vote in the statehouse to elect a straight Republican ticket for vacant judgeships. Among the victors were both Whipper and Moses, the former of whom was Elliott's good friend and former law partner. The senate concurred with the house's slate of judges.

Outraged, the governor retaliated by refusing to sign the commissions for Whipper and Moses to take their seats. One historian called this a "legally questionable" tactic, as Chamberlain held no veto power over the judicial elections and was obligated to sign the commissions. This incident further deteriorated the already fraught relationship between Chamberlain and the state's Black Republicans. It also provided the justification Redeemer Democrats needed to overthrow the Republican power structure by any means necessary.

In South Carolina lore, this turning point became known as "Black Thursday," a day in which the *Charleston News and Courier* held the "Black Band" of Republican elected officials solely responsible for ramming through two unpopular judicial nominees. The *Cincinnati Commercial* observed, "The whites have wanted sufficient excuse to rise up and overthrow the African government under which they live; and now they have it."[36]

This event also became a flash point in April 1876, when the party selected delegates for the Republican National Convention, a process over which Elliott presided. During the proceedings, Judge Thomas Mackey, a white Republican who supported the Democrat Wade Hampton for governor, accused Elliott of being the "head and front" of "the banded robbers that have plundered the state."

True to his hotheaded nature, Elliott reacted by pulling a pistol on Mackey. While the dramatic event ended without bloodshed, it demonstrated the rancorous divisions within the Republican Party ahead of an election that was growing more tumultuous by the day. These divisions threatened to erode the political and civil rights that Blacks had gained during Reconstruction just as much as did the Redeemer Democrats' violence and treachery.[37]

At a separate Republican nominating convention for state offices, Elliott gave a fiery speech warning Black Republicans not to trust Chamberlain and refused to vote in favor of the sitting governor's renomination. However, many Republicans supported Chamberlain for his expressed outrage over the Hamburg Massacre and his request for additional federal protection. In the end, Chamberlain won the party's nomination. Ironically, the party also nominated Elliott, who now considered Chamberlain his bitter enemy, to run on the same Republican slate as attorney general.[38]

ELECTION DAY

With the backdrop of internal Republican Party divisions and external Redeemer outrage, Election Day 1876 was what a modern House historian would call "one of the most tumultuous in South Carolina history."[39] There were twenty to thirty thousand more Black registered voters than white ones in 1876, and they overwhelmingly voted Republican. This knowledge fueled the Redeemer Democrats' continued strategy to use unlawful means to win the election.[40]

With Blacks making up an overwhelming majority in South Carolina's low-country counties, Redeemer Democrats concentrated most of their efforts to employ the Gary Plan upstate. Edgefield remained an area of focus for their violence and intimidation, which they used to keep hundreds of

Black men from voting. To bolster these efforts, however, they also solicited votes from white men they brought into the county from Georgia, as well as underage voters from the surrounding area. In the end, the number of votes cast in Edgefield exceeded the number of eligible voters in the county. This obvious fraud also occurred in neighboring Laurens County.[41]

Thomas Nast's political cartoon published in *Harper's Weekly* depicting two white men forcing a Black voter to cast a Democratic ballot at gunpoint, 1876. (Courtesy of the Newberry Library, Digital Collections)

In the predominantly Black Beaufort County, which happened to be the home of Robert Smalls, the congressman discovered a Redeemer effort to trick illiterate voters. At the time, candidates and political parties printed and distributed ballots to citizens. The Redeemer Democrats had given illiterate Beaufort voters ballots listing their slate of candidates, claiming it was the Republican ticket. After learning of the deception, Smalls crisscrossed the county, visiting every precinct to deliver the correct ballots in person. He narrowly defeated George Tillman, the future governor's brother, with just fifty-two percent of the vote.[42]

During my elections to Congress, I, too, have had to contend with political dirty tricks. Benedict College, a private historically Black college in Columbia, has been the repeated target of these efforts. During my first congressional election in 1992, a near riot broke out at the Benedict precinct when "poll watchers" brandished fake police badges and demanded students not be allowed to vote if their voter registration cards, which of course bore their college addresses, didn't match the address on their driver's license. Tea Party "poll watchers" used similar tactics at the college in 2010.[43] It is no coincidence that the target of these efforts—and the targets of baseless MAGA lawsuits after their candidate's loss in the 2020 presidential election—were all Black precincts.

CHAOTIC ELECTIONS, TUMULTUOUS RESULTS

The Redeemer Democrats' tactics threw South Carolina's congressional races and statewide elections into chaos—though the Republicans were able to eke out some victories.

In 1876, Joseph Rainey won reelection to a fourth term by a margin of just fifteen hundred votes against his challenger, the Democrat John S. Richardson, a far cry from his overwhelming victory only two years earlier.[44] Richardson challenged the results, but despite the Democratic-controlled Committee on Elections declaring the seat vacant due to voting "irregularities," the full U.S House of Representatives failed to act on the committee's recommendation, allowing Rainey to remain in office for the full term.[45]

Richard Cain also ran during the 1876 election, this time for the newly drawn Second Congressional District seat that represented an area with a sixty-five percent Black majority. Because Redeemer Democrats knew they were outnumbered, the political fraud and intimidation wasn't as rampant in the district. Cain won with sixty-two percent of the vote, and despite a perfunctory challenge by his Democratic opponent, the House upheld his election.[46] Finally, according to the vote tallies, Robert Elliott had won his race for attorney general outright.

However, the race for governor was in heated dispute. Taken at face value, the Democrat Wade Hampton had defeated the Republican Daniel Chamberlain by a slim margin of just over one thousand votes. But Republicans cried foul over the Edgefield and Laurens County votes, whose overall tally exceeded their total number of registered voters. This set off months of political turmoil.

Initially, the five-member majority-Republican State Board of Canvassers threw out the vote in the disputed counties, changing the outcome of the governor's race and control of the House in favor of Chamberlain. In response, the Democrats appealed to the State Supreme Court, asking it to throw out the Charleston County vote due to the intimidation of Black Democrats, citing an incident prior to Election Day in which Black Republicans threw bricks at Blacks participating in a Democratic parade. The court ordered the Board of Canvassers to send the vote totals to them for review.

Knowing the five-member court had two Democrats and three Republicans, including two white men with close relationships to the Democrat Hampton, the canvassers followed the advice of their attorney, Elliott, and defied the order. They met on November 22 to certify the election *without* the Edgefield and Laurens County votes and issued certificates of election to all the Republican statewide candidates, the Republican legislative candidates from the disqualified counties, and the Republican slate of presidential electors.[47]

On November 26, the day the constitution set for a new General Assembly to convene, both the Republicans certified by the canvassers *and* the Democratic opponents from the disputed counties showed up at the capitol to be sworn in. Anticipating a confrontation, Chamberlain had ordered a regiment of federal troops that remained in South Carolina to stand guard inside the building. The guards required each man claiming to be a member of the General Assembly to show his election certification and denied entry to those who could not produce the document. All the Democrats, those with certificates and those without, then left the grounds and reconvened at the nearby Carolina Hall on the campus of the University of South Carolina. They declared themselves the legitimate legislature.

Then, on December 6, the General Assembly, convened by Chamberlain, elected him to another term as governor; his inauguration was held the following day. But on the day that he took the oath of office, a defiant Hampton held a rally of Redeemer Democrats, roaring, "The people have elected me Governor, and, by the Eternal God, I will be Governor." A week later, on December 14, the competing Democratic house elected *Hampton* governor; he took the oath of office in front of Carolina Hall, where the Democratic legislature met. From a stand constructed for the occasion, Hampton claimed victory and thanked the people for supporting him "with a lofty patriotism never surpassed, with a patience never equaled, with a courage never excelled, and with a sublime sense of duty, which finds scarce a parallel in the history of the world... and consecrated themselves to the sacred work of redeeming the prostrate state."[48]

Frank Leslie's Illustrated Newspaper cartoon depicting the two men claiming to be South Carolina's governor in a lopsided power struggle, January 6, 1877. (Library of Congress, Prints and Photographs Division, LC-DIG-ds-15070)

And so it was that, for four months, South Carolina had two competing governors and legislatures, each claiming to be the legitimate government. Knowing that the bulk of state taxes came from white residents, Hampton slyly instructed them to remit their payments to his government rather than Chamberlain's. They eagerly complied. Out of money and quickly losing public support, Chamberlain's government survived only due to the protection of federal troops, which remained on guard inside the statehouse.[49]

THE GREAT BETRAYAL

The disputed election in South Carolina had reverberations beyond the state's borders. Because both parties had claimed victory, South Carolina's Electoral College votes were also under question. In fact, in a reflection of the tumult that was still festering post–Civil War, similar scenarios had occurred in Louisiana and Florida, the other former Confederate states that had not been "redeemed" prior to the 1876 election; their Electoral College votes were also cast in doubt. Each state therefore presented two sets of electors to certify the presidential election.

The three states had been allocated a total of twenty electors. Excluding these, the Democratic candidate Samuel Tilden, who had won the popular vote, found himself just one vote shy of the 185 *electoral* votes needed to win the presidency over the Republican Rutherford B. Hayes, who had 165 electoral votes. With neither candidate reaching the threshold, the election was thrown into the House of Representatives.

To determine the winner, Congress established a fifteen-member Election Committee, made up of members of the House, the Senate, and the Supreme Court. On an eight-to-seven vote along party lines, the committee awarded the twenty contested electors to Hayes, enabling the Republican to win by one electoral vote.

Many history books use the benign-sounding "Compromise of 1877" when referring to this ominous event. I call it what it was: "the Great Betrayal." A one-vote deficit in the Electoral College and in the committee set in motion the events that would lead to the Redemption of the remaining Republican-controlled Southern states and its aftermath that continues to this day. Many feel, I among them, that this is what the perpetrators of the January 6, 2021, insurrection were trying to replicate when they attempted to disrupt the certification of Joe Biden as president. They sought to contest enough electors in targeted states that it would throw the election into the House of Representatives. Furthermore, when Vice President Mike Pence refused to go along with their unscrupulous plan, the MAGA devotees resorted to violence, taking yet another page from the Redeemers' playbook. Here I will restate the Spanish philosopher George Santayana's warning: "Those who cannot remember the past are condemned to repeat it."

After the inauguration of President Hayes and the Forty-Fifth Congress's swearing-in on March 4, 1877, South Carolina's Black Congressmen, Rainey, Cain, and Smalls, met with their party's leader at the White House. On March 10, they pled the case for continued federal protections in their home state. Instead, Hayes told them he believed "the use of the military forces in civil affairs was repugnant to the genius of American institutions and should be dispersed with if possible."

With the rightful control of South Carolina's government still undecided, Hampton, the Democratic governor, also made a trip to visit the newly inaugurated Republican president, during which he promised to maintain the peace and protect the rights of African Americans in South Carolina. On April 3, 1877, President Hayes gave the order to withdraw federal troops from the statehouse in Columbia—a decision that would seal the political fate of Blacks in South Carolina for a century.[50]

CHAPTER 8

REDEMPTION TAKES HOLD

—— 1877–1879 ——

"We are circumscribed within the narrowest possible limits on every hand, disowned, spit upon, and outraged in a thousand ways."

—Alonzo Ransier

T HE PROGRESSIVE MOVEMENT THAT characterized the Reconstruction era hit a wall as members of the First Eight found themselves battling forces hell-bent on reconstructing the pre–Civil War South. A combination of brute force and drumbeating about "Black inferiority" and "Radical Republican corruption" soured the wins achieved by African Americans since their emancipation. All the while, the federal government seemed content to play spectator, not referee.

But the chaos had not erased their advances. Though the Redeemers were content to claim Republican ineptness, as the South Carolina historian Walter Edgar would later write, the Black Republicans "had been effective, especially in the last four years of Reconstruction."[1] Their successes, in fact, were a threat to the Redeemers' vision for a white supremacist state, and they did have reason to feel hopeful; their fellow Republican, Rutherford B. Hayes, had been awarded all twenty of the disputed electoral votes and had been declared the nineteenth president of the United States by one vote.

But the dispute over the governor's election loomed large. The incumbent

Republican Daniel Chamberlain and the Redeemer Wade Hampton were both still claiming victory in the contest. Their former colleague Robert Brown Elliott, who had been confirmed as the state's attorney general, saw no path for his party to both hold on to power and follow the rule of law. He joined other members of the Republican government in writing to Governor Chamberlain, advising him to concede the election. The letter's authors warned that prolonging the results would only worsen partisan tensions, to the detriment of the people—and worse, could precipitate "a physical conflict that could have but one result to our defenseless constituency," writing, "We cannot afford to contribute, however indirectly, to such a catastrophe, even in the advocacy of what we know to be our rights."[2]

On April 11, 1877, as the bell tolled noon at Columbia's City Hall, federal troops officially withdrew from the South Carolina State House.[3] Governor Chamberlain followed, leaving his office as his federal protectors departed. Before conceding, however, he issued an address to South Carolina Republicans, saying, "The government of the United States abandons you, deliberately withdraws from you its support, with the full knowledge that the lawful government of the state will be speedily overthrown." He blamed the North for being "weary of the long Southern problems."[4]

Frank Leslie's Illustrated Newspaper drawing of Columbia citizens welcoming the return of Wade Hampton on April 6, 1877, just before federal troops were withdrawn from the state capitol, published April 21, 1877. (Library of Congress, Prints and Photographs Division, LC-USZ62-93269)

Despite the bitterness of Chamberlain's tone, he left office without a fight, a peaceful transfer of power in direct contrast to the violence and lawlessness that had pervaded the 1876 election, which had resulted in nearly 150 deaths.[5] The Redeemer Democrat Wade Hampton was officially the governor of South Carolina, and the era of "Redemption" had begun.

A TROUBLING ERA

Members of the First Eight were immediately impacted by the political changing of the guard from the mostly Black Republicans to the mostly white Redeemer Democrats. With Chamberlain's departure in April 1877, Republicans who depended on political patronage found themselves out of power and without work.

Alonzo Ransier, once the lieutenant governor and the highest ranking African American elected official in the state, was forced into manual jobs to earn a living. Ransier—a congressman who had fought for Black Americans' right to an education—spent the last years of his life as a night watchman and street cleaner. In his autobiography, *Up from Slavery,* Booker T. Washington recalls seeing Ransier in Charleston after the end of Reconstruction, hauling bricks to white masons who taunted him with "Hurry up, Governor!"[6] Ransier, described by a U.S. House historian as "a man of great courage and sagacity," died destitute in a Charleston boardinghouse in 1882 at the age of forty-eight, all but forgotten to history.[7]

Ransier, in many ways, reminds me of John Lewis. Both were men of quiet strength and unwavering commitment. They pursued justice through nonviolent protest and never compromised their principles. Neither man was the loudest voice in the room, but when they spoke, they commanded attention. John received great recognition when he was still alive and was much honored after his passing, even lying in state in the U.S. Capitol. Ransier, on the other hand, died in obscurity. I hope this book helps him receive some of the respect and recognition he deserves.

Another member of the Eight, Joseph Rainey, still held his seat in Congress at the time of President Hayes's "Great Betrayal" in 1877. But as his fourth term began, he acknowledged the gains made during Reconstruction were in danger of slipping away. He lamented that the chaos unleashed by the Redeemers during the 1876 election had destroyed what remained of the biracial Republican Party in South Carolina.[8]

Meanwhile, a newcomer to Republican politics, Thomas Ezekiel Miller, was just getting his bearings on the South Carolina political scene. First elected to the state House of Representatives from Beaufort County in 1874, this member of the next generation of Republican leadership and future congressman had experienced life a little more uniquely than the other members of the First Eight and, like Elliott, the circumstances of his birth were not fully known.

Portrait of Thomas Miller, date unknown. (Courtesy of SC State Historical Collection & Archives, Miller F. Whittaker Library, South Carolina State University, Orangeburg, South Carolina)

By most accounts, including his own, Miller was biologically white. Born on June 17, 1849, he was adopted by free Black parents in Ferrebeeville, Beaufort County, near what is now Ridgeland, Jasper County. According to one biographer, however, some of Miller's own descendants believe this isn't the whole story, but hold that Miller was "the son of a white man and a white girl, whose family would not allow her to keep her baby," and his Black adoptive parents were actually his foster parents. Still other accounts report that his mother was of mixed race and that the light-skinned Miller was one-sixty-fourth Black.[9]

Miller, however, acknowledged late in life, during a Works Progress Administration interview in 1936, that his mother was believed to be the daughter of Judge Thomas Heyward, one of the signers of the Declaration of Independence, and his father was a wealthy white man. Whatever his origins, in 1851, when he was around two years old, Miller's adoptive Black parents moved the family to Charleston, where opportunities were better for them.

When Miller was nine years old, his adoptive mother died, and he had to find work. The following year, the *Charleston Mercury* hired Miller to distribute newspapers at local swanky hotels, including the Mills House. There, his path probably crossed with Rainey's, whose barbershop was in the hotel and whose clientele couldn't have envisioned that their newspaper boy and their Black barber would one day serve in Congress. On the contrary, they probably overwhelmingly agreed with the sentiments they read in the reactionary newspapers Miller sold them.

Miller could read these newspapers as well. A very intelligent young man, motivated by his late mother's high expectations of him, he attended the schools available to free Blacks in Charleston. He quickly proved his capability, and at age eleven, he was entrusted to deliver the newspapers at railroad stations between Savannah and Charleston. In 1864, three years into the Civil War, that railroad took him on as an assistant conductor, a position that would prove fortuitous.

Miller, now just fifteen years old, had to wear a Confederate uniform while working on the railroad, as it was owned and operated by the government. When Union forces captured the train, the crew, including Miller, were sent to a prison stockade in Savannah, where he spent two weeks. Many of the prisoners died in the prison's harsh conditions, but, as one of the few survivors, Miller was taken to the local hospital, where he came to the attention of New York's Twenty-Fourth Negro Regiment. They arranged to take him to Hudson, New York, to finish high school.[10] From there, Miller would follow another Beaufort Black leader, Robert Smalls's son-in-law Samuel Bampfield, to Lincoln University, an HBCU in Chester County, Pennsylvania, that would later produce such great minds as Langston Hughes and Thurgood Marshall.[11] At this point, Miller could have remained in the North, taking advantage of his skin tone and living a comfortable, productive life while "passing," or living as white. Instead, he chose to return to South Carolina to help the community he knew and loved best.

I, too, contemplated leaving South Carolina after college. In fact, Emily and I got married in Paterson, New Jersey, because we thought we would live in that state. Many of our college classmates took part in the Great Migration, in which Blacks left the oppressive South for the urban centers of the North and Midwest, looking for more opportunities and a better life. Emily and I once took a cursory search through our college yearbook and estimated that over seventy-five percent of our classmates left the state after graduation.

As I reflect on Miller's return to South Carolina, I can't help recalling the counsel of one of my high school teachers, Edna Lukens, who taught me Bible classes at Mather Academy. Ms. Lukens was one of two white teachers I had at Mather, and they provided some of my early, positive, and impactful interactions across racial lines. After reading an essay I'd written about my postgraduation plans she became disturbed about my intentions to leave the state. Ms. Lukens told me, "The only way South Carolina will get better is if young, gifted, educated people like you are willing to stay here and make it change." I imagine that Miller felt a similar motivation.[12]

Upon his return home, Miller continued his education studying law at the newly integrated University of South Carolina. The board of trustees changed the school's charter in 1869 to prohibit discrimination on "race, color and creed," and by 1877, the student body was equally Black and white. In fact, during the Reconstruction era, South Carolina was the only

Southern state to integrate its public college. However, this didn't sit well with the Redeemers, nor did it sit well with many of the white faculty, who left their positions in protest. In response, the university hired its first African American professor, Richard Greener, who also was the first Black graduate of Harvard University.

Miller was admitted to the bar in 1875, just before the Redeemers took control of the government, a changing of the guard that led to the closure of the University of South Carolina. (It was reopened several years later as an all-white institution.) Miller had returned to Beaufort in 1872 — and it was around this time that he won his first elective position as a county school commissioner and began his career in public service.

In the violent and fraudulent election of 1876, Miller won a seat to represent Beaufort in the South Carolina House of Representatives. But when President Hayes betrayed the state and removed the federal troops, the Redeemer Democrats demanded that the Republicans who had worked with the Chamberlain House, including Miller, take an oath to "purge themselves of contempt" in order to assume their seats under the incoming governor. Two Black Republicans resigned in protest and the Redeemer Democrats threw out two others.

In another effort to increase their grip on power, the Redeemers also nullified the Charleston County election results. They held a new election in the county, which the Republicans didn't contest, possibly due to the malaise brought on by their complete political defeat, or due to their naïve belief that Hampton was sincere when he called for fair representation for Blacks in Charleston, resulting in the Democratic Party nominating three African Americans in their slate of seventeen candidates. As a result, Democrats won all seventeen house seats, reducing the total number of Republican seats from fifty-five to thirty-seven, adding a significant cushion to what originally was a narrow Democratic majority in the house. The senate, however, remained under Republican control.[13]

Miller tried to be collegial with Governor Hampton. During his second term in the house, they cut a deal that created a new county from the northern area of Beaufort County to be named after Hampton himself.

The Redeemer Democrats, who were frustrated by the Republican stronghold in Beaufort, would benefit by carving out an area of the county that favored them. In return, Hampton promised Miller he would support a Black Democrat's candidacy for the state senate in the next election. Miller trusted the candidate, a former Republican, and was heartened by Hampton's promises to work with Blacks. But after establishing Hampton County, the Redeemer Democrats passed a rule barring any Black person who had not voted for Hampton in the 1876 election from joining the party, nullifying the deal Miller had made with the governor. Not as consequential as the "Great Betrayal," but a betrayal nonetheless. Still, years later, in a 1927 letter, Miller praised Hampton, writing, "It is impossible to express in words the great worth of that very distinguished, faithful, patriotic, self-sacrificing humanitarian."[14]

DEMOCRATIC RULE

When Wade Hampton assumed the governor's office, he called a special session of the legislature that immediately began repealing Republican initiatives. One of the first targets was a law that provided pensions for the widows and families of victims of political violence. As many of the Redeemers were themselves purveyors of this violence, it stood to reason that they would oppose this legislation.

The University of South Carolina was another target. In protest of its recent integration, the Redeemers closed the college—but not before revoking its scholarships for low-income students. One of those scholarship recipients was another future Black congressman, George Washington Murray, an emancipated enslaved man with whom I share a county of birth, and to whom I may be related, according to folklore. Murray, who had enrolled in classes in October 1874, was a sophomore when the Redeemers closed the university in 1877, cutting his education short.[15] Denying education is a common tactic in the history of subjugating Blacks in South Carolina and the nation. That theme continues to this day through our state constitution, which the South Carolina Supreme Court ruled in 1999 "requires the General Assembly to provide the opportunity for each child to receive a minimally adequate education."[16] "Minimally adequate" is a code phrase for "substandard." By setting this very low bar for the state to meet its educational obligation, the court has perpetuated the inequities that have existed in public schools dating back to the era of the First Eight, beginning with the debate over education at the 1868 South Carolina Constitutional Convention.

The Redeemer Democrats also set up a committee to investigate Republican corruption. They had been laying the groundwork for this effort for years, and the chaos of the Reconstruction-era administrations had only promoted their narrative. Still, the Redeemer Democrats' own attorney general acknowledged that their "findings," described in a seventeen-hundred-page report, "would not stand a test as legal evidence, but the moral evidence would be crushing."[17]

Despite this, the Redeemers moved forward with aggression. Robert Elliott, who had surrendered his claim as attorney general in April 1877, following the withdrawal of federal troops from the state, responded by opening a law office in Columbia to defend Republicans charged with corruption.

Finally, also during the very active first special legislative session, a house committee investigated the Black state supreme court justice Jonathan Jasper Wright. Testimony, given in secret, led to a resolution of impeachment under the pretext of drunkenness. In response, Thomas Miller charged the committee with paying bribes to the witnesses who testified, but Wright, under mounting pressure, resigned. As he left the bench, Wright reported, "Governor Hampton said, in accepting my resignation, that he placed no belief in the charges, and that as a jurist I was one of the purest."[18]

In July 1877, the Redeemer Democrats charged another Republican target, Congressman Robert Smalls, with bribery. In October, Smalls was arrested and spent two nights in jail before posting bail and taking a leave of absence from the Forty-Fifth Congress to defend himself at trial. He reported that the chairman of the legislative investigative committee told him to resign his office, threatening, "These men have the court, they have got the jury, and an indictment is a conviction." Smalls refused.

The state's star witness against Smalls was Josephus Woodruff, the former clerk of the senate from whom Smalls had allegedly accepted the bribe while serving in the state senate four years earlier. However, Woodruff himself had left South Carolina after confessing to pilfering $250,000 in state funds. He had been brought back and given immunity to testify against Smalls. While he had no incriminating evidence linking the congressman to the crime, his word was enough for the jury, who convicted Smalls.[19]

Prior to his sentencing, Smalls reported that the editor of an Aiken newspaper visited him on behalf of Governor Hampton and the Democrats. According to Smalls, the emissary had attempted to pay him off, declaring, "Smalls, we don't want to harm you. Get out of the way.... We want this government, and we must have it. If you vacate your office, we will pay you $10,000 for your two years' salary." Smalls allegedly responded, "Sir, if you want me to resign my position you must call meetings all over the Congressional District and get those people who elected me to pass resolutions requiring me to resign, and then you can have the office without a penny."[20]

Ultimately, despite his conviction, Smalls was able to serve out his term in Congress and run for reelection. As the conservative press covered the events, it expressed confusion over the love the Black community still had for Smalls. The *Charleston News and Courier* called Smalls "Beaufort's Brown Idol," and lamented, "It is astonishing to witness the increasing influence of the negro. He seems to possess the confidence of his race to a degree that no other negro can hope to attain. The men, women and children seem to regard him with a feeling akin to worship."[21]

Later, President Hayes and Governor Hampton would eventually strike a deal to pardon Democrats charged with political crimes related to the violence in the 1876 election, which became official in April 1879. In exchange, Smalls and two other Republicans convicted because of the

Democrats' "investigations" were pardoned. However, Smalls didn't ask for, nor did he want, the pardon. He wanted to fight the charges before the U.S. Supreme Court, but never got the chance.[22]

I know how Smalls felt. He knew of his innocence and wanted vindication from the court. During my student protest days, I was arrested several times and spent a few nights in jail. In fact, I met my wife in an Orangeburg, South Carolina, jail during my first arrest in 1960.[23]

In 1974, after being vetted for the gubernatorial appointment as state human affairs commissioner, the chief of the state Law Enforcement Division informed me that the only blemishes they found on my record were my arrests for civil rights activities — or, as John Lewis would say, getting into "good trouble." He informed me that the legislature had empowered him to expunge those records, but he needed a letter from me requesting him to do so. I refused, telling him, "I consider those arrests to be badges of honor." I intend for any future generations that stumble upon my arrest records to know of my willingness to step outside my comfort zone, as was the case with so many of the First Eight, even if it made me a "criminal" in the opinions of some.

CORRUPTION AND CAPITULATION IN THE 1878 CAMPAIGN

As the 1878 election neared, desperate to expand their grip on power, Redeemer Democrats revisited the dirty tricks from the 1876 election. The Republicans split over whether to field candidates for statewide offices for fear it would encourage the Redeemers to repeat their 1876 reign of terror — this time without federal troops in place to protect Republicans. Elliott and Smalls, two of the most influential leaders in the Republican Party, opposed nominating statewide candidates, preferring to focus on those running for the General Assembly. Their position prevailed, and the party platform stated it was "inexpedient" to put forth a full slate of candidates "without incurring great personal risk."[24]

Without a Republican challenger, Hampton was guaranteed another term as governor. Smalls tried to encourage the Democratic incumbent to keep the promises he'd made to Blacks in the state, of "free men, free schools and free ballots."[25] In June 1878, Hampton visited Claflin College (now University), a private United Methodist African American institution, to demonstrate his support for educating Black youth. The following month at a Republican meeting, Smalls praised Hampton's "just and liberal course...which had recommended him to the confidence of the people."[26] However, the governor did not return the courtesy.

On November 6, 1878, Election Day, Laura Towne, a white Penn School teacher and a friend of Smalls, wrote in her diary of the congressman's belief that a recent, harrowing Red Shirt encounter in the Hampton County town of Gillison had been incited by the governor, who declared Smalls "no man for Congress," adding a warning to Democrats that his election would strengthen the Republicans' hand in choosing the next president.[27] As a result of Hampton's incendiary comments, Towne recounted, eight hundred Red Shirts led by former Confederate "colonels, generals, and many leading men of the state" swamped Smalls's Republican rally, demanding equal time for Democrats to speak.

Given his experiences in the previous election with the Red Shirts in Edgefield County, Smalls refused to speak. Instead, he and forty of his armed supporters retreated into the store behind the platform where the speeches were to take place. Democrats surrounded the store and fired into the building. Unable to flush out Smalls and his entourage, the Red Shirts tried to break down the door and threatened to burn the building down with the occupants inside. Smalls directed his protectors not to fire unless the vigilantes entered the building, and they complied. This restraint averted what could have been another massacre. If they had taken the bait, the Red Shirts would have used the "provocation" to justify extreme violence.

As this drama played out, other Democrats proceeded to give speeches. This delay gave Republicans, who had come to hear Smalls speak, time to alert others that he was in grave danger. A thousand Black men and women, armed with guns, axes, and hoes—any weapon they could find—showed up to protect Smalls.

Seeing they were outnumbered and outsmarted, the Red Shirts dispersed, leaving twenty men behind to "attend to" Smalls at the train station. But they underestimated Smalls, and he got away by going ahead of the train and jumping on as it passed. At every stop, a group of armed Blacks waited to protect him, and Smalls returned home safely.[28]

The Redeemer Democrats' attacks on Smalls were indicative of their political violence across the state. They took every opportunity to demonstrate their control and remind Republicans of their willingness to retain it by any means necessary. This became abundantly clear one month before the 1878 elections, when they used the state militia to fire cannons filled with bags of ten-penny nails into a Republican event in Sumter County.

Alarmed by this brazenness and the use of government forces to menace citizens for their political beliefs, Joseph Rainey met with President Hayes, arguing that the incident demonstrated the need for the return of federal troops to ensure a fair election. Rainey, seeking to appeal to Hayes as a fellow Republican, presented the case that state military officials were working on behalf of Democrats. But the president held firm to the promise he made to the Redeemers and refused Rainey's request for protection, maintaining his betrayal.

Using state-sponsored troops to attack citizens for their political views was not a strategy confined to the post-Reconstruction era. In the 1960s, some Redeemer-controlled states used snarling dogs and cattle prods to quell people's rights to free speech and peaceful assembly. During my days as a student civil rights activist, my peers and I faced law enforcement officers wielding powerful water hoses and batons. In 1968, student protesters at my alma mater were shot—and three of them killed—by state Highway Patrolmen during a protest over integrating a bowling alley. That notorious incident came to be known as the Orangeburg Massacre.

Unfortunately, this state-sanctioned violence has persisted. Federal law enforcement officials deployed tear gas, rubber bullets, and flash-bangs to disperse a crowd gathered near the White House—to nonviolently protest the brutal modern-day lynching of George Floyd at the hands of Minneapolis police officers for the crime of using a counterfeit twenty-dollar bill. That day, President Donald Trump declared himself "your president of law and order" and called on governors to use National Guard troops to "dominate the streets" to stop the growing Black Lives Matter protests across the country.[29] In contrast, when Trump incited his supporters to storm the U.S. Capitol on January 6, 2021, to stop the certification of his election loss, he refused to timely call in National Guard troops to end the violent assault on the law enforcement officials who were protecting those of us doing our jobs on Capitol Hill.

The use of law enforcement or military officers against the citizens of this country is antithetical to our Constitution and is indicative of an existential threat to our democratic principles. But it happens often and is another example of modern-day politicians following the Redeemer Democrats' playbook, which were used against members of the First Eight and other Black Republicans of their era.

ELECTION DAY 1878

Election Day 1878 was described by one historian as "another panorama of fraud, intimidation, and violence." As intended, the Redeemer Democrats' unlawful actions succeeded in taking down Black members of Congress.[30] Perhaps their greatest victory was ousting Smalls, their primary target. He lost his reelection bid to George Tillman, the brother of future governor Benjamin "Pitchfork" Tillman, whose family Smalls called "the personification of red-shirt democracy."[31]

Redeemer Democrats had played the long game with Smalls's trumped-up bribery conviction; and their violent, short-term tactics took to heart the declaration of a white newspaper editor in his congressional district: "Any measure that will accomplish the end will be justifiable, however wicked they might be."[32] Knowing his loss came as a result of dirty tricks, Smalls considered contesting the election in

Congress, but decided against it: The Democrats also controlled the U.S. House.

The election also saw another loss for a member of the Eight. During the nominating process, Republicans passed over Richard Cain and instead nominated Edmund Mackey for the Second Congressional District. Some of Cain's opponents accused him of working too closely with whites, something that Cain called a "gross insult to me." In the end, Mackey fared no better than other Republicans, losing in the general election to the Democratic candidate.[33]

To achieve these victories in Republican strongholds, Democrats not only employed straightforward violence and intimidation; they also took creative means, such as abolishing most majority-Republican precincts, an act that forced voters to travel as far as twenty miles to cast a ballot.[34] They also tampered with the ballots themselves. During this era candidates were responsible for printing their own ballots, and in Joseph Rainey's district, the Redeemers used very thin tissue paper, which a House historian later said enabled them "to combine, fold, and insert multiple ballots in the ballot box" at the same time.

That contest was a rematch between Rainey and the Democrat John S. Richardson, whom Rainey had defeated by fifteen hundred votes in the previous election. This time, Richardson "won" by more than eight thousand votes. Rainey chose not to challenge the outcome. He retired as the longest-serving Black congressman of the nineteenth century, having spent nearly ten years in the House over five terms. He would later say of his final election that he had been "legally elected but...defrauded and tissued out of [his] seat." On December 3, 1878, before he left Congress, Rainey introduced a law to make the use of tissue ballots a felony, but in a lame duck session, the measure never went to a vote.[35]

On his final day in Congress, Rainey delivered a speech that became known as "The Destruction of a Free Ballot." From the floor of the House, he lamented, "The Republican Party in South Carolina was destroyed in 1876–77; not by desertion of thousands of [Blacks] who went over to the Democrats...but for the want of a simple guarantee of protection in the exercise of their acquired rights. The Government that had bestowed the gift failed to sustain and protect them in the enjoyment of the same." He then went on to address the relative corruption of both parties, warning, "The destruction of a free ballot by the Democrats is an evil of greater magnitude than the extravagance of the Republicans. The one will eventually destroy the Republic by sapping the foundation of its sacred institutions, while the other is but a comparatively slight and temporary evil, which can easily be repaired."[36]

When Rainey left Congress on March 3, 1879, it was with the belief that he would be "the last of our race that held membership in the U.S. House of Representatives." While this did not bear out, Rainey rightly understood that the future of Black representation in Congress was in jeopardy — as was the recording of its history. It would require an "impartial historian," he said, to capture the truth of the Black fight for liberty, which was as "fundamental and much prized by [his] race . . . as the soul is to the body."[37]

CONGRESSIONAL CHANGES

When the Forty-Sixth Congress was sworn in on March 4, 1879, it marked the first time no Black congressman would serve from South Carolina since Rainey arrived. It also marked the end of the first generation of Blacks to serve in Congress, although Smalls would make a comeback.

As Redemption took hold, these former Black officials had to find other ways to serve the cause, and other means of supporting themselves and their families. Rainey, who by this time was an expert in House procedure, had been promised the position of clerk of the House when he left office, but the Redeemer Democrats' majority prevented him from getting the position. Instead, he received a political appointment as a U.S. Treasury Department special agent in South Carolina, which he held for two years. Rainey then returned to Washington to work in the financial industry, but his business failed within five years. In declining health, he returned to his hometown of Georgetown,

South Carolina, where he died of congestive heart failure in 1887, at the age of fifty-five.[38]

The *Washington Evening Star* wrote that Rainey was "one of the most intelligent representatives of the colored race in the South."[39] The *Chicago Tribune* honored him with an obituary, writing, "He was in politics during a period of extraordinary corruption in public affairs in this State, but he was about the only one whose skirts were clean. He was well thought of by the Democrats of the State."[40]

In recent years, being the first of the "First Eight" has brought Rainey significant recognition and acclaim. Thanks in part to yours truly, his portrait now hangs just outside the room named in his honor in the Capitol, and the U.S. Post Office in his hometown of Georgetown bears his name. His great-granddaughter Lorna Rainey, with whom I occasionally interact, recently authored a children's book to celebrate his legacy.

I feel a kinship with Rainey for the significant place he holds in history. He broke the color barrier with his election in 1870; I experienced a similar situation when I was elected in 1992, ending a ninety-five-year gap in Black congressional representation from South Carolina. And to this day, I share a concern he once expressed: States like South Carolina use their significant Black populations to bolster their number of seats in Congress, while simultaneously suppressing equal participation and equitable representation. Whereas states are allocated an equal number of senators, two each, the number of House members are allocated according to the population. As I write this book, South Carolina is allocated seven seats in the U.S. House of Representatives, and I am the only Black person, and the only Democrat. Yet South Carolina's population is approximately twenty-four percent Black, and at least forty-three percent of the state usually vote Democratic.

After the Redeemers' success in South Carolina, Richard Cain realized the progress he had helped achieve in the state was slipping away. He left the state shortly after leaving Congress in 1877, to serve as the AME Bishop for the Texas-Louisiana Conference. There, he helped found Paul Quinn College, the oldest HBCU west of the Mississippi River. He also served as the college's president for a short time before returning to

Washington to become the AME bishop for the Mid-Atlantic Conference. Cain passed away in the nation's capital at the age of sixty-two, fortunate to have largely escaped the torment of the Redeemer Democrats.

Cain lived in South Carolina for only fifteen years, but he made a lasting impression on its political and religious communities. "Black nationalist ideology was the touchstone of his political activism," one biographer wrote of Cain; and indeed, this was a trait that led him to demand more for his African American constituency. But his real contribution, in my not-so-humble opinion, is the nexus he fostered between politics and the Black church.

The AMEC movement Cain built during Reconstruction survived the political chaos that followed and continues to inform and nurture Black religious and political leaders. This is what drew me as a young man to join the AMEC, and to this day, Cain's work influences mine. His philosophy and my dad's practices laid the foundation for my Pastor, Parish, Precinct Project, which builds on the connection between the Black church and civic engagement.

While several of the first generation of the First Eight would never serve in public office again, their thirst for freedom and hunger for political independence did not end by any means. Another generation stepped up to navigate the challenges facing the future of the Republican Party they belonged to during a time of chaos and conflict.

The leaders of that new generation, Thomas E. Miller and George Washington Murray, stepped up masterfully. Thanks to the Redeemer Democrats' creative devices and racial gerrymandering, their political achievements were limited, but, as will become evident in the chapters to come, their pursuits of educational and economic opportunities never wavered.

CHAPTER 9

THE ASSAULT FROM WITHOUT AND WITHIN

—— 1880–1884 ——

"Like a rope of sand."

—Robert Brown Elliott

W HEN THE FORTY-SIXTH CONGRESS convened, Redeemer Democrats continued to use intimidation and force as they sought to
strip Blacks of the rights they had gained during Reconstruction. The
Redeemer-controlled legislatures throughout the former slave states used
a plethora of creative devices to suppress the vote. And a sympathetic U.S.
Supreme Court issued ruling after ruling that made their actions legal.

In these early years of the post-Reconstruction period, Robert Brown
Elliott recognized that Blacks were being reduced to "citizens in name and
not in fact."[1] These challenging times also increased friction among Republicans in South Carolina, the vast majority of whom were Black, causing
them to turn on one another, greatly diminishing the party's strength.
Among those caught in the political party turmoil were Elliott, Miller,
Smalls, and Murray. These men could not have anticipated the inadvertent
roles they would play in the demise of the Reconstruction era's Republican
Party, and its impact on the future of Blacks in the United States.

By the 1880 election, the factions within the party had caused a serious rift. Thomas Miller, the man described by one historian as "so light
as to be almost indistinguishable from white," a relative newcomer to

Republican politics, aligned himself with the veterans of the party, who became known as the Regulars.[2] At the state convention that year, the Regulars put forth a full slate of nominees, believing the party would collapse if they did not organize statewide. They chose an elderly white man, John Winsmith, as their candidate for governor, and Miller for lieutenant governor.

Meanwhile, change-oriented Republicans, who became known as the Reformers, argued that the party should focus only on organizing for local elections. They thought a statewide Republican slate would energize the Redeemer Democrats and increase their turnout at the polls, leading to a resounding defeat and the further decline of the "party of Lincoln."

The former congressman Elliott spoke for an hour against the Regulars' plan. He compared the party's predicament to that of the Democrats during Reconstruction, when Republicans were too strong for the opposition to mount a successful campaign. Redeemer Democrats now had the strength, in force and the judiciary, although not in numbers. Republicans struggled internally over how to respond. The Democrats' creative devices, reinforced by their perfected plantation tactic of "divide and conquer," proved very effective. Elliott blamed internal Republican Party divisions for causing it to crumble "like a rope of sand."[3]

Elliott's argument stalled the Regulars' plan, resulting in a stalemate. George Washington Murray, attending his first state Republican convention, watched the delegates' disarray with an impatience and frustration that would become his signature. As the debate dragged on, it became clear to him that they were too paralyzed to take meaningful action. The process was futile—and so Murray made a motion to adjourn. To his surprise, most of the delegates agreed, and the delegates disbanded.[4]

The final decision fell to the Executive Committee, which was chaired by Elliott. Given his position on the matter, the Republicans ultimately did not nominate statewide candidates; instead they focused on local and legislative elections and the Fifth Congressional District. This would be blamed as a major contributor to the "complete disintegration of the Republican Party" in South Carolina for many decades to come.[5]

These divisions remind me of a powerful lesson my dad used to teach my brothers and me about not letting minor differences break us apart. One day, my two brothers and I allowed a verbal disagreement to devolve into a physical altercation. We were not aware that our dad was observing us. He called us over to him and was holding a piece of corded string in his hands. He handed that piece of string to each of us in turn and asked us to break it. One by one, Charles, John, and I failed to do so. Despite our best efforts, the string remained intact.

My father then retrieved the string and began rubbing it in his hands. The longer he rubbed, the more friction he created. And the more friction he created, the more unraveled the cord string became. In short order, the string was in three pieces. He handed each of us a piece and asked us to try again. This time, we successfully and easily broke the strings apart. With a calm but serious manner, he looked at us and said, "Sons, let this be a lesson to you for as long as you live: Don't let the little disagreements among you cause so much friction that they separate you, because if you do, the world will pop you apart and you may never know why."[6] He didn't need to say any more. And he didn't.

That powerful lesson is one I have shared with others throughout my life to caution families, community-based organizations, and political groups of the consequences that might occur when little disagreements are allowed to cause too much friction—something the "party of Lincoln" would come to learn all too well. If we are to succeed in our current pursuit of "a more perfect Union," we must learn the value of working cooperatively and collectively.

THE 1880 ELECTION

Amid the Republican Party disarray, Robert Smalls, who had been out of office for two years, ran again for the Fifth Congressional District. It didn't take long for the party's infighting to affect his campaign. The Beaufort County Republican chairman declared he would not support Smalls because he "was totally unfit for the position," referencing his questionable conviction on bribery charges. The *Charleston News and Courier* seized on the Republicans' waning support for Smalls, praising the party for being "ashamed" of one of their most important leaders and demonstrating this "sign of their awakening sense." This intraparty strife, in combination with the Redeemers' continued malicious tactics, proved too much for Smalls to combat. He received just forty percent of the vote in the general election, losing once more to the Redeemer Democrat incumbent George Tillman. This time, however, Smalls decided to contest the race before a slim Republican majority in the U.S. House of Representatives.[7]

Smalls testified before the House committee about the extensive irregularities that had occurred during the election, including widespread instances of Redeemer Democrats stuffing ballot boxes and throwing out Republican votes. He reported that in Hampton County, poll managers were stripped of Republican ballots, making it impossible for his constituents to vote. In some instances, polling places were opened at odd hours to confuse voters. He also gave examples of the Redeemer Democrats' efforts to intimidate Republican voters, citing Edgefield County, where Red Shirts forcibly took control of polling places on the eve of the election and "rode through the town discharging guns and pistols." In Aiken County, Red Shirts positioned a loaded cannon just outside a polling place.[8]

Knowing things didn't look good for them, House Democrats tried to stop the vote that would determine Smalls or Tillman as the winner. One hundred and forty-four members refused to show up, hoping to keep the House from reaching a quorum. This attempt backfired. In the end, the House threw out the votes in four counties that employed these creative devices, and Smalls won the most important vote, that of the U.S. House of Representatives, 141 to 5. Had the Democrats all voted against Smalls, he would have lost. Contesting the election took significant time, and Smalls finally took his seat for his third term in the House on July 19, 1882, with less than eight months remaining in the Forty-Seventh Congress.[9]

ELLIOTT'S LAST STAND

After another election marred by violence and dirty tricks, in January 1881 Elliott led a delegation of Black leaders to meet with the Republican president-elect James Garfield to address the oppression of African Americans in the South. Elliott called for the incoming president, with whom he had served in Congress, to protect those rights that had been "illegally and wantonly subverted" by the "imperious will of an unscrupulous minority." A *New York Times* account of this visit said, "All who had met Elliott...had been impressed with [his] unusual, good sense, sagacity and patriotism." But Garfield, like Hayes before him, refused to act.

At the time, Elliott held a political appointment as a low-level customs inspector in Charleston. Perhaps to separate Elliott from his political power base, and certainly to further "the Great Betrayal," when the Garfield administration took office, Elliott was transferred against his wishes to New Orleans in May 1881. Eleven months later, he lost that job. Left with no money to return home, he remained in New Orleans trying to eke out a living as a lawyer, but struggled; "redemption" had taken hold in Louisiana as well.[10]

Elliott died of malaria on August 9, 1884, in New Orleans, two days shy of his forty-second birthday. Even in death, the *Charleston News and Courier* could not find the grace to acknowledge Elliott's gifts and contributions. Instead, the conservative newspaper's headline read, "Another of the South Carolina Thieves Gone to His Account." By contrast, the *New York Globe*, a widely read Black newspaper, ran an obituary for "Gen. R.B. Elliott, Statesman, Jurist and Orator." But perhaps the most compelling, complimentary assessment of Elliott's life came from Frederick Douglass, who extolled, "From under that dark brow there blazed an intellect and a soul that made him for high places among the ablest white men of the age."[11]

Decades later, a tribute came from W.E.B. Du Bois, a leading Black thinker at the turn of the century. Du Bois named Elliott one of the Talented Tenth, his theory that the most capable Black men had the responsibility to lead the rest of their race to a better life through education and work. Of Elliott and other select Reconstruction-era Black elected leaders, Du Bois wrote, "Through political organization, historical and polemic writing and moral regeneration, these men strove to uplift their people."[12]

I admire Elliott for his persuasive and impressive oratory, which made the seemingly impossible sound possible. As was the case for so many African Americans in the Reconstruction South, his passion and promise were cut short. To me, Elliott is an example of the "what ifs" of this tragic period. We will never know what more he, and countless others, could have accomplished, had his career in public service been allowed to continue and flourish.

MURRAY'S POLITICAL RISE

As many first-generation Black leaders made their exit from South Carolina's political scene, George Washington Murray, the 1880 Republican convention disruptor, stepped into the spotlight. But his path to political leadership differed significantly from those of the seven Black South Carolina congressmen who preceded him.

Born enslaved in Rembert, Sumter County, Murray wrote in his congressional biography that "emancipation found him a lad of eleven summers: bereft of both parents, thrown upon the rugged shores of early emancipation." His colorful prose greatly exceeded the length of those biographies written by his congressional colleagues.

His physical presence also distinguished him. Murray's biographer described him as he joined the U.S. House as "a Black man of the darkest hue" and thereby "more noticeable than the earlier lighter-skinned Black representatives," a trait made all the more apparent by his great height.[13]

Murray's striking comportment and lofty language reflected the dignity he possessed as a self-made man. Despite his early years in slavery,

Portrait of George Washington Murray, circa 1893. (Library of Congress, Prints and Photographs Division, LC-DIG-bellcm-07982)

and as an emancipated orphan, Murray acquired enough education on his own that when he attempted to enroll in the Rafting Creek public school in Sumter County, he was so advanced the school hired him to be the teacher at the age of eighteen. Even after enrolling in the newly integrated University of South Carolina in 1874, Murray continued to teach at Rafting Creek, and did so for fifteen years.

But Murray primarily earned his living as a farmer. He began farming as a teenager and had a plot of land about twenty miles northwest of my hometown of Sumter, near the Spring Hill community where my paternal grandmother and her siblings were born and raised.

During Murray's time, Black students were allowed to attend school for only three months of the year, which enabled him to tend to his farm and livestock while maintaining his job as a teacher. Murray's work ethic and determination made him successful. By the time he became involved in politics at the age of twenty-six, Murray owned sixty-four acres of land and buildings valued at $1,500, equivalent to nearly $47,000 today.[14] He never strayed far from home and committed himself to making life better for himself and his community.

WORSENING CONDITIONS

While Murray remained grounded in South Carolina, many other Blacks in the post-Reconstruction era did not believe the state offered them any reason to stay. The "Exoduster" movement took hold between 1878 and 1880, and many African Americans migrated to the Midwest and as far away as Liberia in hopes of carving out a more humane and prosperous future.

In the fall of 1881, while serving as one of two Black state senators, Thomas Miller proposed the appointment of a committee to study this phenomenon, calling out "the grievances under which our people are laboring, to the extent that they are compelled to leave their homes and native state" at a time when labor and economic development were sorely needed. Through this investigation, Miller wanted to draw attention to the Redeemer Democrats' use of lynchings as extrajudicial punishment, their supporters' enthusiasm for the tactic, and its subsequent contribution to the Black exodus. But the Redeemers, still in control of the Senate, postponed consideration of the resolution indefinitely.[15]

Although statistics on lynchings weren't kept until 1882, from then until the end of the century, not a single year passed in South Carolina without such an extrajudicial killing. By one account, seventy-three lynchings occurred during those years, though even this may not have captured the full extent of the phenomenon.[16]

Smalls understood that the steady rise in lynchings contributed significantly to this outward migration. He tried to keep fearful Blacks from leaving the state, inviting them to move to Beaufort County because of its significant Black majority. Indeed, fifteen hundred African Americans had already come to the county in 1878 and 1879 alone, drawn to the safety of community.[17]

However, most Black South Carolinians believed the future looked bleak. One told the *News and Courier*, "For ten years we have tried to make money and have not been able to do so. We are poorer now than when we began, we have less, in fact, we have nothing... There is no use trying to get along under the old conditions any longer, and we have just determined to go somewhere and take a new start."[18]

Black leaders felt just as helpless in their efforts to protect the rights of African American voters. In addition to the use of violence and intimidation, Redeemer Democrats in the state legislature tortuously drew congressional district lines to limit the number of Blacks in the legislative body. When it came to Black voter disenfranchisement, there seemed to be no limit to their imagination.

TORTUOUS GERRYMANDERING

In 1882, two years after the decennial census, the legislature redrew the congressional district lines, as required. The census had reported a sixty percent African American population in South Carolina, and the state's total population had grown sufficiently to increase its representation in Congress from five to seven seats. Less than a decade earlier, four of the five members of Congress from South Carolina were Black: Rainey, Elliott, Ransier, and Cain.

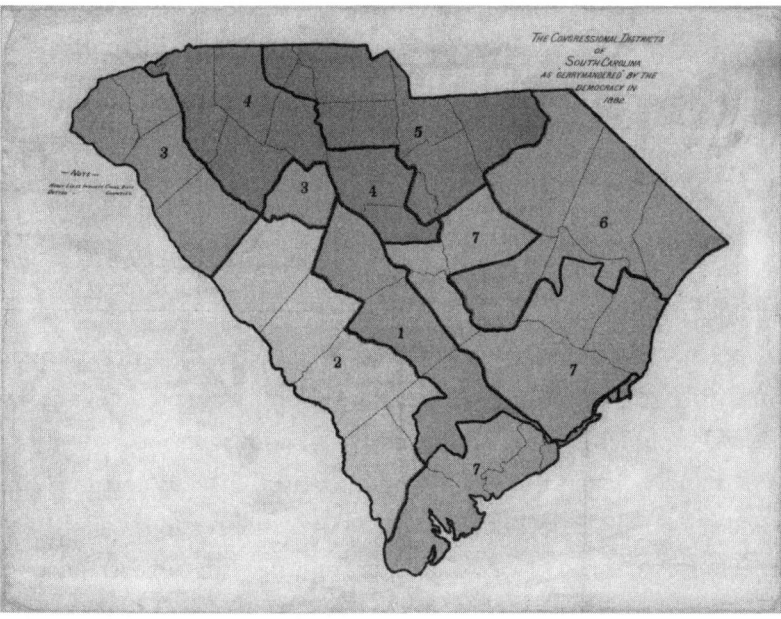

The Redeemer Democrats' gerrymandered Congressional district map, 1882. (Library of Congress, Geography and Map Division, 2015588077)

But with the change in power dynamics, Redeemer Democrats sought to turn the tables to their advantage.[19] Totally disregarding the principle of one man, one vote, they packed the larger Black communities into one congressional district, the Seventh. The new district took in all or parts of the coastal counties of Beaufort, Charleston, and Georgetown, then up a narrow corridor that reached into Sumter County one hundred miles inland. It resembled and was nicknamed the Shoestring District. Blacks made up eighty-one percent of eligible voters in this Seventh District. The map also grouped the congressional aspirants Smalls, Miller, and Murray into this single district, making the other six districts winnable for Redeemer Democrats.[20] Today, we refer to this creative device as "packing."

Ironically, the congressional district that guided my historic election in 1992 was drawn in response to this tortuous gerrymandering, a practice begun by Redeemer Democrats in the 1880s to limit Black representation and religiously adhered to by the legislatures in South Carolina and other Redeemer states for more than a century.

Before the decennial reapportionment in 1992, the U.S. Justice Department informed these states that a 1982 amendment to the Voting Rights Act of 1965 required district lines to be drawn that ensured African American voters would be able to elect candidates of their choice to Congress. In other words, the "packing," and later "cracking" (to widely distribute Black voters so they wouldn't have enough votes to influence the outcome of an election), that the Redeemer-controlled states began in the 1880s would not be tolerated in the 1990s.

At the time of my candidacy, Blacks constituted nearly thirty percent of South Carolina's population, yet the state's congressional delegation was one hundred percent white. Following the "Exoduster" movement in the late 1870s and '80s and the Great Migration in the 1920s and '30s, South Carolina's population declined, resulting in a congressional allotment of just six House seats in 1992. And, as was done with the Seventh District in 1882, the state legislature in 1992 made the Sixth District highly winnable for a Black candidate—but the other five districts nearly impossible for a white candidate to lose.

THE EXPLOSION OF CREATIVE DEVICES

Racialized voting and tortuous redistricting were not enough for Redeemer Democrats, who seemed determined to add as much insult to injury as they could possibly muster.

In 1882 one of the early devices they employed in South Carolina was the Eight Box Law. This required voters to correctly place individual ballots for each elective office into a designated box. If a voter put their ballot in the wrong box, their vote was thrown out. This amounted to a literacy test that was rigged against Black Americans, who had significantly lesser educational attainment for obvious reasons. In 1880, nearly seventy-nine percent of all Black South Carolinians were illiterate, compared to just twenty-two percent of whites.[21]

Miller led the Senate opposition to the legislation, chiding Redeemer Democrats for their assertion that the law would ensure fair elections and protect both white and Black voters. "Is there a Senator here who believes [this]?" he challenged. "No, Senators, it is a libel on our intelligence."

The Eight Box Law proved very effective. It skirted federal election laws because on its face it was race-neutral, which made it more effective in practice: Redeemer-employed poll workers could easily direct illiterate whites to the correct boxes while misguiding illiterate Black voters, and that is what they did.

Another piece of legislation, also targeting Black Americans, required all to re-register to vote by June 1, 1882; if they failed to do so, they were disqualified from registering forever. Further, if the voter moved—even if within the same precinct—they had to pay to re-register; otherwise, they would also be disqualified. Like with the Eight Box Law, election registrars bent the rules in favor of whites. If the registrar didn't want to register a voter for any reason, the voter would have to appeal in a confusing and lengthy process designed to encourage them to drop the matter entirely.[22] These devices resulted in a dramatic drop in effective Black voting in South Carolina, from fifty-eight thousand in 1880 to less than fourteen thousand by 1888.[23]

Still more tactics prevailed. The *New York Daily Tribune* reported on the experience of a Hampton County Republican, who said that Democrats, but not Republicans, were mailed registration certificates even if they had not gone in person to their polling places, as was required by law. The county registrar also challenged the ages of many Black voters, whose cases had to be heard before the board of registration. That board then met in secret without public notification, and simply disqualified the Black voters after they failed to appear.[24] In other instances, registrars asked Black voters to interpret sections of the U.S. Constitution; if they could not do so to their satisfaction, they would not be registered to vote.

As egregious as these devices were, over time, the Redeemers' tactics grew even more creative and sophisticated—so much so that they influenced generations to come. Most people have heard of tactics such as asking potential Black voters the number of jellybeans in a jar or the number of bubbles in a bar of soap—two tactics that have been used in my lifetime—but there were other, more complex strategies too, such as at-large voting districts, numbered posts, and fifty-percent-plus-one runoff requirements. And, just in case a threatening number of Black voters were made eligible, a fail-safe method called "full-slate voting" was employed. When I ran for the state legislature in 1970, I had to cast a total of eleven votes, one for myself and one each for ten of the other candidates running for the office, in order for my ballot to be counted.

The Redeemers' tactics worked as intended. In 1872, ninety-six Blacks were elected to the South Carolina legislature; by 1890, there were just seven.[25] In 1873, four of South Carolina's five House members were Black; when I ran for Congress in 1992, there were none and there had not been any since 1897, a ninety-five-year gap.

THE 1882 ELECTION

With the newly gerrymandered Seventh Congressional District in place and a plethora of new laws restricting voter participation, the Republicans held their nominating convention in September 1882. Robert Smalls, undeterred by his previous loss because of the Redeemers' tactics, sought the nomination for the Shoestring District. Given its new configuration, which gave it an eighty-two percent Black voting majority, winning the district's Republican nomination would be tantamount to winning the general election.

Two other candidates challenged Smalls for the nomination — Samuel Lee, the first Black speaker of the South Carolina House of Representatives, and Representative Edmund Mackey, a white Republican who had previously defeated Cain in the Second District.

Murray, for his part, had thrown his lot in with Lee. Despite being a political newcomer, he served as a delegate to the 1882 nominating convention and continued to demonstrate his proclivity to agitate. He took to the floor and threatened to "turn the district to the Bourbons," a disparaging term for fiscally conservative Democrats, if the convention didn't nominate Lee. While it was a hollow threat, Murray's determination to "trouble the waters" reflected the disarray of the Republicans at that time. The convention descended into paralysis.

After a week of voting and two hundred and fifty ballots, the nominating process was once again hopelessly deadlocked. Smalls withdrew, throwing his support to his political ally Mackey, and, on the two-hundred-and-fifty-first ballot, the white candidate became the nominee for "the Black District."

In response, the Murray and Lee faction charged malfeasance, and petitioned the Republican State Committee to reject Mackey's nomination due to fraud. But because Mackey also served as the committee's chairman, the protest went nowhere. Lee ran instead as an Independent Republican, but ultimately lost to Mackey by more than eight thousand votes in the general election, in which the Democrats didn't run a candidate because they had no chance of winning.[26] But in a twist of fate, Mackey died unexpectedly while in office on January 27, 1884. A special election was held to fill the seat for the remainder of the term — an election that was won by none other than Robert Smalls.[27]

THE 1883 COLORED PEOPLE'S CONVENTION

Intraparty strife was far from over, and that much became clear during a State Convention of Colored Men in Columbia on July 18, 1883. The convention sought to draw attention to the rapid erosion of Black civil rights, and Miller, Murray, and Smalls served as delegates.

The convention recognized the Republicans' role in securing citizenship rights for Blacks and their "partial enjoyment" of those rights to date. But its delegates also underlined the party's betrayals when it came to Black advocacy, and its failure to appoint African Americans to any office of "honor, emolument or trust" in the past six years, despite their voting loyalties. However, they held their greatest condemnation for the Redeemers, and made this plea:

> We wish the American people to understand...that we are cursed with the most damnable form of State Government to which a free people have ever been subjected. By legislation, the right to enjoyment of an honest vote and a fair count has been taken from us. The right of a fair trial by an impartial jury is denied us...The lynching of our people for suspected offences has become prevalent...we feel called upon to denounce in unmeasured terms such flagrant and so far unpunished violations of law.

That September, Miller and Smalls attended the National Convention of Colored Men in Louisville. As the delegates gathered, an editorial appeared in the *Indianapolis Journal* as a preemptive effort to dismiss their concerns. It reflected the widely held attitude in the white community that Blacks, freed from the bondage of slavery, were now citizens and should be able to provide for themselves without government assistance. The editorial read in part:

> The delegates must know that the time has come for the colored man to take his place in the race of life according

to his deserts. Once there was a necessity for his receiving the fostering care of the government to protect him from the tyranny and rapacity of his former master, but that necessity no longer exists as an imperative force. He must care for himself and can reasonably expect to enforce no claim upon the government not common to all American citizens.[28]

Frederick Douglass served as chairman of the Louisville convention, and in his address refuted the editorial's argument that Blacks were now equals before the law. "In all the relations of life and death, we are met by the color line," he declared. "We cannot ignore it if we would and ought not if we could." And while he struck a positive tone of racial reconciliation, noting his "faith in [the white race], in reason, in truth, and justice," he too acknowledged the growing political discontent within the Black community, saying, "If the Republican party cannot stand for and demand justice and fair play, it ought to go down. We were men before that party was born, and our manhood is more sacred than any party can be. Parties were made for men, not men for parties."[29]

His attitude reflected the same frustration expressed a decade earlier by Robert De Large and Alonzo Ransier at a Charleston rally that cost them support within the Republican Party.

Undeterred by the potential consequences, the Black men at the Louisville convention overwhelmingly rejected a resolution to support the Republican president, Chester Arthur, in large measure because he had reformed the political patronage system by instituting a "merit"-based system, which prevented Blacks from securing many of these coveted positions. The opposition to President Arthur's reelection no doubt caused a greater rift within the party.

Lithograph of ten notable African American men published around the time of the National Convention of Colored Men, including Frederick Douglass, Joseph Rainey, Robert Elliott, and the University of South Carolina professor Richard Greener, 1883. (Library of Congress, Prints and Photographs Division, LC-DIG-pga-02252)

THE HIGH COURT CAPITULATES

Three weeks after the National Convention of Colored Men, the fears of Miller, Smalls, and other delegates were realized when the U.S. Supreme Court declared most of the Civil Rights Act of 1875 unconstitutional. The high court handed down an eight-to-one decision in the Civil Rights Cases, finding that Congress did not have the power to criminalize the discriminatory actions of a private person or business.

Rainey, Elliott, Ransier, and Cain had argued passionately for the act, which had enshrined protection for Black citizens, prohibiting states from depriving them of their rights to life, liberty, or property without due process. Now, however, the Supreme Court had declared that Congress could not enact legislation that "nullifie[d] and ma[de] void all state legislation, and state action of every kind, which impair[ed] the privileges and immunities of citizens."

The *Chicago Tribune* praised the ruling for preventing Blacks from being held "above the white man," declaring it an end to their status as "wards of the government." Another Northern newspaper summarized the reactions to the decision across the country, reporting, "The whites are represented as jubilant and the Negroes as perplexed and depressed."[30]

However, Smalls, who was serving in Congress at the time of the ruling, was concerned about the impact it would have on the companion civil rights law he had championed in South Carolina in 1870. The Democrat-controlled legislature in the state had just reenacted the law in 1882 in keeping with the federal statute. Smalls's fears didn't materialize immediately, but the law remained on the books only until 1889, when the South Carolina legislature repealed it as they continued their long-game efforts to redeem the state back to the social and political conditions that existed prior to Reconstruction.[31]

To add insult to injury, on April 14, 1884, the U.S. Supreme Court issued another devastating ruling in the Slaughterhouse Cases, which narrowed the scope of the Fourteenth Amendment to cover only federal citizenship rights, saying it didn't apply to state laws. John C. Calhoun—that avid defender of slavery—and his theory of states' rights were being resurrected by court order.

THE 1884 ELECTION

In 1884, as the assault on Black civil and political rights continued to take its toll, the Republican Party, still home to most African Americans, held its nominating conventions for the next round of elections. But, as one observer put it, these conventions had long become "empty gestures" rather than effective organizing operations.[32] This time around, the party had decided to officially nominate a slate of statewide candidates; but even then, in a reflection of flagging party faith, the man nominated as lieutenant governor acknowledged it was an "empty honor."[33]

Murray, meanwhile, participated in the nominating convention for the newly drawn Seventh Congressional District. And although he had begun his career aligning with the faction of the party known as the Regulars, by the 1884 election cycle he began to clash with members of this alliance.

At the county convention, Murray injected himself into a heated debate about the Seventh Congressional District nomination. Samuel Lee, whom he had supported for the post just two years earlier, was the chair of the convention and gaveled Murray out of order. Murray preceded to parade around the convention floor, demanding to be heard and causing a spectacle.

Lee admonished all the attendees that the press was watching and that these antics would fuel the narrative of Republicans in disarray. Though Murray relented, he retaliated by opposing Lee's proposed lineup of candidates, referring to Lee's supporters as "low down scoundrels." Murray's slate was rejected by the delegates, but his audacious actions earned him the reputation as a vocal critic within the establishment wing of the party. This emerging notoriety didn't help Murray in his first bid for elective office. He sought nomination as a legislative candidate but received only 106 votes, the lowest vote total of any of the candidates, far behind the nominee's nearly 2,000 votes.[34]

In the general election that year, "Regular" Republican Smalls ran again for the Forty-Ninth Congress against the Democrat William Elliott, a Confederate veteran. During the campaign, Smalls leaned in on his status as a war hero and implored African Americans to support him rather than a man who "had fought with the Confederacy against them." Employing its usual incendiary political rhetoric, the *Charleston News and Courier* responded to Smalls's appeal by referring to Blacks on the Sea Islands as his "slaves." "Is it any wonder," the paper mused, "the easily led, credulous and highly emotional colored man votes for the party which he is told protects him from the oppression of white Democrats?" The newspaper reflected the norms of the day, with most publications openly taking sides in the political debate. Its rhetoric feels very similar to what is common in the political arena today. During the Smalls campaign, for example, the *News and Courier* called on "Democrats to take the stump and expose [the Republicans'] misrepresentations" so every Black voter would know Democrats "are his best friends."

To strengthen the resolve of African American voters to go to the polls in the face of all the obstacles, Black ministers urged their parishioners to "fight for their rights." Their angle worked. Despite the heated rhetoric of the campaign, the election took place more peacefully than anticipated, and Smalls won by four thousand votes.[35]

In December 1884, Smalls, ever prescient, made one of the first *Congressional Record* references to Jim Crow, the popular 1820s blackface minstrel character that was demeaning to Blacks. During a floor debate, Smalls objected to an amendment that would allow railroads to provide "separate but equal" accommodations for Black and white passengers. Smalls knew from personal experience that the "Jim Crow car," as he called it, he was forced to use on Georgia trains was not equal to the cars he used in his home state, which still abided by an 1870 law he'd enacted that required equal accommodations.[36]

Smalls could not have known, at that time, the extent to which "Jim Crow segregation" would be injected into the daily lives of African Americans. But it is certainly another notch in the "Most Consequential South Carolinian" belt that I have awarded him.

PART III

JIM CROW

CHAPTER 10

TILLMANITES TAKE CONTROL

—— 1885–1894 ——

"We need protection . . . the chiefest of which is the
right to live."

—Thomas E. Miller

ETWEEN 1885 AND 1894, South Carolina's economy, still grounded
in the "good ol' days" of the antebellum period when cotton was
king, faced challenging times. The Gilded Age, the period following the
Civil War, resulted in rapid industrial and technological advancements
in most of the country, but created widening disparities between the rich
elite and the working poor. In South Carolina, those disparities were
even more pronounced as the agrarian-based economy faced unique
challenges of its own. An overproduction of cotton, persistent droughts,
and a plague of army worms caused devastating crop losses. As a result,
from 1886 to 1888, more than a million acres—equal to eight percent of
all the state's farmland—were auctioned off due to failure to pay taxes.
Yet the state's Democratic leaders insisted the economy was doing well
and that those who complained were ignorant.[1]

As is the case today, the state of the economy influenced opinions about
those in political control. As the party in power, Redeemer Democrats found
themselves challenged within their own party by a populist movement; but
the Black Republicans, as the outgoing party, were made scapegoats too,

accused of creating the state's economic woes. Further still, their hard-won place in South Carolina's political and social structure continued to be undermined by the growing efforts to return to a system of Black servitude and white supremacy, an era that became known as Jim Crow.

Despite these circumstances, George Washington Murray, a farmer by trade, successfully navigated the challenges his profession faced. He even began expanding his land holdings in 1888, purchasing more than three hundred acres near the Rafting Creek farm he had owned since the 1870s.[2] His star was on the rise professionally and politically.

The higher profile he had acquired during the 1884 convention, while troubling to some Republican Party leaders, elevated Murray's status among his local peers. In 1885, the Sumter County Republican Party elected Murray chairman, the first of three terms he would serve in the post.[3] He was now among the leaders of the Republican Party in South Carolina during its precipitous decline in power. The next generation was beginning to take up the mantle—but a familiar player from the party's old guard was still holding on.

SMALLS'S STRUGGLE FOR THE SEVENTH DISTRICT

In 1886, Robert Smalls, the incumbent in the gerrymandered Shoestring District, ran for a sixth term in Congress. Ten years after the bloody election that effectively ended Reconstruction, Smalls's once-revered status as the "King of Beaufort" had been tarnished by challenges from within and without. The Redeemer Democrats, even more determined to oust this Republican icon, rallied their low-country operatives to "work to remove this danger."

As was the trend, the trouble was not limited to forces outside the party. Infighting among Black Republicans also threatened his reelection bid, as the "pure Blacks" who worked the farmland on St. Helena Island, once Smalls's political base, rebelled against his belief that the district would be better served if it was represented by men "who could read and write and had some attainments derived from travel or as waiters." The farm laborers, who were largely illiterate, pointed to this as Smalls's preference for light-skinned, mixed-race Blacks, and threatened to vote for the Democratic candidate, William Elliott.

The *Charleston News and Courier* reveled in this development and crowed that Smalls was "undoubtedly uneasy" as his chances for reelection were "getting smaller and beautifully less." The Redeemer Democrats were unsure of their candidate's ability to win "the Black district," and thus resorted to familiar dirty tricks, throwing out poll boxes and hundreds of votes for "irregularities," something the *Greenville News* reported as "the county boards [acting] within the law." These tactics, combined with the dissatisfaction within Smalls's political base, resulted in William Elliott claiming victory with fifty-six percent of the vote. Still, the *Greenville News* admitted that the outcome might be called into question and would put the state "before the country as being party to a plain deliberate and wanton fraud."

Smalls, with the support of the Massachusetts senator Henry Cabot Lodge, a proponent of Black voting rights, challenged Elliott's election. The Democrat claimed victory, arguing that Smalls's Black supporters had deserted him. Smalls countered, "The vote is the same today and more, but the Democrats have improved their methods of preventing votes from getting into the box."[4] The House voted to seat Elliott, and Smalls returned home to Beaufort at end of the Forty-Ninth Congress in March 1887. With his defeat, the U.S. House of Representatives became an all-white institution, prompting *The Washington Post* to observe, "The negro is not only out of Congress, he is practically out of politics."[5]

FARMERS' DISCONTENT

For all the Redeemers' efforts to limit Black political power, there was one man among them who stood out, who made it his mission to erase all African American gains. Benjamin Tillman was the youngest of eleven children of an Edgefield County plantation and slave owner. He had lost his father at the age of two and his mother just ten years later, so was raised by his siblings in a family that Robert Smalls once described as "the personification of red-shirt democracy."[6]

Indeed, Tillman had been an integral part of Martin Gary's Red Shirt movement and had even participated in the Hamburg Massacre. He had lost an eye to a tumor as a young man, which perhaps aggravated the anger he felt due to the earlier tragedies in his life. As an adult, Tillman developed a fiery political persona that earned him the nickname "Pitchfork."

"Pitchfork" Ben Tillman began his career in politics organizing the Edgefield Agricultural Society in 1885. His speeches to the group blamed farmers' problems on "renting [land] to ignorant lazy negros" and being "hoodwinked by demagogues" in the Redeemer Democrats' regime. The Charleston News and Courier elevated this rhetoric by publishing a series of rants written by the virulent racist in 1885.

With his growing platform and what the South Carolina historian Walter Edgar referred to as his skill as an "expert manipulator of crowds," starting in November 1886 Tillman began holding annual Farmers' Conventions, ostensibly to seek relief for the white agrarian community. But in reality, Edgar noted, these meetings were an effort to grow a political organization to serve Tillman's ambitions.

A Democrat himself, Tillman tapped into the discontent of farmers, who were frustrated by the claims of Redeemer Democrats that the economy was robust while people were losing their land and their livelihoods. To demonstrate commonality with the masses, Tillman described himself as a "dirt farmer"; he was, in fact, a successful farmer who had inherited land and fortune, which he'd secured by diversifying his crops. But the messaging worked, and he became the voice of the disgruntled farmers and their reform movement.[7] In fact, this narrative persisted long after his death. In 1940, the year of my birth, a statue of Tillman was dedicated on the grounds of the South Carolina State House. It includes an inscription hailing Tillman as a "leader of the common man."

A portrait of "Pitchfork" Benjamin Tillman from 1910, by which time he was serving in the U.S. Senate. (Library of Congress, Prints and Photographs Division, LC-DIG-ggbain-13454)

The tactics of Tillman and his followers should be familiar to anyone observing politics in America today. The MAGA movement and their attacks on the 1964 Civil Rights Act, the 1965 Voting Rights Act, Affirmative Action, and Diversity, Equity, and Inclusion (DEI) programs resemble the rhetoric and actions of the "Tillmanites." To me, the parallels are eerie and clear.

At the time of this writing, the MAGA movement is following a policy blueprint, the infamous *Project 2025*, a guide for the "next conservative president." Its proposals undermine civil and political rights, educational opportunities, and the constitutional guarantees of due process and equal protection. Unlike Martin Gary's Red Shirt plans, this manifesto does not explicitly state that its purpose is to diminish the rights of African Americans. However, that nefarious intent is obvious.

One example is its directive to amend Title VII of the Civil Rights Act of 1964—which prohibits employment discrimination based on race, color, religion, sex, or national origin—in order to prohibit the collection of data by race.[8] While this may seem innocuous on the surface, as a former South Carolina Human Affairs commissioner who spent eighteen years adjudicating cases of employment discrimination, I know that prohibiting data collection would make it more difficult to empirically detect the results of systemic biases, such as poverty and employment rates among racial and ethnic minorities. If successful, this prohibition would take the country back to the post-Reconstruction-era efforts that eliminated civil rights protections.

Another *Project 2025* directive undermines programs designed to address our nation's ten generations of slavery and subsequent decades of Jim Crow discrimination. Particularly, it seeks to eliminate DEI programs, meant to level the playing field for historically underrepresented communities, and teachings about our nation's history of discrimination, which they have mislabeled as "critical race theory," or CRT. MAGA proponents claim that CRT is "actively disrupting the values that hold communities together such as equality under the law and color-blindness," which evidence shows is achieved through openly discussing and educating people on issues of discrimination rather than suppressing them.[9] If successful, *Project 2025* will turn back the clock on the progress that has been made, resulting in devastating impacts on race relations and the pursuit of equity and opportunity for all—which is, of course, the point.

While the discrimination at the core of these policies is more implicit than the vitriolic words and deeds of Tillman and his followers, it is no less harmful. Co-opting the anger of the working class (having been born into an elite class himself) and stoking racism as a wedge issue were Tillman's modi operandi. He perfected bombastic bullying, disenfranchised Black voters, and, most notoriously, imposed segregationist policies under Jim Crow. And today, as the nation watches, MAGA and President Donald Trump are pursuing an agenda that eerily echoes Tillman's rhetoric and the Redeemers' efforts. And if they are allowed to succeed, the consequences could be equally damaging.

MURRAY'S STAR RISING

The 1888 presidential campaign was a chance for George Washington Murray to demonstrate his political acumen. He campaigned vigorously for the Republican Benjamin Harrison and presided over a gathering in Sumter County that celebrated Harrison's victory, despite his loss in South Carolina by more than fifty-two thousand votes to the Democrat Grover Cleveland.

In his address to the more than two thousand Blacks gathered, Murray chided the Redeemer Democrats and blamed the decline of the Republican Party on "ballot-box frauds." He went on to proclaim that the American eagle would leave the South "where it was not healthy for it to live" and go to other states where Republicans were not threatened or harassed. His comments earned him the moniker "the Black bold eagle of South Carolina," which would follow him the rest of his political career.[10]

In another bold move, Murray penned a fifteen-page letter of advice to President Harrison. The letter cautioned the president against his reported plan to appoint Independents rather than Republicans to political patronage jobs—a tactic meant to rebuild the party in South Carolina by attracting disillusioned white Democrats. This, Murray warned, would devastate the party's loyal base, who had risked their personal safety to support Harrison's candidacy. When the president made his South Carolina appointments, he picked a few Independents but ultimately gave most of the positions to Regular Republicans like Robert Smalls, whom he named customs collector in Beaufort. However, whether this minor victory for loyal Republicans could be attributed to Murray's influence was in question, because Harrison also passed him over for the position of Sumter postmaster.[11]

Later, in December 1889, Murray successfully secured a political patronage position as customs inspector in Charleston by appealing to a Sumter colleague who had been tapped as the Charleston customs collector. This proved to be a significant opportunity for Murray; working in the Charleston Customs House put him at the epicenter of Republican politics in the state.[12]

REGULAR REPUBLICANS

As Murray continued to grow his political persona, Thomas Miller also sought to expand his influence in the Republican Party. In October 1888, as a member of the Republican Executive Committee, Miller signed a letter to South Carolina's Democratic governor John Richardson urging him to appoint at least one Republican election commissioner in each county and congressional district in "the act of simple justice and in the interests of a fair, full and honest election."

Two days later the governor denied the request from Miller and his colleagues, whom he called "the comatose...remnants of the Republicans in this state." The governor blamed the "disgraceful scenes and unscrupulous manipulations of elections" on Republicans, declaring "happily, [those days] of the past...can never return...to curse the blight with their horrors the peaceful, prosperous course of all the people of South Carolina."[13]

Richardson went on to declare the state's elections "the freest and fairest in the world." This defiant tone despite all the evidence to the contrary is reminiscent of dishonest political rhetoric today. Many modern-day Republicans employ this practice, believing that if you repeat something that is untrue often enough, people will begin to believe it.

Having no choice but to proceed under the circumstances, Miller did what he thought best for his party during these trying times and convinced Smalls not to run again for the Seventh Congressional District after his "loss" in the previous election. Smalls acquiesced, making way for Miller, who in turn showed his reverence for the contributions of his predecessor by calling him "the greatest politician of any one of us."[14]

Though they were caught off guard by Miller's nomination, the Redeemer Democrats still ran their campaign full of voter suppression and intimidation to maintain control of the "Black district." The *Charleston News and Courier* rallied the Redeemer Democrats' voters, urging them to vote early and often. On Election Day, Elliott, the Redeemer Democrat incumbent, "won" by about thirteen hundred votes.

As the Republicans often did in these situations, Miller challenged the outcome before the U.S. House of Representatives, which held a slim Republican majority, arguing that the Eight Box Law and voter intimidation suppressed the votes of Black Republicans. The data backed him up: In 1888, the number of Black voters dwindled to just under fourteen thousand, compared to the ninety-two thousand that voted in 1876, a dramatic decrease due to the Redeemer Democrats' tactics.[15]

The challenge took most of the Fifty-First Congress to resolve. Miller's case finally came up on the floor of the House on September 23, 1890, nearly two years after the election. On the same day, the House voted to seat Virginia's first Black congressman, John Langston. Resorting to a familiar maneuver, the House Democrats attempted to thwart Langston's confirmation vote by leaving the floor to prevent a quorum; once more, they failed. Given the success of seating Langston, the Speaker of the House unexpectedly called for a vote on Miller's case. Democrats protested, but the vote proceeded, and Miller prevailed with a vote of 157 to 1.[16]

THE ULTRACONSEQUENTIAL 1890 ELECTION

By 1890, having accomplished their goal to overthrow Radical Reconstruction, cracks began to emerge in the once-unified Democratic Party. The populist Tillman challenged the leadership of the old guard, known as the "Bourbon" or Conservative Democrats' wing. Tillman had amassed quite a following through his farm alliance organizing, and his supporters, known as the Tillmanites, pushed for their leader to be nominated for governor. Meanwhile, the aging Confederates who made up the rest of the party backed the rebel colonel, Alexander C. Haskell. Tillman ultimately prevailed, securing the nomination over what he described as the "broken down aristocrats" who saw things "through antebellum spectacles." Stung by what they viewed as disrespect and disobedience, the conservative wing of the party refused to support Tillman's candidacy for governor.[17]

The Democrats' division was a gift to the Republicans, finally giving them an opportunity to unify and assert their political power. But at the Republican State Convention, delegates were once more divided over whether the party should put forward its own slate of statewide candidates or fuse with one of the Democratic factions. Murray, who chaired the convention, played a role in delaying the decision by ignoring a request for a roll call vote, and sent the issue to the Executive Committee to decide later. While the Republicans were biding their time, Haskell announced in September 1890 that he would run against Tillman for governor on the "Straightout Democratic" ticket made up of only conservative Democrats. This turn of events reignited the internal Republican debate.

A group of Black Republicans convened in Columbia in October to formulate their strategy against the competing Democratic candidates. Among the eighty delegates, Murray spoke about Haskell being well-educated and friendly to Blacks. This infuriated another delegate, who countered that Haskell, who might very well be their opponent in the general election, represented the orchestrators of the racial violence of the 1876 campaign, which had ended with Wade Hampton as governor.

After a raucous debate, the gathering of Black leaders eventually agreed not to field a candidate and instead to support Haskell's candidacy. In the same resolution, they also condemned Republican Party leadership for its previous inaction, which Murray objected to as a party leader. Tempers flared and a scuffle ensued after Murray refused to take his seat while the fiery debate continued. The meeting ended as shouts and hisses drowned out Murray's protestations at being ruled out of order. It was clear there was as much division within the Republican Party as there was among Democrats, and Murray had emerged as the chief instigator of the chaos.[18]

Ultimately, Tillman trounced Haskell in the election, as white voters refused to support a candidate who they thought Blacks were supporting. The brunt of the defeat fell hardest on the Republicans.

DIVISIVE CONGRESSIONAL RACE

The divisions in the Republican Party also played out in the race for Congress in the Seventh (Shoestring) District. A three-way contest developed among the Republican Party chairman, a white man named Ellery Brayton who didn't reside in the district; Miller, the incumbent; and Murray, a newcomer making his first run for Congress. And once again, colorism became an issue in the campaign.[19]

The press loved stoking this division, referring to the light-skinned Miller as "the Canary" and the dark-skinned Murray as "the Black Eagle." Miller received more support in coastal communities where individuals of mixed race were held in high esteem, while Murray fared well in his inland home county of Sumter.

At the party's nominating convention, Miller bested both Murray and Brayton, taking more than half the vote. Brayton's supporters claimed fraud, and he ran for the seat as an Independent Republican. In the general election, Miller ran against Brayton and the Democratic nominee, William Elliott, and received the most votes, in defiance of the Tillmanites' best efforts. (Among other antics, they'd raided Sumter County's Rafting Creek precinct, where they destroyed three ballot boxes and the voter registration book.)

However, the state's Democratically appointed election officials quickly overturned Miller's victory through a series of technicalities. At that time, candidates provided their own Election Day ballots, and Miller's ballots were found to be one-sixteenth of an inch narrower and one-eighth of an inch shorter than the regulations allowed. Election officials also claimed that instead of the prescribed white ballots, Miller's ballots had a "yellow tinge." He'd also printed the word "for" before the office title "representative," which also didn't follow the rules.[20] It was a crushing disappointment for the Republicans and for Miller, who would have to wait for the start of the next Congress to contest the election before the House of Representatives. But first, he needed to return to Washington to participate in the remaining three months of his term under the Fifty-First Congress.

MILLER'S BRIEF CONGRESSIONAL SERVICE

Back in the nation's capital, Miller took the opportunity to address the outcome of his reelection bid during a speech on the House floor, reaffirming his victory by declaring, "I was elected."

Miller knew his statements challenging the nullification of his election might diminish his chances of winning the contest for the Seventh District, but he believed it was his responsibility to tell the truth. He continued:

> I shall not be muffled here. Muffled drums are instruments
> of the dead. I am in part the representative of the living; of
> those whose rights are denied; of those who are slandered by
> the press, on the lecture platform, in the halls of legislation,
> and oftentimes by men in the livery of heaven, and I deem it
> is my supreme duty to raise my voice, though feebly, in their
> defense.[21]

In his speech, one of only two he delivered on the House floor, Miller referenced the failure of Congress to pass the Election Bill of 1890, known as the Lodge Bill, which sought to provide federal oversight of elections and protect against voter violence and intimidation. The legislation, had it been passed, would have resulted in very different election outcomes across the former Confederate states.

During the Fifty-First Congress, Republicans held the presidency and both the House and Senate for the first time since the end of Reconstruction. However, in the most recent November election, Democrats had recaptured the House for the Fifty-Second Congress by a wide margin. That meant if Congress failed to enact the Lodge Bill in the lame duck session, it would be shelved indefinitely. Thus, after the election, the House acted with urgency and passed the legislation by just six votes, sending it to the Senate. Miller urged them to follow suit, imploring, "We need protection... the chiefest of which is the right to live."[22]

In his remarks, Miller also responded to comments made by a Georgia senator that Blacks had demonstrated their inability to govern during Reconstruction and that they were to blame for the South's economic decline. Miller gave a lengthy, scathing rebuttal:

> The presence of the negro does not retard the development of the South. It is not his fault that the South has remained bottled up, yes, literally bottled up within her circumscribed sphere feasting upon sectional hate, seeking to destroy all that is good in our institutions, falsifying and misrepresenting her countrymen.... There is no people in the world more self-opinionated without a status; no people in the world so quick to misjudge their countrymen and misstate historical facts or political economy, and impugn the motives of others. History does not record a civilized people who have been contented with so little and can feast for so long upon a worthless buried past. While crying for mercy and attempting to speak as ambassadors of peace, there are no people in the world more vituperative than her leaders.[23]

I find much resonance in Miller's remarks and could deliver a similar floor speech today about our current political discourse and the "vituperative . . . leaders" of today's Republican Party. Even more poignant, history has now shown us the danger of political power in the hands of those "contented with so little" who "feast for so long upon a worthless buried past." Having the benefit of knowing how this tragic story played out, I can confirm that all of Miller's fears came to pass.

Yet Miller's pleas went unheeded as the Senate spent thirty-three days paralyzed by a Democratic-led filibuster making it unable to enact the Lodge Bill. This marked the first instance in which the Senate used the filibuster to stop civil rights legislation, a procedure that currently requires the votes of sixty Senators to end debate. This became the go-to maneuver by Southern Democrats in the 1950s, many of whom would be

Republicans now. In modern times, Republicans have set records for the use of the filibuster.

The next time Miller would appear before Congress was to challenge the results of the election. However, in the Fifty-Second Congress, Democrats held a two-to-one majority over the Republicans in the House. And they used their partisan advantage to further the Great Betrayal by delaying a hearing on Miller's appeal. It wasn't until the last month of the two-year term that Miller got to plead his case, and it fell on deaf ears. The House seated the Democrat William Elliott despite Miller's overwhelming victory at the ballot box.[24] South Carolina once again had no Republican and no Black representation in Congress.

TILLMAN TENETS

After his election, "Pitchfork" Ben Tillman wasted no time asserting his agenda. In his inaugural address, he declared his win a "triumph of democracy and white supremacy over mongrelism and anarchy, of civilization over barbarism." He asserted his desire to convene a constitutional convention to rewrite the state's governing document, and believed he had a mandate to do so, but ultimately could not secure the two-thirds Senate majority needed to move forward.[25]

This failure should have galvanized the Republicans into action against the Tillman agenda. However, the opposition party proved more divided than ever. As organizing began for the 1892 election, the Reformers and the Regulars even went so far as to hold separate conventions to elect delegates to the national gathering. Miller, Smalls, and Murray participated in the Regulars convention in Columbia on April 19, 1892.

The *Charleston News and Courier* disparaged the convention participants, describing them as representatives of "every species of colored man....A face which glistens in its blackness is seen next to that of a mulatto who can scarcely be distinguished from that of his neighbor, a white man." In a demonstration of continued party divisions, Miller on behalf of the Regulars referred to the Reformers' convention as "a small, weak, and inconsequential band of men... drawn together by selfish greed."[26]

While Republicans were far from unified, the divisions that existed in the previous campaign amongst Democrats remained. Tillman's supporters, who had used Martin Gary's Red Shirt tactics to great effect in 1876, employed the same strategy against their intraparty opponents in 1892. This intimidation of fellow Democrats, in combination with the Republicans' infighting, resulted in Tillman running unopposed for governor, attempting to secure a second term in office. With the nomination secured but never being one to accept responsibility for his failures, Tillman blamed the ineffectiveness of his first term on the "driftwood" legislature and called on voters to defeat the lawmakers who disregarded "the will of the people" by opposing him.[27]

The Republicans decided to focus their energy on winning the Seventh Congressional District and a handful of legislative seats. Murray, whose profile had risen during the 1890 election season, began campaigning in April for the "Black" congressional seat, vying for the nomination against Miller, Smalls, and Brayton, the white candidate who had run as an Independent Republican in the 1890 race.

Murray again pointed to his darker complexion to distinguish himself from his lighter-skinned opponents and appeal to the many "full Africans" in the district. This time, he emerged as the victor. The Port Royal newspaper, however, dismissed his chances of winning the general election, calling him "an obscure colored man."[28]

Although Murray's complexion had successfully distinguished him from the pack, it didn't necessarily translate to universal acceptance among Blacks. After a political rally featuring Murray on the coast, it was reported that some Blacks left in disgust, saying "if they couldn't have a colored man most like a white man, they would rather have a white man, and they would vote for" the conservative Democrat challenger, E. W. Moise.[29]

Indeed, Republicans had a rough election night; what little power they had left was further diminished, as their representation in the state legislature fell from six seats to three. Even the Black Shoestring District, which should have been the bright spot, remained too close to call.

When the count ended eight days later, Murray had the votes to be declared the winner. However, thirteen hundred ballots in Berkeley County necessary to secure his victory were thrown out, just as Miller's had been previously for being the wrong size. Murray had to argue his case before the State Board of Canvassers, made up of five Tillmanites, who would decide the outcome of the election. One would expect a unanimous decision for Moise, but that would ignore the split within the Democratic Party.

The Tillman Democrats saw an opportunity to retaliate against the Bourbon Democrats, and they took it. And so, though the Board of Canvassers represented the most racist faction in South Carolina politics, they ruled in favor of Murray — to them a better option than Moise, who represented the Democratic Party's old guard.

Thus Murray's election dispute, along with further dividing the Democrats, brought together warring factions of Republicans—at least temporarily. In fact, the attorneys who represented Murray before the Board of Canvassers were two of his prior adversaries, Thomas Miller and Samuel Lee.[30]

With his victory, Murray could now focus on how he would represent not only the African American residents of his district, but Blacks from across the country. He was the lone Black member of the United States House of Representatives.

MURRAY ENTERS CONGRESS

George Washington Murray's first action as a Member of Congress in 1893 was inauspicious. As the first order of business, the new House members had to select their seats in the chamber. Each member received a number based on where their name fell in the alphabet. When a marble with their number was pulled from a container, they chose their seat from those available. Murray's number was called early, and press accounts of the day reported he selected a good seat. However, despite its prime location, the seats surrounding him weren't taken until the last numbers were called—a grim welcome indeed.[31]

Murray's entry into the hallowed halls of the U.S. Capitol revealed a lot about the challenges and isolation he would face. But before he could get up to speed, Murray had to hurry home to deal with a natural disaster in Beaufort County. On August 27, 1893, a hurricane with winds reaching 120 miles per hour made landfall on Hilton Head. The devastating storm killed as many as twenty-five hundred people in the South Carolina sea islands. Murray and Smalls joined in the effort to collect money, food, and clothing for those left homeless by what would have been a Category 3 hurricane by today's measures.

Predominately Black communities were more severely impacted by the disaster, but Governor Tillman refused to render aid to them, arguing they could not "be treated as we would white people." This inaction prompted Murray, on September 11, 1893, to introduce a joint resolution in the House instructing the federal government to provide food and medical assistance to the affected communities. The resolution was sent to the Appropriations Committee, but it never received consideration.

At that time, FEMA (Federal Emergency Management Agency) had yet to be established, so the federal government didn't provide aid to states to help with natural disasters. Eventually, at the urging of community leaders, the governor asked Clara Barton, head of the fledgling American Red Cross, to provide aid. Having spent nine months on Hilton Head during the Civil War, Barton was familiar with the area. Still, she didn't arrive in Beaufort County until six weeks after the storm struck. But even at seventy-one years old, she energetically organized a relief effort, raising money, rebuilding homes, and providing food for more than thirty thousand people.[32]

When Murray returned to Washington for congressional business, the topic at hand was a personal priority. Up for debate in the House was legislation to remove impartial federal election supervisors and deputy marshals from polling places in the South. Murray opposed the legislation, which was a clear method of voter suppression, but felt the need to stroke Tillman's ego—likely because he owed his seat to Tillman's election board—and began his speech with an olive branch to his state's Democratic administration. He claimed there was no administration "more honest and truer to the principles of right"; but he knew that revoking this weak federal protection would hammer the last nail in the coffin of Blacks' right to vote.

Having lauded the Democrats, Murray then criticized the measure, saying it "must have been conceived in sin and born in iniquity." Addressing the millions of African Americans nationwide that he felt it was his duty to represent, Murray told them to "mark the name of every man casting an affirmative vote and regard him as their perpetual enemy."[33]

Knowing that his words alone might be futile, however, Murray then publicly implored President Cleveland to intervene, to thunderous applause from his Republican colleagues. Despite this, the bill passed both houses of Congress, and President Cleveland signed it into law in February 1894.[34]

Murray's performance, although failing to achieve his aims, earned him praise from the Black press. *The Washington Bee* called him "the best representative that has been in the House."[35]

THE 1894 ELECTION

In 1894, Murray returned to South Carolina to seek another term in Congress. The state legislature had redrawn the congressional district lines, this time gerrymandering them with the intent to "crack" rather than "pack" Black voters. Instead of concentrating it, this plan diluted Black voting power by dispersing African American communities among all the districts so they couldn't achieve a majority in any. Murray's home base of

Sumter County and heavily Black Orangeburg County remained in the reconfigured Seventh District, which no longer resembled a shoestring. "Cracking" became the South Carolina method all the way up to 1992.

Because of the overwhelming Black majority along the coast, the new First Congressional District, which also included Beaufort and Charleston, could not be fully "cracked." This provided the only real opportunity for a Republican victory. Murray thus opted to move to Charleston, where he had previously served as a customs inspector, and to seek reelection in the newly drawn district, which had twenty thousand more Black voters than white.

Robert Smalls, who had lost his position as customs inspector under President Cleveland's administration, had also decided to run for the district. Smalls and Murray had a longstanding rivalry, and the race quickly grew bitter. They fought, most notably over who had done the most to aid victims of the 1893 hurricane. Murray also re-raised their differing skin tones, intoning that voters ought to elect "a typical Black man" to Congress and not a candidate of mixed race like Smalls. When Smalls challenged the way Murray had secured the Republican nomination, Murray complained his opponent seemed "more desirous of accomplishing my defeat than even [the Democratic opponent] Elliott."[36]

But there were also self-inflicted problems in Murray's campaign. That same year, Murray was invited by Booker T. Washington to deliver an address at Tuskegee Institute, the agricultural and mechanical training school in Alabama where Washington served as principal. His campaign opponents seized on a passage in his address in which he lamented that many well-educated Blacks were waiting tables or working in barbershops.

Two Black barbers published a letter defending the value of their trade. Murray reacted defensively, attacking "the persons who tried to distort my words" as "either fools or rogues." The *Charleston News and Courier* piled on, writing that "a good barber, whatever the color of his skin, is really of more account than a poor congressman." To be sure, considering the importance of the barbering profession in Black political circles, Murray's words were an avoidable misstep during an already bruising campaign.[37]

When the results were declared on Election Day, Murray had lost the campaign to Elliott, the perennial Democratic candidate. Likely thanks to Democratic tactics of voter suppression, just four percent of the district's population had voted on Election Day.[38] Murray once again prepared to contest the election, using the evidence Republicans collected. This time, the Tillman-controlled state elections board did not rule in his favor, forcing Murray to take his challenge to Congress.

At the hearing before the House Elections Committee, Murray brought a stack of evidence reported to be twelve inches thick. Upon review, the Elections Committee found that Elliott had "stood like a stone wall between [Blacks] and the ballot box in many instances." The committee also found that ballots from precincts with large Black majorities in the district had not been opened. As a result, Murray won the support of the House, and he took the oath of office for his second term with just seven days left in the first session of the Fifty-Fourth Congress.[39]

Despite this victory, Murray didn't return to Washington for the remaining two sessions of his term. Instead he turned his attention back home, where, via a public referendum, Governor Tillman, whose term was ending, had finally gathered enough support for a constitutional convention, setting in motion his plan to completely repeal Black civil and political rights.

The referendum had passed by fewer than two thousand votes, and one white Tillman foe warned, "Remember that a Constitutional Convention has been called through fraud of the blackest character." The *Charleston News and Courier* concurred, printing a headline, "A Machine Election — White Men Cheat White Men in South Carolina."[40] Despite the documented fraud, Tillman's handpicked successor moved forward, setting an August 1895 election to select delegates to rewrite the state constitution. And all the while, Murray, a Republican Party leader and one of the few remaining Black elected officials in South Carolina, committed himself to "arouse [their] people up to a realization of the situation and what they can do to help themselves."

Future history books would perpetuate a narrative that Blacks of the era had resigned themselves to a future of "reasonable white supremacy." However, Murray's last stand against the full implementation of Jim Crow debunks that myth.[41] There was too much at stake for himself and his people. This well-known agitator wasn't done getting into "good trouble."

CHAPTER 11

THE FIRST EIGHT ERA ENDS

———— 1895–1935 ————

"The house is afire, get your buckets of water and put it out."

—George Washington Murray

I N FEBRUARY 1895, REPUBLICANS held an organizational meeting to address the direness of their situation. Things had deteriorated so rapidly that "the very life of suffrage in [the] state" was at stake, they said, along with "other cherished rights." They called upon Black ministers to encourage their congregants to register to vote and turn out in force to select delegates who would advocate for them.[1] As they had since before the Civil War in South Carolina, Black clergy had significant influence and integrity in the African American community and proved to be effective political organizers.

The widespread fraud that occurred during the constitutional convention referendum provided the evidence George Washington Murray needed to win his challenge before Congress to represent the First Congressional District. Despite his victory, Murray took leave from his duties in Washington to lead what his biographer called "the Black militant opposition to disenfranchisement." He embarked upon a speaking and legal fundraising tour sponsored by the Black Ministerial Union throughout the state, telling audiences that he needed $1,200 to pay Washington lawyers to challenge the Redeemer Democrats' voter registration laws in court, proclaiming, "The house is afire, get your buckets of water and put it out."[2]

In my lifetime of social and political activism, the NAACP, the Legal Defense Fund, the American Civil Liberties Union, and the Leadership Conference on Civil Rights have been at the forefront of legal challenges to racial discriminatory laws, but back then, such organizations did not exist — which was why Murray had taken it upon himself to lead the charge. But African Americans didn't universally support Murray's plan to stop their disenfranchisement. Thomas Miller, Murray's longstanding intraparty political foe, published a public letter chiding Murray for making promises that he knew he couldn't keep. In it, he also wondered why Murray would pay Washington lawyers when there were capable Black lawyers like himself and Samuel Lee in South Carolina. In response, Murray lashed back at Miller, questioning his motives for the public attack and arguing that his critics could have acted earlier, but chose not to.

Then as now, media outlets relished the differences of opinion and did all they could to drive wedges in the Black community. The *Palmetto Post*, a pro-Tillman paper, delighted in reporting the Miller-versus-Murray antagonism, saying, "By the time the Canary gets through with the Blackbird, the latter will be willing to shed his feathers." But the public feud didn't dissuade Murray from continuing his course of action, and Miller for his part focused on registering Black voters to elect more friendly delegates to the constitutional convention.[3]

Murray's efforts did produce a lawsuit in the U.S. Circuit Court. He challenged a new special voter registration law that required Blacks who wanted to register to vote in the constitutional convention's delegate election to have been previously registered under the onerous 1882 voter registration law, or provide a full accounting of their life history since 1882, including sworn affidavits by two "reputable" people affirming that history. They had just a fourteen-day window in which to accomplish this and convince the white registrar to accept their application.

In the subsequent lawsuit, *Wiley v. Sinkler,* the Black voter Daniel Wiley, accompanied by Murray, had attempted to vote in the 1894 election, but the election official D. L. Sinkler turned him away for lack of a registration certificate. In the lawsuit, Wiley asked for $2,500 in damages for the violation of the Fifteenth Amendment protection against denying a citizen's right to vote "on account of race, color, or previous condition of servitude." The case languished in the courts for years and was ultimately decided in Sinkler's favor.[4]

Harper's Weekly cartoon depicting whites preventing African Americans from voting, 1874. (Library of Congress, Prints and Photographs Division, LC-USZ62-127754)

Mills v. Green followed. This case was filed by twenty-six-year-old Lawrence P. Mills, a Black man who met all the state's registration requirements, and charged W. Briggs Green, the Richland County election supervisor, with blocking his right to register to vote. Unlike the Wiley case, however, things worked in the Black voter's favor—at least at first.

A federal judge ruled the registration laws were written "to abridge and destroy the greatest number of votes of the citizens of African descent, while at the same time interfering with as few as possible of the votes of the white race," and ordered a permanent injunction.[5]

But the celebration was short-lived. A month later, the U.S. Court of Appeals in Richmond overturned the decision, saying the federal court's jurisdiction in political matters pertained only to property rights. And though Murray continued to support legal challenges, the *Mills v. Green* ruling was cited as precedent and resulted in other cases being dismissed.[6]

In one final effort to rally Blacks across the country against the coming constitutional convention, a group of sixty Black leaders, including Murray, met in Columbia. The gathering produced an open letter published in Columbia's *The State* newspaper on July 11, 1895, called "An Appeal to Uncle Sam." The authors urged "the strong arm of the national government" to enforce the constitutional right of Blacks in South Carolina to vote. The writers declared they would not be vanquished. "We will fight the flesh, the devil and all his imps through every court and power in the nation before we shall be robbed of our rights by anarchistic nullifiers."[7]

Despite these resistance efforts, an August election selected delegates to the constitutional convention that began the following month. Only ten thousand Blacks were able to register to vote in the election.[8] As a result, only six Black delegates were elected, five from Beaufort County and one from Georgetown County. They included Miller, Smalls, and William Whipper—the latter two being the only African Americans who had the distinction of serving in both the 1868 constitutional convention that established South Carolina's Reconstruction government and the 1895 convention to undo the progress of its predecessor. In contrast, there were a total of 154 white delegates—112 Tillmanites and 42 Conservative Democrats.[9]

With such overwhelming odds, Smalls, Miller, and three of their fellow Black delegates made one last attempt to warn of what was to come. They sent a letter to the *New York World*, published just after the convention began, with the intent "to stir the conscience of the world" about the impending revocation of Black voting rights in South Carolina. Taking a tone more conciliatory than Murray's earlier appeal, they argued that African Americans posed no threat to white supremacy because "even in the days of Republican ascendancy all the great offices, and the majority of all the offices, were held by white men, and no one ever thought of making that a Negro government."[10]

REWRITING THE SOUTH CAROLINA CONSTITUTION

Ben Tillman, now a U.S. senator, and his allies knew that to continue "lawfully" disenfranchising Black voters, they had to devise ways to do so within the confines of the Fifteenth Amendment. Still, he didn't hide from the tactics used by Redeemer Democrats to end the period of Reconstruction in South Carolina. Speaking at the convention, Tillman smugly declared, "By fraud and violence, if you please, we threw it off. In 1878 we had to resort to more fraud and violence, and so again in 1880. Then the Registration Law and eight-box system had evolved from the superior intelligence of the white man to check and control this surging, muddy stream of ignorance."[11]

The 1895 constitution expanded upon those creative devices to further disenfranchise Black voters; Tillman even served as the chair of the Committee on the Rights of Suffrage so he could oversee the implementation of this top priority.

The committee wrote provisions that limited voter eligibility to men who paid at least three hundred dollars in property taxes and could read and interpret the constitution.[12] Smalls knew that white election officials would administer this literacy test unequally, subjecting Black Republicans to an impossible standard while allowing white Democrats, whether Bourbon or Tillmanites, to pass with a very low bar. He offered a "fair and honest" alternative, a more straightforward, reasonable literacy test that many African Americans could pass. The white delegates, who had no interest in being fair, rejected his proposal.[13] Once Tillman's provisions were enacted in the new constitution, these barriers remained in place in South Carolina until poll taxes were outlawed in 1951 and the federal Voting Rights Act was passed in 1965.

Tillman, true to his incendiary reputation, resurrected the trumped-up bribery charges against Smalls as he railed against "those years of good stealing." Smalls didn't let the slight go unanswered. "I stand here the equal of any man," Smalls declared, drawing a stark contrast between his and his opponents' biographies. "I fought in seventeen battles to make glorious and perpetuate the flag that some of you trampled under your feet. Innocent of every charge attempted to be made here today against me, no act of yours can in any way blur the record I have made at home and abroad."[14]

Miller also defiantly responded to the accusation that Blacks were responsible for government corruption during Reconstruction. "We were eight years in power. We had built schoolhouses, established charitable institutions, built and maintained the penitentiary system...rebuilt the bridges, and reestablished the ferries," he declared, "In short, we had reconstructed the state and placed it upon the road to prosperity."[15]

By these measures, South Carolina's government during the period of Reconstruction was very successful in restoring the institutions vital to a functioning society. Their success made them a target. *The Columbia Daily Register* gave credit to Miller and his Black Republican colleagues at the convention, writing that "abler representatives the colored race could not have had if the state had been raked over with a fine-tooth comb."[16]

MORAL VICTORIES

Knowing the African American delegates didn't have the numbers to stop the enactment of a regressive constitution, Miller decided to focus his efforts on securing greater educational opportunities for Black South Carolinians.

In 1862, President Abraham Lincoln had signed into law the first of two land grant for education laws authored by Representative Justin Morrill of Vermont. The first Morrill Act authorized the sale of federal land to fund the creation of colleges to "benefit the agricultural and mechanical arts." When Thomas G. Clemson, the son-in-law of the ardent defender of slavery John C. Calhoun, died in 1888, he left eighty thousand dollars for the state to start a whites-only agricultural college on his estate in Oconee County. Tillman, then the governor of South Carolina, took this opportunity to designate Clemson College, now Clemson University, as a federal land grant college under the first Morrill Act. The school's white-only charter incented Morrill, who had become a senator, to author a second law.

The second Morrill Act required states to demonstrate that their existing land grant institutions didn't discriminate based on race or to establish a separate institution for Black students. This led to what are now called the 1890 land grant colleges, nineteen HBCUs in the South created to comply with the "separate but equal" requirement.

With this history in mind, at the 1895 constitutional convention, Miller, who was in Congress when the second Morrill Act passed, saw a way to expand educational opportunities for Black students. He offered an amendment establishing a separate state-supported institution for African American students, and Tillman readily agreed. In addition to being a moral victory, this amendment would soon provide a professional opportunity for Miller as well.

The 1895 constitution was ratified on December 4 by a vote of 116 to 7. Thirty-four of the delegates were absent. Two Conservative Democrats voted with five Black Republicans against ratification. Miller made two motions to put the constitution up for a public vote; both times the measure was rejected. The constitution became effective on January 1, 1896, the thirty-third anniversary of the Emancipation Proclamation.[17]

The consequences were enormous for the Black delegates from South Carolina and their constituents. Smalls refused to sign the constitution, which he believed legalized "the frauds perpetrated upon the election franchise in this state since 1876."[18] When told his travel expenses would not be paid if he didn't sign, Smalls simply replied, "I'd rather walk [home] than put my name to a constitution with such an article on suffrage." While he could not stop the devastation from happening, Smalls acquitted himself in a way that one editorial writer characterized as a "brilliant moral victory."

The writer went on to say that Smalls demonstrated that white opposition to Black political power "is not born so much of their regard for their numbers as their intellectual ability. It is not Negro ignorance but Negro intelligence that is being feared." Despite the ratification of the new constitution, Smalls went almost immediately on the campaign trail around the country in support of William McKinley for president. At every stop, he railed against his home state's efforts to nullify political participation for African Americans.[19]

Though Smalls's efforts were heroic, history shows that the new constitution ultimately achieved its purpose. Just one year later, South Carolina had only fifty-five hundred Black registered voters.[20]

A LAND GRANT INSTITUTION FOR BLACKS

When the constitutional convention concluded, Miller resumed his work in the South Carolina House of Representatives. In early 1896, he introduced legislation to establish the independent Colored Normal Industrial Agricultural and Mechanical College of South Carolina, which implemented the directive included in the new state constitution. The legislation designated a state appropriation of five thousand dollars annually for the college and mandated that it could admit only Black students and employ only Black faculty and staff.[21]

Miller's bill was quickly enacted, and, on March 4, 1896, the new 1890 land grant institution was established in Orangeburg. In 1954, the name was changed to South Carolina State College, and in 1992 to South Carolina State University. It remains the only public, historically Black liberal arts college in South Carolina, and I am among its more than thirty thousand proud alumni.[22]

Three days after the new 1890 land grant institution began operations, Miller resigned his seat in the state house of representatives and became the first president of the college, an accomplishment made possible through the victory he had secured in the 1895 convention. He would go on to guide the college through its formative years. The well-educated lawyer and politician took great pride in leading an institution that offered opportunities to the second generation of Black students born after emancipation, opening doors for those who had been denied access to education for so long. The campus thrived under his care, and in 1903, an oversight legislative committee report praised Miller for accomplishing "wonders with the amount of money he has had to work with. We believe he is striving hard for the upbuilding of his race."[23]

Yet it was Miller's involvement in politics that ended his college presidency in 1911. In the previous year's election, Miller had openly opposed the ardent segregationist Democrat Coleman Blease as he ran for governor of South Carolina. Blease believed spending money on the education of Black students resulted only in "ruining a good plow hand and making a half-trained fool" — a disingenuous statement for many reasons, not least because at the time, South Carolina spent just $1.90 per Black student compared to the $17.02 spent on each white student.[24] When Blease prevailed in the general election, he demanded Miller's resignation. Miller left the college he loved and had nurtured through its first fifteen years, making it clear to the governor and others that he had no regrets.

Today the opposition to funding HBCUs continues. In his first term as president, Donald Trump questioned the constitutionality of HBCUs receiving federal funding for construction projects, proclaiming, "It benefits schools on the basis of race."[25] What that statement fails to acknowledge is that these predominantly Black institutions were established because for centuries, African Americans in the South were prohibited from attending public higher education institutions, with the sole exception of the Reconstruction-era University of South Carolina. And even when established they have been historically underfunded: In 2024, the U.S. Department of Education reported that sixteen public HBCUs had a total of $13 billion in funding disparities compared to the white majority institutions in those states, including South Carolina.[26]

HBCUs serve an essential purpose. They educate nearly fifty percent of our nation's Black teachers, seventy percent of our Black doctors and dentists, and eighty percent of our Black lawyers.[27] I liken their role to the art of cutting and polishing diamonds in the rough. Many Black students arrive on HBCU campus in need of remedial education due to their underfunded — and in South Carolina, often "minimally adequate" — public school educations.[28] As the late, great astronaut Ronald McNair of Lake City, South Carolina, once told me, "When people introduce me, they always talk about my Ph.D. from MIT. Nobody talks about what really launched me. If I had not gone to North Carolina A&T, where I received personal attention and had the benefit of small classes in a nurturing environment, I wouldn't have been prepared to succeed at MIT."[29]

Ron had the talent and the tenaciousness to take him to the elite corps of American astronauts, but he, like so many African Americans whose opportunities have been limited by racial discrimination, needed that which HBCUs offer: professors and administrators whose similar backgrounds and experiences helped cut and polish him into the valuable diamond he became, before the space shuttle *Challenger* disaster cut short his promise. I have heard similar stories from others, and I am a living testimony to the importance of HBCUs as well.

THE LAST OF THE FIRST EIGHT

Reeling from the decimation of Blacks at the hands of the 1895 South Carolina Constitutional Convention, the Republican Party fractured in two. In 1896, Smalls and Miller joined the Regular Republicans' convention. Murray, meanwhile, participated in the Reformers' nominating convention known as the "Lily Whites," a misnomer, as the delegates included 54 white men and 250 Blacks. The Reformers nominated Murray for reelection to the First Congressional District, while the Regulars nominated Cecil Cohen, a white Charleston railway mail clerk.

Incensed by the intraparty opposition, the candidates launched another bruising campaign. Cohen attacked Murray, saying he was nominated illegally by a faction of the party that failed to gain recognition of its delegates to the national convention. Murray countered that he secured the endorsement of the Republicans' national congressional committee; his supporters piled on and accused Cohen of planning to drop out of the race if he received an appointment to be a postmaster. As a result of the intraparty fighting, Murray focused his energy more on defeating Cohen than on his once-again Democratic opponent, William Elliott.

Unsurprisingly, Elliott won. He received more than forty-six hundred votes, defeating Murray by a two-to-one margin. But Murray took pride in besting Cohen with nearly 2,500 votes to his intraparty opponent's paltry 173.[30] Murray attempted again to challenge the election and prepared reams of evidence of Black voter disenfranchisement to support his case, but Republicans in Congress, weary of deciding the outcome of disputed Southern contest after Southern contest, delayed hearing the case and ultimately failed to act.

Still, Murray had a plan. Falling back on his disruptor roots, Murray returned to Washington for the end of the Fifty-Fourth Congress and caused a stir by threatening to contest the presidential electors from South Carolina if Congress didn't investigate the widespread disenfranchisement of Black voters in his home state. He claimed to have evidence of 100,000 legal voters who had been prohibited from casting their ballot. South Carolina Democrats accused Murray of attempting to "prejudice the country against the election laws of the south" and force them "to submit to negro domination."[31]

But Republicans didn't like Murray's tactics either, believing he was jeopardizing the chances of their presidential candidate, William McKinley. Indeed, by this point Murray's own party was tiring, a mindset encapsulated by this statement from the Republican Samuel W. McCall: "A full generation has passed since the colored men were enfranchised, and I do not know how long they can expect us to coddle them and fight to secure their electoral rights while they neglect to learn to read and write."[32]

Murray succumbed to the pressure and agreed not to challenge the electors. Instead he submitted a petition to Congress, signed by several hundred South Carolinians, calling for an investigation; in February 1896 he introduced a resolution with the same message. When Senator Tillman threatened to filibuster Murray's resolution, the House leadership struck a face-saving deal and agreed to hold hearings on the resolution, though they intended to bury it. Murray, Smalls, and Ellery Brayton, usually bitter rivals, presented a united front, and provided testimony from various factions within the South Carolina Republican Party.

With only weeks to go in the Fifty-Fourth Congress, as expected, no substantial action was taken. The House expressed concern over the disenfranchisement of Black voters, but its only action was to issue a "statement of the charges and allegations without findings," then to refer the matter to the incoming Fifty-Fifth Congress, effectively washing their hands of the matter. Murray's last stand had come to an end.

His longtime critic Thomas Miller, now serving as president of South Carolina State College, didn't pass up the opportunity to weigh in. Miller called Murray "a heartless traitor" for not contesting the presidential electors as he threatened, then criticized him for publicizing his grand plans and "cowardly deserting them before the battle was on" by retracting his challenge. Murray retorted that Miller fought against the new constitution as a delegate at the convention, but once it was enacted began praising it around the state to secure his position as president of the new constitutionally established Black college. Theirs proved to be a rivalry that would not end.[33]

DANGEROUS WORK

With the Republicans back in control of the federal executive branch, Murray tried to exert his political influence one more time to get his friends appointed by the president to political patronage jobs in South Carolina. McKinley ignored Murray's requests and appointed other Republicans, including reinstating Smalls as customs inspector in Beaufort.

However, political patronage jobs for Blacks in South Carolina could be dangerous work. The first Black postmaster appointed in the town of Lake City by President McKinley was Frazier Baker. In February 1898, a mob of several hundred white men demanded Baker step down from the post. They set fire to his home, in which the post office was located. When Baker emerged from the burning house with his infant daughter in his arms, the two were gunned down and died instantly. Baker's wife and five other children escaped into the nearby woods, but many of them were wounded. The surviving family members eventually resettled in Boston.

Outraged by these horrific murders, Murray joined a delegation from South Carolina to meet with President McKinley. While the president expressed sympathy, he took no action. Several men were tried for the murders in South Carolina, but the case resulted in a hung jury.[34]

MRS. FRAZER BAKER AND CHILDREN,
Family of the Murdered Postmaster at Lake City, So. Carolina.

Surviving members of Lake City Postmaster Frazier Baker's family who escaped to Boston after his lynching, 1898. (Library of Congress, Prints and Photographs Division, LC-DIG-ds-14128)

Like so many victims of racial violence in South Carolina, Frazier Baker and his story disappeared from public consciousness. I learned about his lynching from his grandniece, Fostenia Baker, who was a college classmate of mine. Fostenia was very passionate about getting recognition for her granduncle, and soon after I got elected to Congress, she started lobbying me on his behalf. His story haunted me, and although it took some time to accomplish, I eventually secured congressional approval to rename the Lake City Post Office in honor of Frazier B. Baker, to ensure his sacrifice would be remembered. I proudly stood with Fostenia and her family at the dedication on February 22, 2019. I did not know of Murray's involvement with Frazier Baker until I was far along with this project. It made me even prouder to know that I completed the effort that Murray began, which President McKinley had originally rejected.

MURRAY REFUSES TO FADE AWAY

In 1898, railing against the obstacles placed in his path, Murray tried once more to regain his seat in Congress, again running against the Democrat William Elliott. The *Charleston News and Courier* described the race as one between "a capable, conscientious and thoroughly tested white man, and an ignorant and unworthy negro."[35]

In the election, Murray tried to beat the Democrats at their own game. He wrote an incendiary letter and he told a friend, "I used the word 'n—' so as to make the language as contemptible and as much like that of the most prejudiced Democrat as possible," and signed it "A Disgusted Democrat," with the intent of distributing it widely the night before the election, hoping to spur more Blacks to vote. However, a Murray supporter in Beaufort mishandled the document, exposing the plot. Still, even if executed properly, Murray's "dirty trick" likely would have had little impact. On Election Day, he received just over fifteen hundred votes, significantly off from his 1892 electoral victory with a total of nearly five thousand. Elliott won the 1898 election handily by a two-to-one margin.[36]

Discouraged by the lack of congressional action during his previous election appeal, Murray didn't turn to them this time and instead sent letters to the state Board of Canvassers with his objections, but didn't pursue any other avenues.[37] It was clear that his political career was ending. What was not clear, at the time, was that the disenfranchisement of Black voters would end African American representation in Congress from South Carolina for nearly a century.

Although Murray's time in Congress had come to an end, he continued to demonstrate "a determined effort to overcome his state's racist discrimination," and turned his attention to pursuing justice for African Americans outside of policymaking.[38]

Murray helped found and served as president of the Negro National Protection Association in Washington. He toured the country attempting to uplift the condition of Blacks by spreading the association's message, one that he had been delivering throughout his public life: Blacks would overcome prejudice through economic empowerment, property ownership, and racial pride. The association was eventually folded into the Afro-American Council, a precursor to the National Association for the Advancement of Colored People (NAACP), a renowned organization in which I hold two life memberships and that continues to advocate for Black Americans to this day. Yet even with this far-reaching achievement under his belt, Murray was not done with his advocacy work just yet.

A PERSONAL CONNECTION

While I share significant kinship with all eight of the Black Congressmen who preceded me, I feel a special kinship with Murray. First, if not foremost, he and I are historical bookends: Murray, as the last of the First Eight, marked the end of Black congressional representation from South Carolina and the beginning of the long, dark period of Jim Crow. Nearly a century later, I became the ninth and the first to emerge from that era and once again provide the African American citizens of South Carolina political representation in Congress.

Secondly, both our roots run deep in the soil of Spring Hill, near the little town of Rembert, South Carolina. Murray was born in that rural community, as were my paternal grandmother, Phoebe Lloyd, and her siblings. In fact, the spring that gave the area its name was on her brother Enoch's property.

Third, according to Murray's biographer, in the 1890s, he fathered a son out of wedlock named William, about whom little is known. This revelation intrigued me on a personal level because of certain family rumors I'd heard growing up, suggested parallels between my family and Murray's that were too eerie to ignore.

My dad was born in 1897. He had two older brothers, William, born around 1892, and Charlie, born in 1895. Uncle Charlie and his family lived in Camden; we visited them often, and occasionally there would be discussions about their long-lost brother, William. Both brothers had lost contact with him after World War I. But my dad was always chasing leads as to his whereabouts. In the 1950s, we found him in Rowland, North Carolina.

Dad always said that his father died two months before he was born, and his mother, Phoebe, died when he was two or three years old. But he would always follow this with the caveat "or so they told me," which led me to believe he had his doubts about this explanation of his parents' absence.

Murray biographer John Marszalek wrote of *his* William, "Murray's out-of-wedlock son William lived most of his life at sea and out of touch with the rest of the family. He suddenly reappeared one day and lived the remaining years of his life in Norfolk near his physician half-brother."[39]

Both Williams' lives were shrouded in mystery, both had deep connections to Spring Hill, and the years of their birth correlate. Could the two Williams be the same person—and could Murray have been his father? Could he, in fact, have secretly fathered all three of Phoebe's sons? I have researched census records and found entries for my grandmother, Phoebe, and her three sons. I have never found any record or mention of a father or a male presence in the household. Murray's physical appearance aligns with those of my father and his brothers. Was my father's brother, William, Murray's out-of-wedlock son? Did George Washington Murray have a second family? When, where, and how did Phoebe get the name Clyburn? A lot of questions, and I have never been able to get straight answers.

During my 1992 congressional campaign, I was invited to keynote the "Family and Friends Day" program at St. Matthews United Methodist Church, one of the Lloyd family churches near Spring Hill. My cousin Johnny Lloyd, Enoch's grandson, brought the subject up and suggested that I talk to his mother. I called her later that night, and she seemed extremely evasive. When I called her back several days later and questioned her about what her son had told me, she lamented, "Now, James, back then, a lot of things happened without the benefit of marriage," which I took to mean Phoebe's sons were born out of wedlock.

That discreet response alluded to the rumors I heard throughout my youth that it was possible that my relationship with Murray may be by blood "without the benefit of marriage." I regret that I never pressed my aunt or other relatives for more information, and now any relatives who would possess knowledge of this relationship have passed on. And as most African Americans know, our genealogical records are rare, and I have not found any documentation to prove or disprove any theories.

I have reached out to several known Murray descendants, and they have been gracious in talking with me. Still, I am no closer to answering the question of whether Murray could have fathered my Uncle William, and possibly Uncle Charlie and my father, as well. At any rate, as I often say to the Clyburns I encounter in my travels—all of whom seem to trace their roots back to Kershaw County—I have no idea if we are related by blood or marriage, but it is a safe bet that we are related by soil.

It is very clear, however, that I have a political kinship with George Washington Murray. We share similarities in character, drive, and philosophy. Murray spoke out at political gatherings whether his remarks were welcome or not. He didn't shy away from confronting political opponents or standing up for what he believed was right. And when he saw the rights of Black South Carolinians being eroded, he fought against the injustices with every ounce of his being, no matter how difficult it seemed.

Murray was also a pragmatic politician who adjusted his positions when he needed to achieve a greater goal. He made efforts to work with the opposing side, though he was often met with clenched fists. He believed that in the face of few to no opportunities, economic empowerment equaled Black power. He was immensely proud and lectured on the need for the African American community to chart its own course. While I may never know the breadth of our relationship, Murray and I are kindred souls, related through the values and virtues shared by two men with deep roots in the soil of Sumter, Kershaw, and Lee Counties, South Carolina.

MURRAY FLEES SOUTH CAROLINA

Even out of office, Murray remained dogged in his efforts to ensure that as many African Americans as possible could vote in South Carolina under the onerous new restrictions.

Years earlier, he had begun purchasing land and reselling parcels of his property through lease agreements with Black tenant farmers. By 1902, Murray had as many as two hundred tenant families on nine thousand acres of land, mostly in Sumter County — and under the property ownership clause of the 1895 constitution, the men leasing this land qualified to vote. Confident in this logic, Murray wrote to the Black register of the U.S. Treasury Department in 1901, encouraging him to replicate this property ownership scheme across the country.[40]

Yet it was one of his lease-to-own property contracts that subjected Murray to "Redeemer justice." Two Black tenant farmers charged him with fraud. With the help of a white witness, a white judge, and an all-white jury, he was convicted on questionable charges and sentenced to three years' hard labor and a $250 fine. While free on bond, Murray fled South Carolina to avoid the harsh sentence. He set up a trust managed by his attorney holding eight hundred acres of land, and he left orders to pay his debts and cover the living expenses of his family who remained behind. At the age of fifty-five, Murray secretly moved to Chicago to restart his life.

ERA'S END

George Washington Murray devoted his later years to traveling the country, preaching his prescription for lifting the Black community from prejudice and poverty. He touted the need for "Black ideals," saying that the community must provide their own salvation by supporting Black-owned businesses, owning land, and instilling racial pride. African Americans, he argued, had unconsciously accepted the white narrative that they were inferior; he believed that his race "had all the elements of success except the proper pride in itself." Murray eventually collected his speeches and writings into two self-published books, *Race Ideals: Effects, Causes and Remedy for the Afro-American Race Troubles* and *Light in Dark Places.*[41]

On April 21, 1926, Murray died from cancer at the age of seventy-two. At his funeral, he was eulogized by a Chicago neighbor and former Black Mississippi congressman, John R. Lynch, and the anti-lynching advocate Ida B. Wells-Barnett. Despite his achievements in life, it is believed Murray died penniless, as he was buried in the poorest section of Lincoln Cemetery in Chicago. In 1940, the Murray family had his remains reinterred in an unmarked plot in the newly opened section of the cemetery established by the Oddfellows, a fraternal organization that helped bury deceased community members.[42] There were at least two Oddfellow Lodges in Sumter — Carolina and Vashti — the latter of which was chartered in 1892. I have not been able to determine whether Murray was a member of the Oddfellows, but his reinterment seems to indicate that he may have been associated with them in some way.

While Murray could not remain in South Carolina and be buried in his native soil, Robert Smalls, when he returned to Beaufort after the Civil War, lived out the balance of his days in the home where he was once enslaved. Smalls remained employed as the customs collector for the

Beaufort port until 1913, when two white Southern Senators opposed his reappointment to the political patronage job. He left the position in poor health. Two years later, on February 23, 1915, Smalls died at the age of seventy-five from complications of diabetes at his home in Beaufort. He had lived a truly remarkable life, which the New-York Daily Tribune had captured as early as September 10, 1862, after the full impact of his escape aboard the Planter was understood. The article it published that day read, "[Smalls] is a hero—one of the few who history should be delighted to honor. He has done something for his race and for the world of mankind." The article continued, "He has added new proof to the evidence...that negroes have skill—and courage and tact, and that they will risk their lives for the sake of their liberty."[43]

I have already discussed my connections with Miller and Murray, but as it happens, I also have an interesting connection to Smalls, which I'll share here.

Throughout his years of activism, Smalls's closest confidant and next-door neighbor, for a long time, was a man named J. Irving Washington. His grandson, J. Irving Washington III—whom everybody affectionately called J.I.—became a clandestine mentor to those of us South Carolina State students who were founding members of the Student Nonviolent Coordinating Committee (SNCC). Later, when I got involved in statewide politics, many of the planning meetings for my campaigns were held in the home of J.I. and his wife, Gloria. I was proud to sponsor the legislation renaming Orangeburg's main post office in his honor. Their daughter now serves on the board of my foundation.

The connections do not stop there. J.I.'s sister Julia was married to M. Maceo Nance, the fifth president of South Carolina State, and their son Robert has been my district director for my entire career in Congress. Finally, one of the Washingtons was my debate professor at South Carolina State—and another member of that family is my friend and supporter, the actress Kerry Washington.

For these reasons, I feel a great affection for Smalls—and I am certainly not alone in this. Accolades continued to pour in for him long after his death. One biographer called Smalls "South Carolina's elder states-man," and another acknowledged, "He was a major participant in every important event from the beginning to the end of Black political partici-pation in South Carolina."[44] Throughout his life, Smalls was driven by his most famous quote, declared during the 1895 constitutional convention. Engraved on a bronze bust of him in Beaufort's Tabernacle Baptist Church courtyard are these words: "My race needs no special defense, for the past history of them in this country proves them to be the equal of any people anywhere. All they need is an equal chance in the battle of life."[45]

At his funeral, which *The Savannah Tribune* reported was "the largest ever held in this city," he was eulogized as "a great citizen" and "one of the greatest Negroes."[46] Those accolades are true, but they should not be limited to a single race; I maintain that Smalls was the most consequential South Carolinian who ever lived, irrespective of color.

Finally, Thomas Miller outlived all his First Eight colleagues. After being forced from the presidency of South Carolina State, Miller retired to Charles-ton. There he supported America's efforts in World War I and helped recruit more than thirty thousand Black soldiers, much like Smalls's efforts during the Civil War. He also served on a Black subcommittee of an all-white state committee to help citizens prepare during the war.[47]

Miller and his wife later spent much of the 1920s in Philadelphia, where one of their daughters lived. *The Tribune* called the former congressman "a celebrated character" in the city. Miller and his wife moved back to Charles-ton in 1934, and in his later years, he lost his sight. He told a Works Progress Administration biographer that he had written "a true history of Congres-sional Reconstruction and the part Negroes played in it in South Carolina."[48] There is no record, however, that his written account was ever published.

As he reflected on his life during the WPA interview, Miller stated his belief that the only chances he got in life were through "foresight and the determination to grasp every opportunity that came within his reach." But he also acknowledged the challenges he faced and the enemies he made.[49] Miller died in 1938 at the age of eighty-eight, just two years before I was born.

I first learned of Miller when I was a student at South Carolina State.

There were rumors about his parentage, and seeing his picture among the other former university presidents, it became rather obvious that he was much less African than nearly all the students and professors on that campus. A widely discussed story about Miller focused on the inscription on his tombstone, and there were various versions of what it said. I resolved to find Miller's gravesite, and even though I lived in Charleston for a decade after graduating from South Carolina State, I never made an earnest attempt to find it until Juneteenth 2023.

His tombstone in Charleston's Brotherly Association Cemetery was not hard to find. It's in the southeast corner and is, by far, the largest one there. But the inscription is not exactly as any I had heard. I took pictures, and one of them is published here. In addition to biographical information about his wife and son, the much-discussed inscription reads:

I SERVED GOD AND ALL THE PEOPLE,
LOVING THE WHITE MAN NOT LESS, BUT
THE NEGRO NEEDED ME MOST.

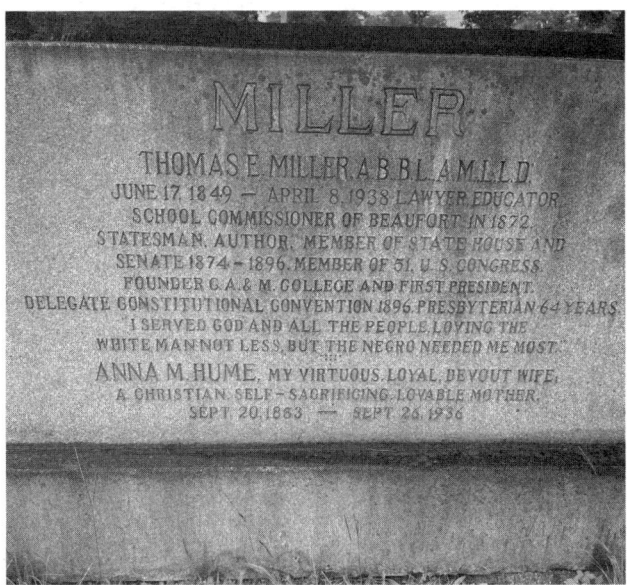

Thomas Miller's tombstone in Charleston's Brotherly Association Cemetery, 2023. (Courtesy of James E. Clyburn)

The message on Miller's tombstone sums up the life of this post-Reconstruction-era Black congressman, whose obvious lack of melanin prompted the white press to derisively refer to him as the Canary. Given a practice of the times and his admitted knowledge of his possible parentage, Miller could have easily opted to live as a white person—as many did. But he found the tug of his upbringing and life experiences too strong. It speaks volumes to me that despite the complicated role race and color played throughout his life, Miller remained dedicated to the fight for racial equity and equality that were the plight of the only family he knew.

Back in 1895, as South Carolina prepared for their constitutional convention, members of the First Eight saw no mystery in what was at stake. Ben Tillman had explicitly told them of his target, "the question of the suffrage and its wise regulation."[50] Black leaders knew the rewritten constitution would put an end to what little remained of their political power in the state. Despite their best efforts, they were unable to stop it. And yet Thomas Miller, George Washington Murray, and Robert Smalls, even after being forced out of public office, found other ways to improve their lot and nurture their communities.

Although they expressed no illusions about the situation they were in, I feel certain that they and other members of the First Eight could not have imagined that the political pendulum would swing as far to the right as it did. Nor could they have imagined that ninety-five years would pass before a ninth Black South Carolinian would be elected to serve the state in the United States Congress. And, growing up in Jim Crow South Carolina, although my mother assured me that it could, I never thought it would be me.

Throughout my career, I have done my best to avoid the pitfalls that entrapped the First Eight, who did not have the history from which to learn as we have. Today, reminiscent of the arc of Robert Smalls's life, I find myself working to protect the gains I fought for as a student activist during the civil rights activities of the 1950s and '60s; and now, as a congressman, working to resist the orchestrated attempts to reverse that progress and derail our trek to a more perfect Union. Yet the example the First Eight set for me and future generations to follow shows that we must never give up. I will continue to follow their lead in our shared pursuit for as long as I am able.

And when the time comes, inspired by Thomas Miller, I've asked my daughters to engrave on my headstone: "He did his best to make the greatness of America accessible and affordable for all." It is the motto that represents who I am, and I hope, like Miller's epitaph, it summarizes the principles instilled in me by the hopes and dreams of the First Eight, and incentivizes those who take up the torch.

EPILOGUE

W HEN I DEVELOPED THE concept for this book several years ago, my intent was to recognize and honor the contributions of South Carolina's first Black congressmen, men not widely known but whose shoulders I stand upon. But when I finally began working on this book, which was a two-year labor of love, the country I was writing about had changed dramatically, and the parallels between then and now came into sharper relief. As a result of the tumultuous and challenging times in which we now live, this book has become much more than an introduction to heroic figures who have been lost to history. It is now a cautionary tale.

The question at the heart of this book—indeed, the question the First Eight wrestled with through the decades—concerns the contradiction at the core of the American promise. How to reconcile the ideal that "all men are created equal"—a phrase synonymous with the country itself—with the violence and inequality that are emblematic of its very founding?

In wrestling with this contradiction and their own individual circumstances, the Eight never sought special treatment; and while they used the phrase often, they never sought *equal* treatment. Though they spent their lives fighting to enshrine the rights of African Americans, they also recognized, time and time again, that they stood in *contrast* to those who were previously their enslavers. They did not enjoy the benefit of generational wealth or education from the finest schools, if at all. And what little wealth and limited freedoms they had were subjected to whimsical actions and arbitrary rules.

Their arguments were always about equity, being treated according to their needs. These pioneering men sought the right to "life, liberty, and the pursuit of happiness," and, except for the brief period known as Reconstruction, to borrow from the great poet Langston Hughes, their dreams were not deferred; they were denied.

Considering this, I decided to address this epilogue to those who will come after me; to those who may feel some responsibility for helping to guide the country's future, whether as public officials, private citizens, community servants, or just conscientious voters. We are an incredibly diverse country that, for the most part, is dedicated to the proposition of "one nation under God, with liberty and justice for all." Whether by birth or choice, the citizens of this great country — and we are a great country — simply want a fair chance to realize the American dream. Our challenge, it seems to me, is to do what is necessary to make the greatness of this country accessible and affordable for *all* its citizens.

Over the past several years I have often been asked, "Have you ever seen divisiveness like this before?" My answer is always the same: No, none of us has. But it's not because the country has never been divided like this before. It's because none of us was around during the 1860s and 1870s. There are frightening similarities between the Reconstruction and post-Reconstruction eras and the events we are experiencing today. In fact, I subscribe to the notion that those responsible for the events that played out on January 6, 2021, developed their playbook from General Martin Whitherspoon Gary's 1876 manifesto.

Redeemer Democrats, the party of the Confederates, reacted violently to Abraham Lincoln's presidency and the outcomes of the 1864, 1868, and 1872 presidential elections. They, of course, had seceded from the Union and launched a bloody Civil War. When they did not like the outcome of this war, one among them murdered the president, while others used vigilante violence to suppress and intimidate voters and murder their political opponents.

Today, the Redeemers and their supporters—whose politics centered on returning to their antebellum way of life—have been replaced by MAGA Republicans and their supporters, who want to "Make America Great Again" by, yes, remaking it in the image of the antebellum era. Just as in the time of the Redeemers, deeply partisan reporting, polarized rhetoric, and hostile reactions to election results now run rampant.

Like the Redeemers, MAGA supporters blame "others" for their discontent. Red shirts have been replaced by red caps. The KKK and rifle clubs have been replaced by the Proud Boys and Oath Keepers. The false narratives they spin against their enemies have infiltrated the highest levels of government, where MAGA Republicans are resurrecting the violent chaos of decades past. New names, same old game. The refrain "Anything that has happened before can happen again" may have more currency for me and my colleagues today than it did back in the 1960s, when I repeated it to my students almost daily.

If we want to see a different outcome this time around, however, we must heed Elliott's 1872 plea that "the very dangers that menace our rights are intended to admonish us to be vigilant in guarding them." In other words, those who infringe upon our rights are a reminder to every citizen that we must never turn complacent. We must safeguard our collective rights and our democracy. As the arc of history during the First Eight's lifetimes shows us, there are no guarantees; freedom can be fleeting. Elliott's entreaty was not just a warning for his time; it is a note for all time.

Today, like the visitors to my office who prompted the writing of this book, I imagine the names Joseph Rainey, Robert De Large, Robert Elliott, Alonzo Ransier, Richard Cain, Robert Smalls, Thomas Miller, and George Washington Murray hold no meaning for most Americans. The loss of these men's contributions is both tragic and intentional. Redeemers, who successfully erased Black political and civil rights from our nation's consciousness, also erased the records and the impacts of African Americans from our history books. They sought to suppress any achievements made by individuals of a race they deemed "inferior." We are witnessing this today as the MAGA administration seeks to rewrite America's story once again. African American history is our nation's history. The truth remains the truth. The more we tell the stories of our past, the less effective attempts to alter them will be.

As the torch is passed to you, the next generation, I urge you to heed the lessons to be learned from the First Eight. The "precepts and examples" of their experiences highlight the resistance and resolve, the promise and purpose, and the faith and fortitude they constantly displayed. Their stories are our stories. And as the struggle they undertook continues, some one hundred and fifty years later, collective and comprehensive efforts are needed from those who believe in the promise of America to write a new ending.

Congressman James E. Clyburn
March 2025

PROFILES OF THE FIRST EIGHT

JOSEPH HAYNE RAINEY
B. JUNE 21, 1832 *D.* AUGUST 1, 1887

First Black to serve in U.S. House of Representatives
Represented the 1st Congressional District
- 41st Congress (Dec. 12, 1870–March 3, 1871)*
- 42nd Congress (March 4, 1871–March 3, 1873)
- 43rd Congress (March 4, 1873–March 3, 1875)
- 44th Congress (March 4, 1875–March 3, 1877)
- 45th Congress (March 4, 1877–March 3, 1879)

ROBERT CARLOS DE LARGE
B. MARCH 15, 1842 *D.* FEBRUARY 14, 1874

Struggled to straddle the color line in South Carolina
Represented the 2nd Congressional District
- 42nd Congress (March 4, 1871–January 24, 1873)*

ROBERT BROWN ELLIOTT
B. AUGUST 11, 1842 *D.* AUGUST 9, 1884

First of two Black Speakers of the South Carolina House of Representatives
Represented the 3rd Congressional District
- 42nd Congress (March 4, 1871–March 3, 1873)
- 43rd Congress (March 4, 1873–November 1, 1874)*

RICHARD HARVEY CAIN
B. APRIL 12, 1825 D. JANUARY 18, 1887

First Black minister to serve in U.S. House of Representatives
Represented the At-Large District
- 43rd Congress (March 4, 1873–March 3, 1875)

Represented the 2nd Congressional District
- 45th Congress (March 4, 1877–March 3, 1879)

ALONZO JACOB RANSIER
B. JANUARY 3, 1834 D. AUGUST 17, 1882

First of two Black lieutenant governors of South Carolina
Represented the 2nd Congressional District
- 43rd Congress (March 4, 1873–March 3, 1875)

ROBERT SMALLS
B. APRIL 5, 1839 D. FEBRUARY 23, 1915

A genuine Civil War hero
Represented the 5th Congressional District
- 44th Congress (March 4, 1875–March 3, 1877)
- 45th Congress (March 4, 1877–March 3, 1879)
- 47th Congress (July 19, 1882–March 3, 1883)*

Represented the 7th Congressional District
- 48th Congress (March 18, 1884–March 3, 1885)*
- 49th Congress (March 4, 1885–March 3, 1887)

THOMAS EZEKIEL MILLER
B. JUNE 17, 1849 *D.* APRIL 8, 1938

First president of (now) South Carolina State University
Represented the 7th Congressional District
- 51st Congress (September 24, 1890–March 3, 1891)*

GEORGE WASHINGTON MURRAY
B. SEPTEMBER 22, 1853 *D.* APRIL 21, 1926

Last Black to serve in the U.S. House of Representatives from South Carolina in the nineteenth century
Represented the 7th Congressional District
- 53rd Congress (March 4, 1893–March 3, 1895)

Represented the 1st Congressional District
- 54th Congress (June 4, 1896–March 3, 1897)*

---

* Did not serve full term due to special election, contested election, or resignation

Image Credits:

Rainey, Library of Congress, Prints and Photographs Division, LC-DIG-cwpbh-04424; De Large, Library of Congress, Prints and Photographs Division, LC-DIG-cwpbh-00549; Elliott, Wikimedia Commons/Public Domain; Cain, Library of Congress, Prints and Photographs Divsion, LC-DIG-bellcm-00707; Ransier, Library of Congress, Prints and Photograph Division, LC-DIG-cwpbh-00613; Smalls, Library of Congress, Prints and Photographs Division, LC-DIG-cwpbh-03683; Miller, Courtesy of S.C. State Historical Collection & Archives, Miller. F. Whittaker Library, South Carolina State University, Orangeburg, S.C.; Murray, Library of Congress, Prints and Photographs Division, LC-DIG-bellcm-07983

ACKNOWLEDGMENTS

The great orator Robert Brown Elliott once said, "History has been to me the delight and study of my life." That is a sentiment I share with him. I have always loved history, and I have great respect for those who dedicate their lives to ensuring that our past is preserved and promoted so that we may learn its lessons. This book is rooted in research that was necessary to bring the lived experiences of *The First Eight* into clear focus. I relied on the works of many historians, some of whom I have the honor of knowing personally, to glean the stories that bring these men to life. Without their work, this work would not have been possible.

We all know that no one who has achieved any success in their lives has done it alone. I could not have completed this project without the tremendous support of my family, friends, and colleagues. For this book, I leaned on several new entrants into this growing circle—David Larabell, Alex Littlefield, and Morgan Wu. David provided his expertise to ensure this book would reach the widest audience with the guidance of a top-notch publishing house. Once Little, Brown committed to the project, Alex and Morgan provided encouragement and a skillful eye that helped shape an idea I toyed with for many years into this fully formed book. Their contributions have been invaluable.

I must also thank a diverse group of friends and acquaintances from various stages of my career, some of whom agreed to read this book and provide feedback. You see their comments on the back cover of *The First Eight,* and I am grateful for their willingness to share their perspectives despite each of them leading very busy lives. To Ralph Dawson and Jaime

Harrison, who provided the Foreword for this book — I owe a great debt of gratitude that extends beyond this current project. Ralph has been in my life for more than sixty years and Jaime for more than thirty. I met these men when they were high-school students, and they grew into sounding boards and confidants, and I often seek their advice and counsel.

As blessed as I have been by family and friends, I have been extremely fortunate to have been surrounded by competent and supportive, professional and personal staffs, but when it comes to this project, there is one who stands out above all others, Hope Derrick. I first met Hope when she was a young reporter at a local television station. I was impressed by her news reporting. Later, she became communications director for the South Carolina Democratic Party, which afforded me the opportunity to observe her message development.

I concluded that Hope and I were kindred spirits, and she was who I needed to help me address the needs and aspirations of my constituents. I approached Hope and she accepted my invitation to join my staff, first in the Congressional District, and later in Washington.

Shortly after joining my staff, Hope became aware of my interest in and respect for the eight subjects of this book, and we often spoke of the interesting relationships I have with several of them. She constantly encouraged me to make this effort, and I kept postponing the undertaking. But when she retired from my Congressional staff and offered to devote some of her time and efforts to the research and editing needed for a book like this one, I had no excuses left. The fits and starts became rewrites and edits and here we are. Without Hope, this project never would have come to fruition. And the pun is intended.

NOTES

1. FREEDOM (1861–1865)

1 "History of the Charleston City Market," Charleston City Market website, undated, retrieved from https://www.thecharlestoncitymarket.com/history on Jan. 22, 2025.

2 Ethan J. Kytle and Blain Roberts, *Denmark Vesey's Garden: Slavery and Memory in the Cradle of the Confederacy* (New York: New Press, 2018), 28–29.

3 Walter Edgar, *South Carolina: A History* (Columbia: University of South Carolina Press, 1998), 354.

4 Jon Meacham, *And There Was Light: Abraham Lincoln and the American Struggle* (New York: Random House, 2022), 207.

5 Andrew Billingsley, *Yearning to Breathe Free: Robert Smalls of South Carolina and His Family* (Columbia: University of South Carolina, 2007), 10–33.

6 John J. Navin, *The Grim Years: Settling South Carolina, 1670–1720* (Columbia: University of South Carolina Press, 2020), 91.

7 Bernard E. Powers Jr., "African Americans" in *South Carolina Encyclopedia*, ed. Walter Edgar (Columbia: University of South Carolina Press, 2006), 5; Kytle and Roberts, 19.

8 Powers, "Slave Trade" in *South Carolina Encyclopedia*, 876.

9 Powers, "African Americans," 5.

10 Billingsley, 42–43.

11 Billingsley, 47.

12 Billingsley, 52.

13 Cate Lineberry, *Be Free or Die: The Amazing Story of Robert Smalls' Escape from Slavery to Union Hero* (New York: Picador), 13.

14 Billingsley, 57–58.

15 Billingsley, 59.

16 Billingsley, 61.

17 Okon Edet Uya, *From Slavery to Public Service: Robert Smalls 1839–1915* (New York: Oxford University Press, 1971), 19.

18 Joel Williamson, *After Slavery: The Negro in South Carolina During Reconstruction: 1861–1877* (New York: Norton Library, 1965), 3.

19 Eric Foner, *Forever Free: The Story of Emancipation and Reconstruction* (New York: Vintage Books, 2006), 45.

20 Edgar, 366.

21 "The Inspiring Story of Mitchelville," Historic Mitchelville Freedom Park

website, undated), retrieved from https://exploremitchelville.org/our-story-2 on Oct. 14, 2024.

22 Jonathan W. White, "Meet the Black Men Who Changed Lincoln's Mind About Equal Rights," *Smithsonian*, January 2020, retrieved from https://www.smith sonianmag.com/history/men-changed-changing-lincolns-mind-180979230/ on Oct. 17, 2024.

23 Billingsley, 1.

24 Lineberry, 110.

25 Billingsley, 70.

26 Lineberry, 114; Budge Weidman, "Black Soldiers in the Civil War," National Archives Educator Resources website, Mar. 19, 2019, retrieved from https://www .archives.gov/education/lessons/blacks-civil-war/article.html on Oct. 15, 2024.

27 Edward A. Miller, *Gullah Statesman: Robert Smalls from Slavery to Congress, 1839–1915* (Columbia: University of South Carolina Press, 1995), 15.

28 Lineberry, 132.

29 South Carolina General Assembly, H.3893 Summary of Robert Smalls (Black History Month), *House Journal*, Feb. 7, 2023, 14, retrieved from https://www .scstatehouse.gov/sess125_2023-2024/bills/3893.htm on Oct. 15, 2024.

30 "African American Civil War Memorial," National Park Service website, undated, retrieved from https://www.nps.gov/afam/learn/historyculture/index.ht-m#:~:text=In%201865%2C%20President%20Lincoln%20said,could%20not%20 have%20been%20won%22.&text=Inscribed%20on%20the%20Wall%20of, Officers%20and%202%2C145%20Hispanic%20surnames on May 3, 2023.

31 National Archives, "The Emancipation Proclamation," National Archives web-site, January 28, 2002, retrieved from https://www.archives.gov/exhibits /featured-documents/emancipation-proclamation#:~:text=President%20 Abraham%20Lincoln%20issued%20the,and%20henceforward%20shall%20 be%20free.%22 on May 3, 2023.

32 Matthew Pinsker, "Emancipation Among Black Troops in South Carolina," Emancipation Digital Classroom website, Dickinson College, Nov. 6, 2012, re-trieved from https://housedivided.dickinson.edu/emancipation/2012/11/06 /emancipation-among-black-troops-in-south-carolina on Apr. 6, 2024.

33 Angela Ards, "Annette Gordon-Reed Explores the Tangled Meaning of June-teenth," *Texas Monthly*, June 2021, retrieved from https://www.texasmonthly.com /arts-entertainment/annette-gordon-reed-on-juneteenth-review on Apr. 8, 2024.

34 National Museum of African American History and Culture, "Celebrating June-teenth," National Archives website, undated, retrieved from https://nmaahc.si .edu/explore/stories/celebrating-juneteenth on Apr. 8, 2024.

35 Billingsley, 82.

36 Billingsley, 84–85.

37 Kytle and Roberts, 34–35.

38 Blain Roberts and Ethan Kytle, "When Freedom Came to Charleston," *New York Times*, Feb. 19, 2015, retrieved from https://archive.nytimes.com/opinionator.blogs .nytimes.com/2015/02/19/when-freedom-came-to-charleston/ on May 4, 2023.

39 Bernard E. Powers Jr., *Black Charlestonians: A Social History, 1822–1885* (Fayette-ville: University of Arkansas Press, 1994), 68.

40 Billingsley, 90.

41 Billingsley, 92.

2. "RECONSTRUCTION BEGUN" (1865–1867)

1 Office of the Historian, U.S. House of Representatives, *Black Americans in Congress 1870–2007* (Washington, D.C., Government Publishing Office, 2008), 72.

2 Office of the Historian, *Black Americans in Congress 1870–2007*, 72.

3 Bernard E. Powers Jr., *Black Charlestonians: A Social History, 1822–1885* (Fayetteville: University of Arkansas Press, 1994), 36.

4 James E. Clyburn, *Blessed Experiences: Genuinely Southern, Proudly Black* (Columbia: University of South Carolina Press, 2014), 104.

5 R. L. Reece, "Color Crit: Critical Race Theory and the History and Future of Colorism in the US," *Journal of Black Studies* (2018): 3–4, retrieved from https://7c2c4239-2cae-4bf7-9d24-e25021092699.filesusr.com/ugd/5fff9b_35b35e913a 25425bac7e96256ae071f8.pdf?index=true.

6 R. L. Reece, "Genesis of U.S. Colorism and Skin Tone Stratification: Slavery, Freedom, and Mulatto-Black Occupational Inequality in the Late 19th Century," *Review of Black Political Economy* 45, no. 1 (2018): 6, retrieved from https://7c2c4239-2cae-4bf7-9d24-e25021092699.filesusr.com/ugd/5fff9b_738c19918f2149 0a904304b5852ed5f4.pdf?index=true.

7 Ethan J. Kytle and Blain Roberts, *Denmark Vesey's Garden: Slavery and Memory in the Cradle of the Confederacy* (New York: New Press, 2018), 13.

8 Robert P. Stockton, "History Obscures People 'of Color,'" *Charleston News and Courier*, date unknown (from the James Holloway Scrapbook, the South Caroliniana Library, University of South Carolina, Columbia, S.C.); Powers, *Black Charlestonians*, 26–27.

9 Walter Edgar, *South Carolina: A History* (Columbia: University of South Carolina Press, 1998), 310.

10 "Century Fellowship Society Souvenir Program 1904," Brown Fellowship Society file 1790–1911, the South Caroliniana Library, University of South Carolina, 5, 7.

11 Bernard E. Powers Jr., "Brown Fellowship Society," in *South Carolina Encyclopedia*, ed. Walter Edgar (Columbia: University of South Carolina Press, 2006), 104.

12 Edgar, *South Carolina: A History*, 310; Powers, *Black Charlestonians*, 65.

13 Thomas Holt, *Black over White: Negro Political Leadership in South Carolina During Reconstruction* (Urbana: University of Illinois Press, 1977), 11.

14 Kytle and Roberts, 56.

15 Office of the Historian, *Black Americans in Congress, 1870–2007*, 72.

16 Powers, *Black Charlestonians*, 82.

17 Cate Lineberry, *Be Free or Die: The Amazing Story of Robert Smalls' Escape from Slavery to Union Hero* (New York: Picador, 2017), 200.

18 Office of the Historian, U.S. House of Representatives, *Black Americans in Congress, 1870–2022* (Washington, DC: Government Publishing Office, 2023), 20–21.

19 Joel Williamson, *After Slavery: The Negro in South Carolina During Reconstruction: 1861–1877* (New York: Norton Library, 1965), 305; Edgar, *South Carolina: A History*, 377–81.

20 William S. Powell, *Encyclopedia of North Carolina* (Chapel Hill: University of North Carolina Press, 2006), retrieved from https://www.ncpedia.org/redeemer -democrats on Oct. 28, 2024.

21 Richard Zuczek, *State of Rebellion: Reconstruction in South Carolina* (Columbia: University of South Carolina Press, 1996), 15.

22 Edgar, *South Carolina: A History*, 384.

23 Richard Zuczek, "Black Codes" in *South Carolina Encyclopedia*, ed. Walter Edgar (Columbia: University of South Carolina Press, 2006), 74.

24 Zuczek, *State of Rebellion*, 16.

25 "Address to the Legislature of the State of South Carolina" from the Proceedings of the Colored People's Convention of the State of South Carolina (Charleston, SC; Nov. 1865), 28, retrieved from https://omeka.coloredconventions.org/files /original/fb7ce2e02cc45786fb4530926135de24.pdf on Oct. 28, 2024.

26 Office of the Historian, *Black Americans in Congress, 1870–2007*, 106.

27 "An Act to Incorporate the Amateur Literary and Fraternal Association of Charleston" (SC Home website, Feb. 26, 1869), retrieved from https://www .carolana.com/SC/Education/1869_02_26_Act_to_Incorporate_Amateur _Literary_and_Fraternal_Association.html on Oct. 25, 2024.

28 William C. Hine, "Black Politicians in Reconstruction Charleston, South Carolina: A Collective Study," *Journal of Southern History* 49, no. 4 (1983): 565, retrieved from https://doi.org/10.2307/2208676 on Oct. 28, 2024; Williamson, *After Slavery*, 312–13.

29 Holt, 9.

30 "Reconstruction Begun," *South Carolina Leader*, Nov. 25, 1865, retrieved from the Library of Congress, www.loc.gov/item/sn83025783/1865-11-25/ed-1/ on Oct. 28, 2024.

31 Powers, *Black Charlestonians*, 82.

32 Peggy Lamson, *The Glorious Failure: Black Congressman Robert Brown Elliott and the Reconstruction in South Carolina* (New York: Norton Library, 1973), 37.

33 Powers, *Black Charlestonians*, 83.

34 Powers, *Black Charlestonians*, 83.

35 Holt, 16–17.

36 Maurine Christopher, *America's Black Congressmen* (New York: Thomas Y. Crowell Company, 1971), 101; Lamson, 180.

37 Powers, *Black Charlestonians*, 84–85.

38 Holt, 10.

39 "History and Culture," Reconstruction Era National Park South Carolina, National Park Service website, Apr. 17, 2024, retrieved from https://www.nps .gov/reer/learn/historyculture/historyculture.htm#:~:text=The%20 Reconstruction%20era%20(1861%20to,transformation%20within%20the %20United%20States on Oct. 30, 2024.

40 "Reconstruction Begun," *South Carolina Leader*, Nov. 25, 1865, retrieved from the Library of Congress, www.loc.gov/item/sn83025783/1865-11-25/ed-1 on Oct. 28, 2024.

41 Proceedings of the Colored People's Convention of the State of South Carolina, Charleston, S.C., Nov. 1865, 21, retrieved from https://omeka.coloredconven tions.org/files/original/fb7ce2e02cc45786fb4530926135de24.pdf on Oct. 28, 2024.

42 "Address of the Colored State Convention to the People of the State of South Carolina," Colored People's Convention of South Carolina, Nov. 24, 1865, retrieved from https://hd.housedivided.dickinson.edu/node/44782 on Feb. 25, 2025.

43 Amy Dru Stanley, "Slave Emancipation and the Revolutionizing of Human Rights" in *The World the Civil War Made,* ed. Gregor P. Downs and Kate Masur (Chapel Hill: University of North Carolina Press, 2015), 290; Letter of George T. Downing and Alonzo Ransier et al. to Charles Sumner, Feb. 1, 1866, Papers of Charles Sumner, series I, reel 35, Princeton University Library.

44 Office of the Historian, *Black Americans in Congress 1870–2022,* 19.

45 Memorial to the United States Congress from the Proceedings of the Colored People's Convention of the State of South Carolina, Charleston, S.C., Nov. 1865, 31, retrieved from https://omeka.coloredconventions.org/files/original/fb7ce2e02cc45786fb4530926135de24.pdf on Oct. 28, 2024.

46 Office of the Historian, *Black Americans in Congress 1870–2022,* 18–19.

47 Philip Dray, *Capitol Men: The Epic Story of Reconstruction Through the Lives of the First Black Congressmen* (Boston: Mariner Books, 2008), 26–27.

48 Holt, 25.

49 Edgar, *South Carolina: A History,* 385; Zuczek, "Black Codes" in *South Carolina Encyclopedia,* 74.

50 Edgar, *South Carolina: A History,* 385.

51 Lineberry, 172–73.

52 Christopher, 97.

3: "WHERE THERE IS NO VISION, THE PEOPLE PERISH" (1867–1868)

1 Henry Louis Gates Jr., *The Black Church: This Is Our Story, This Is Our Song* (New York: Penguin, 2021), 82.

2 Letter by Richard Harvey Cain written at the time of the Civil War, quoted in Zak Mettger, *Till Victory Is Won: Black Soldiers in the Civil War* (New York: Puffin Books, 1997), 2.

3 Gates, 81.

4 Bernard E. Powers Jr., "'I Go to Set the Captives Free': The Activism of Richard Harvey Cain, Nationalist Churchman and Reconstruction-Era Leader," in *The Southern Elite and Social Change,* ed. Randy Finley and Thomas A. DeBlack (Fayetteville: University of Arkansas Press, 2002), 43.

5 Keith O'Shea, Darran Simon, and Holly Yan, "Dylann Roof's Racist Rants Read in Court," CNN website, Dec. 14, 2016, retrieved from https://www.cnn.com/2016/12/13/us/dylann-roof-murder-trial/index.html on Feb. 5, 2025.

6 Bernard E. Powers Jr., *Black Charlestonians: A Social History, 1822–1885* (Fayetteville: University of Arkansas Press, 1994), 21.

7 PBS, "Church on John's Island," Africans in America Resource Bank website, undated, retrieved from https://www.pbs.org/wgbh/aia/part3/3h87.html on Feb. 5, 2025.

8 "Mother Emanuel AME Church," U.S. Civil Rights Trail website, retrieved from https://civilrightstrail.com/attraction/emanuel-ame-church/ on Feb. 5, 2025.

9 Bernard E. Powers Jr., "African Methodist Episcopal Church" in *South Carolina Encyclopedia,* ed. Walter Edgar (Columbia: University of South Carolina, 2006), 7; Ethan J. Kytle and Blain Roberts, *Denmark Vesey's Garden: Slavery and Memory in the Cradle of the Confederacy* (New York: New Press, 2018), 20.

10 David Roberston, *Denmark Vesey: The Buried History of America's Largest Slave Rebellion and the Man Who Led it* (New York: Knopf, 1999), 123, 133.

11 "South Carolina State Arsenal," National Park Service website, Feb. 21, 2018, retrieved from https://www.nps.gov/places/south-carolina-state-arsenal.htm on Feb. 5, 2025.

12 Philip Dray, *Capitol Men: The Epic Story of Reconstruction Through the Lives of the First Black Congressmen* (Boston: Mariner Books, 2008), 40; Office of the Historian, U.S. House of Representatives, *Black Americans in Congress 1870–2022* (Washington, D.C., 2023), 80.

13 Joel Williamson, *After Slavery: The Negro in South Carolina During Reconstruction, 1861–1877* (New York: Norton Library, 1965), 190; Bernard E. Powers Jr., "Richard Harvey Cain," in *South Carolina Encyclopedia*, ed. Walter Edgar (Columbia: University of South Carolina Press, 2006), 119; Gates, 38.

14 Lowcountry Digital History Initiative, "Establishing Black Churches," Morris Street Business District website, undated, retrieved from https://ldhi.library.cofc.edu/exhibits/show/msbd/post-civil-war/establishing-black-churches on Feb. 5, 2025.

15 Dennis C. Dickerson and Bernard E. Powers Jr., "Morris Brown," in *South Carolina Encyclopedia*, ed. Walter Edgar (Columbia: University of South Carolina Press, 2006), 103.

16 Williamson, 206.

17 Gates, 38.

18 Maurine Christopher, *America's Black Congressmen* (New York: Thomas Y. Crowell Company, 1971), 89; Powers, *Black Charlestonians: A Social History, 1822–1885,* 222–23.

19 Powers, "'I Go to Set the Captives Free': The Activism of Richard Harvey Cain, Nationalist Churchman and Reconstruction-Era Leader," 43.

20 Christopher, 89; Lamson, 54.

21 Powers, "'I Go to Set the Captives Free,'" 45.

22 Kevin M. Cherry, *Virtue of Cain: From Slave to Senator* (Takoma Park, MD: Rocky Pond Press, 2019), 72.

23 Office of the Historian, U.S. House of Representatives, *Black Americans in Congress 1870–2022* (Washington, D.C., 2023), 80.

24 Powers, *Black Charlestonians: A Social History,* 234–35; William C. Hine, "The 1867 Charleston Streetcar Sit-Ins: A Case of Successful Black Protest," *South Carolina Historical Magazine* 77, no. 2 (1976): 110–14, retrieved from http://www.jstor.org/stable/27567373 on Feb. 5, 2025; Damon L. Fordham, *Voices of Black South Carolina: Legend and Legacy* (Charleston, SC: History Press, 2009), 29–31.

25 Andrew Billingsley, *Yearning to Breathe Free: Robert Smalls of South Carolina and His Family* (Columbia: University of South Carolina Press, 2007), 116; Richard Zuczek, *State of Rebellion: Reconstruction in South Carolina* (Columbia: University of South Carolina Press, 1996), 40–41.

26 Zuczek, 40.

27 Office of the Historian, National Park Service, *The Life and Legacy of Robert Smalls of South Carolina's Sea Islands* (Fort Washington, PA: Eastern National, 2020), 33.

28 Walter Edgar, *South Carolina: A History* (Columbia: University of South Carolina Press, 1998), 386.

29 Peggy Lamson, *The Glorious Failure: Black Congressman Robert Brown Elliott and the Reconstruction in South Carolina* (New York: Norton Library, 1973), 46–48.

NOTES

30 Dray, 39.

31 Kytle and Roberts, 70.

32 Williamson, 63.

33 Eric Foner, *A Short History of Reconstruction,* updated edition (New York: Harper Perennial, 2014), 73.

34 Reginald F. Hildebrand, "History: Richard Harvey Cain, African Methodism and the Gospel of Freedom," *A.M.E. Church Review,* Jan.–Mar. 2001, 38.

35 Lamson, 55.

36 Dray, 57; Lamson, 55.

37 Lamson, 55.

38 South Carolina Constitutional Convention proceedings 1868, University of South Carolina Coleman Karesh Law Library, retrieved from https://archive.org /details/procedingsofcon00sout/page/212/mode/2up on July 10, 2024.

39 Williamson, 143.

40 Steven Hahn, *A Nation Under Our Feet: Black Political Struggles in the Rural South from Slavery to the Great Migration* (Cambridge, MA: Belknap Press of Harvard University Press, 2003), 260.

41 David Slade and Angie Jackson, "SC Land Slipping Away from Families Amid Fragile Claims and Explosive Growth," *Charleston Post and Courier,* Dec. 5, 2018, retrieved from https://www.postandcourier.com/business/real_estate/sc-land -slipping-away-from-families-amid-fragile-claims-and-explosive-growth/article _3b6f4fa2-dc56-11e8-9145-33ac81ce0616.html on Feb. 5, 2025.

42 Okon Edet Uya, *Robert Smalls 1839–1915: From Slavery to Public Service* (New York: Oxford University Press, 1972), 52.

43 Lamson, 56.

44 Uya, 52–53.

45 Thomas Holt, *Black over White: Negro Political Leadership in South Carolina During Reconstruction* (Urbana: University of Illinois Press, 1977), 152.

46 Office of the Historian, U.S. House of Representatives, *"We Are in Earnest for Our Rights": Representative Joseph H. Rainey and the Struggle for Reconstruction* (Washington, DC: Government Publishing Office, 2020), 8.

47 Lamson, 58–60.

48 Edgar, *South Carolina: A History,* 386; Kytle and Roberts, 69; Williamson, 279.

49 W.E.B. Du Bois, *Black Reconstruction in America, 1860–1880* (New York: Free Press, 1935), 390.

50 Williamson, 348.

51 Lamson, 63.

52 Heather Cox Richardson, "South Carolina's Remarkable Democratic Experiment of 1868," We're History website, Mar. 16, 2018, retrieved from https://werehistory .org/south-carolinas-remarkable-democratic-experiment on Feb. 3, 2025; Cole Blease Graham Jr., "Constitutions" in *South Carolina Encyclopedia,* ed. Walter Edgar (Columbia: University of South Carolina Press, 2006), 217; Williamson, 343.

53 Lamson, 51.

54 Edgar, *South Carolina: A History,* 386.

55 Zuczek, 57; Dray, 80.

56 Edgar, *South Carolina: A History,* 387.

4: FIRSTS (1868–1870)

1 Journal of the House of Representatives of the State of South Carolina (July 6, 1868), retrieved from https://www.carolana.com/SC/Legislators/Documents /Journal_of_the_House_of_Representatives_of_the_State_of_South_Carolina _1868_Special_Session.pdf on Nov. 5, 2024.

2 James E. Clyburn, *Blessed Experiences: Genuinely Southern, Proudly Black* (Columbia: University of South Carolina Press, 2014), 116–18.

3 Walter Edgar, *South Carolina: A History* (Columbia: University of South Carolina Press, 1998), 388.

4 Benjamin Ginsberg, *Moses of South Carolina: A Jewish Scalawag During Radical Reconstruction* (Baltimore: Johns Hopkins University Press, 2010), 100.

5 Thomas Holt, *Black over White: Negro Political Leadership in South Carolina during Reconstruction* (Urbana: University of Illinois Press, 1977), 108.

6 Joel Williamson, *After Slavery: The Negro in South Carolina During Reconstruction, 1861–1877* (New York, W.W. Norton & Company, Inc., 1965), 333; Peggy Lamson, The Glorious Failure: Black Congressman Robert Brown Elliott and the Reconstruction in South Carolina (New York: Norton Library, 1973), 23, 25; Office of the Historian, U.S. House of Representatives, *Black Americans in Congress 1870–2007* (Washington, D.C., 2008), 78.

7 Lamson, *The Glorious Failure*, 29–30.

8 Millicent Ellison Brown, "Robert Brown Elliott" in *South Carolina Encyclopedia*, ed. Walter Edgar (Columbia: University of South Carolina Press, 2006), 297; Williamson, 333; "Letter from Robert B. Elliott to L. Dunneman" (National Museum of African American History and Culture, Aug. 4, 1880), retrieved from https:// nmaahc.si.edu/object/nmaahc_2012.160.152.2?destination=/explore/collection /search%3Fedan_q%3D%252A%253A%252A%26edan_fq%255B0%255D%3 Dname%253A%2522Elliott%252C%252BRobert%252BBrown%2522%26op%3 DSearch on Nov. 5, 2024.

9 Williamson, 176–77; Brown, 297.

10 Maurine Christopher, *America's Black Congressmen* (New York: Thomas Y. Crowell Company, 1971), 70; Lamson, 92–93.

11 Office of the Historian, U.S. House of Representatives, *Black Americans in Congress 1870–2007*, 72.

12 Office of the Historian, U.S. House of Representatives, *Black Americans in Congress 1870–2007*, 75; Lamson, 75.

13 Eric Foner, *Freedom's Lawmakers: A Directory of Black Officeholders During Reconstruction*, 69–70.

14 Ginsberg, 102; Lamson, 69.

15 Ginsberg, 102; Lamson, 80.

16 Office of the Historian, U.S. House of Representatives, *Black Americans in Congress 1870–2007*, 78.

17 William C. Hine, "Benjamin Franklin Randolph" in *South Carolina Encyclopedia*, ed. Walter Edgar (Columbia: University of South Carolina Press, 2006), 773; Holt, 141; Julie L. Mellby, "Radical Members of the South Carolina Legislature" (Princeton University Library website, May 19, 2011), retrieved from https: //www.princeton.edu/~graphicarts/2011/05/radical_members_of_the_south _c.html on Feb. 13, 2025.

18 Lamson, 37.

NOTES

19 Damon L. Fordham, *Voices of Black South Carolina: Legend & Legacy* (Charleston: History Press, 2009), 43–45.

20 Holt, 30.

21 Foner, *Freedom's Lawmakers*, 36.

22 Richard Zuczek, *State of Rebellion: Reconstruction in South Carolina* (Columbia: University of South Carolina Press, 1996), 58, 62.

23 Williamson, 345.

24 Lamson, 82–83.

25 Andrew Billingsley, *Yearning to Breathe Free: Robert Smalls of South Carolina and His Families* (Columbia: University of South Carolina Press, 2007), 120.

26 Bernard E. Powers Jr., *Black Charlestonians: A Social History, 1822–1885* (Fayetteville: University of Arkansas Press, 1994), 239–40; Ginsberg, 111.

27 Powers, *Black Charlestonians: A Social History, 1822–1885*, 233.

28 Lamson, 105.

29 Holt, 106.

30 Holt, 107–8, 117–19.

31 Holt, 108; Dray, 416–17n; Office of the Historian, U.S. House of Representatives, *Black Americans in Congress 1870–2007*, 72.

32 Holt, 196.

33 Williamson, 392–93.

34 Dray, 368–70.

35 Lee Hendren, "40 State Legislators Sign Letter in Support of Clyburn Connector, *The Times and Democrat* (Orangeburg, SC), Apr. 2, 2003.

36 Adam Nossiter, "Race, Politics and a Bridge in South Carolina," *New York Times,* Feb. 25, 2007, retrieved from https://www.nytimes.com/2007/02/25/us/25bridge.html on Nov. 8, 2024.

37 Dray, 79.

38 Christopher, 27.

39 Don Kennon, "Rainey in Bermuda," U.S. Capitol Historical Society blog, Nov. 14, 2011, retrieved from https://uschs.wordpress.com/2011/11/14/rainey-in-the-carribean/ on Mar. 11, 2025.

40 Bobby J. Donaldson, "Meet Joseph Rainey, the First Black Congressman," *Smithsonian,* January 2021, retrieved from https://www.smithsonianmag.com/history/joseph-rainey-first-black-congressman-180976502/ on Nov. 10, 2024.

41 Clyburn, 36.

42 Office of the Historian, U.S. House of Representatives, *"We Are in Earnest for Our Rights": Representative Joseph H. Rainey and the Struggle for Reconstruction* (Washington, D.C.: Government Publishing Office, 2020), 11; Douglas R. Egerton, *The Wars of Reconstruction: The Brief, Violent History of America's Most Progressive Era* (New York: Bloomberg Press, 2014), 278.

43 "The Colored Senator from South Carolina," *Buffalo Morning Express,* Dec. 13, 1870, 1; "First Colored Member of the House," *Fall River (Massachusetts) Daily Evening News,* Dec. 13, 1870, 2.

44 Office of the Historian, *"We Are in Earnest for Our Rights,"* 11.

45 Office of the Historian, *"We are in Earnest for Our Rights,"* 22.

NOTES

5: ALARM BELLS (1871–1872)

1   Peggy Lamson, *The Glorious Failure: Black Congressman Robert Brown Elliott and the Reconstruction in South Carolina* (New York: Norton Library, 1973), 118–19.

2   Lamson, 119, 122.

3   Office of the Historian, U.S. House of Representatives, *Black Americans in Congress, 1870–2022* (Washington, DC: Government Publishing Office, 2023), 421–22.

4   Joanna R. Lampe, "The Insurrection Bar to Holding Office: Appeals Court Issues Decision on Section 3 of the Fourteenth Amendment," Congressional Research Service website, June 1, 2022, retrieved from https://www.congress.gov/crs-product/LSB10750 on Feb. 19, 2025.

5   Lamson, 123–24.

6   Maurine Christopher, *America's Black Congressmen* (New York: Thomas Y. Crowell Company, 1971), 99.

7   "Timeline—The 1870s," *America's Best History* website, 2023, retrieved from https://americasbesthistory.com/abhtimeline1872m.html on Feb. 23, 2025; Brook Thomas, "The Perils of Pardoning: Ulysses S. Grant and the Legacy of the Ku Klux Klan Pardons," *Journal of the Civil War Era* website, Jan. 14, 2025, retrieved from https://www.journalofthecivilwarera.org/2025/01/the-perils-of-pardoning-ulysses-s-grant-and-the-legacy-of-the-ku-klux-klan-pardons on Mar. 17, 2025.

8   Lamson, 123.

9   Austin Sarat, "14th Amendment Disqualification Decision Saves Trump but Damages the Supreme Court," *Justia Verdict* website, Mar. 11, 2024. Retrieved from https://verdict.justia.com/2024/03/11/14th-amendment-disqualification-decision-saves-trump-but-damages-the-supreme-court on Feb. 19, 2025.

10 Eric Foner, *Freedom's Lawmakers: A Directory of Black Officeholders During Reconstruction, Revised Edition* (Baton Rouge: Louisiana State University Press, 1993), 175.

11 Philip Dray, *Capitol Men: The Epic Story of Reconstruction Through the Lives of the First Black Congressmen* (Boston: Mariner Books, 2008), 87–88.

12 Richard Zuczek, *State of Rebellion: Reconstruction in South Carolina* (Columbia: University of South Carolina Press, 1996), 88–92; Lamson, 124; Walter Edgar, *South Carolina: A History* (Columbia: University of South Carolina Press, 1998), 400.

13 Lamson, 127.

14 Office of the Historian, U.S. House of Representatives, *"We Are in Earnest for Our Rights": Representative Joseph H. Rainey and the Struggle for Reconstruction* (Washington, D.C.: Government Publishing Office, 2020), 14.

15 Office of the Historian, *"We Are in Earnest for Our Rights,"* 14.

16 Ethan S. Rafuse, "John C. Calhoun: The Man Who Started the Civil War, HistoryNet.com, Jun. 12, 2006, retrieved from https://www.historynet.com/john-c-calhoun-the-man-who-started-the-civil-war on Nov. 11, 2024.

17 Office of the Historian, *Black Americans in Congress, 1870–2022*, 32.

18 Lamson, 128–29.

19 "Joseph Rainey" from *Notable Black American Men, Book II*, Encyclopedia.com, Aug. 16, 2024, retrieved from https://www.encyclopedia.com/african-american-focus/news-wires-white-papers-and-books/rainey-joseph on Nov. 14, 2024.

20 Office of the Historian, U.S. House of Representatives, *Black Americans in Congress, 1870–2007* (Washington, DC: Government Publishing Office, 2008), 74.

21 Christopher, 99; Congressional Globe, 42nd Congress, First Session (Washington, D.C.: Government Publishing Office, 1872), 230–31.

22 Dray, 78.

23 Dray, 90; Office of the Historian, *"We Are in Earnest for Our Rights,"* 15.

24 Office of the Historian, *"We Are in Earnest for Our Rights,"* 15–16.

25 Dray, 90.

26 Lamson, 132.

27 Office of the Historian, *Black Americans in Congress, 1870–2022*, 32; Edgar, *South Carolina: A History*, 401.

28 Douglas R. Egerton, *The Wars of Reconstruction: The Brief, Violent History of America's Most Progressive Era* (New York: Bloomsbury Press, 2014), 301; Zuczek, 101–2.

29 Zuczek, 103.

30 Dray, 100.

31 Zuczek, 108, 129; Lamson, 131.

32 Zuczek, 108.

33 Dray, 251.

34 Edgar, *South Carolina: A History*, 401.

35 Dray, 136.

36 Eric Foner, *Give Me Liberty! An American History*, vol. 2, 2nd ed. (New York: W.W. Norton, 2008), 577–78; Ibram X. Kendi, *Stamped from the Beginning: The Definitive History of Racist Ideas in America* (New York: Bold Type Books, 2016), 255.

37 Andre E. Johnson, "Further Silence upon Our Part Would be an Outrage: Bishop Henry McNeal Turner and the Colored Conventions Movement," in *The Colored Conventions Movement: Black Organizing in the Nineteenth Century*, ed. P. Gabrielle Foreman, Jim Casey, and Sarah Lynn Patterson (Chapel Hill: University of North Carolina Press, 2021), 305.

38 Proceedings of the Southern States Convention of Colored Men held in Columbia, S.C., October 1871 (Columbia: Carolina Printing Company, 1871), 50, retrieved from https://omeka.coloredconventions.org/files/original/5917d807b04f53e0ab2e80793c114f16.pdf on Apr. 3, 2025.

39 Nicole Hannah-Jones and *New York Times Magazine, The 1619 Project: A New Origin Story* (New York: One World, 2021), 10.

40 History.com editors, "Voting Rights Act of 1965," History.com, Jan. 10, 2023, retrieved from https://www.history.com/topics/black-history/voting-rights-act on Mar. 18, 2025.

41 Martin Luther King Jr., "March on Ballot Boxes," University of South Carolina Center for Civil Rights History and Research, Jan. 18, 2021, retrieved from https://www.youtube.com/watch?v=P70q6wlL0_Y on Dec. 2, 2024.

42 Dray, 167.

43 Christopher, 30.

44 Office of the Historian, *Black Americans in Congress, 1870–2007*, 74.

45 Congressional Globe, 42nd Congress, Second Session (Washington, D.C.: Government Printing Office, 1872), 1442, 1443.

46 Office of the Historian, *"We Are in Earnest for Our Rights,"* 17.

47 Office of the Historian, *Black Americans in Congress, 1870–2007*, 74.

48 Office of the Historian, *Black Americans in Congress, 1870–2007*, 75.

49 Christopher, 97; "Emancipation in Washington, D.C.," National Park Service website, Apr. 14, 2024, retrieved from https://www.nps.gov/articles/000/emancipation-in-washington-dc.htm on Nov. 2, 2024; Lamson, 146–48.

50 Lamson, 148.

51 Office of the Historian, *Black Americans in Congress, 1870–2007*, 28.

52 South Carolina Advisory Committee to the United States Commission on Civil Rights, "Reversing Political Powerlessness for Black Voters in South Carolina: Will Single-Member Election Districts Lead to Political Segregation?" (U.S. Commission on Civil Rights website, Mar. 1991, retrieved from https://www.usccr.gov/files/historical/1991/91-002.pdf on Mar. 20, 2025.

53 Lamson, 195; Benjamin Ginsberg, *Moses of South Carolina: A Jewish Scalawag During Radical Reconstruction* (Baltimore: Johns Hopkins University Press, 2010), 2–3, 171–72.

54 Zuczek, 126–28.

6: POLITICAL TIDES TURNING (1873–1875)

1 Office of the Historian, U.S. House of Representatives, *Black Americans in Congress, 1870–2007* (Washington, D.C.: Government Publishing Office, 2008), 3.

2 Peggy Lamson, *The Glorious Failure: Black Congressman Robert Brown Elliott and the Reconstruction in South Carolina* (New York: Norton Library, 1973), 120–21; Maurine Christopher, *America's Black Congressmen* (New York: Thomas Y. Crowell Company, 1971), 32–33.

3 Office of the Historian, U.S. House of Representatives, *"We Are in Earnest for Our Rights": Representative Joseph H. Rainey and the Struggle for Reconstruction* (Washington, D.C.: Government Publishing Office, 2020), 23.

4 Lamson, 121.

5 Lamson, 120.

6 Andrew Glass, "Supreme Court Decides Dred Scott Case, March 6, 1857," PBS website, Mar. 6, 2018, retrieved from https://www.politico.com/story/2018/03/06/supreme-court-decides-dred-scott-case-march-6-1857-435658#:~:text=The%20Supreme%20Court%20ruled%20that%20since%20Scott,a%20slave%2C%20he%20lacked%20standing%20to%20sue.&text=Citing%20the%20phrase%20%E2%80%9Call%20men%20are%20created,people%20who%20framed%20and%20adopted%20this%20declaration.%E2%80%9D on Dec. 2, 2024.

7 Philip Dray, *Capitol Men: The Epic Story of Reconstruction Through the Lives of the First Black Congressmen* (Boston: Mariner Books, 2008), 169.

8 Office of the Historian, *Black Americans in Congress, 1870–2022*, 30.

9 Jon Meacham, *And There Was Light: Abraham Lincoln and the American Struggle* (New York: Random House, 2022), 207.

10 Office of the Historian, *Black Americans in Congress, 1870–2007*, 81; Dray, 169–70.

11 Office of the Historian, *Black Americans in Congress, 1870–2007*, 78.

12 Dray, 172; Lamson, 175.

13 Dray, 172–74.

14 Dray, 173.

15 Lamson, 178.

16 Douglas R. Egerton, *The Wars of Reconstruction: The Brief, Violent History of America's Most Progressive Era* (New York: Bloomberg Press, 2014), 310.

17 Dray, 175.

18 Eric Foner, *The Second Founding: How the Civil War and Reconstruction Remade the Constitution* (New York: W.W. Norton & Company, 2019), 143.

19 Dray, 177.

20 Office of the Historian, U.S. House of Representatives, *Black Americans in Congress, 1870–2022* (Washington, DC: Government Publishing Office, 2023), 89.

21 Richard Cain, "A Nation of Croakers," in *Reconstruction: Voices from America's First Great Struggle for Racial Equality*, ed. Brooks D. Simpson (New York: Library of America, 2018), 484.

22 Carey M. Roberts, "Preston Smith Brooks," in *South Carolina Encyclopedia*, ed. Walter Edgar (Columbia: University of South Carolina Press, 2006), 100; Charles Sumner, "The Crime Against Kansas," U.S. Senate floor speech, May 19–20, 1856, retrieved from https://www.senate.gov/artandhistory/history/resources/pdf/CrimeAgainstKSSpech.pdf on Nov. 19, 2024.

23 Walter Edgar, *South Carolina: A History* (Columbia: University of South Carolina Press, 1998), 347.

24 Dray, 168.

25 *The Boston Globe* (Boston, Massachusetts), Apr. 15, 1874, 2.

26 Lamson, 193.

27 Lamson, 193.

28 Office of the Historian, *"We Are in Earnest for Our Rights,"* 21.

29 Bobby J. Donaldson, "Meet Joseph Rainey, the First Black Congressman," *Smithsonian*, January 2021, retrieved from https://www.smithsonianmag.com/history/joseph-rainey-first-black-congressman-180976502/ on Nov.19, 2024; Office of the Historian, *Black Americans in Congress, 1870–2022*, 27.

30 Office of the Historian, *"We Are in Earnest for Our Rights,"* 19–20.

31 Benjamin Ginsberg, *Moses of South Carolina: A Jewish Scalawag During Radical Reconstruction* (Baltimore: Johns Hopkins University Press, 2010), 3.

32 Joel Williamson, *After Slavery: The Negro in South Carolina During Reconstruction, 1861–1877* (New York: Norton Library, 1975), 389; Ginsberg, 164.

33 Williamson, 400.

34 Christopher, 103.

35 Office of the Historian, *Black Americans in Congress, 1870–2007*, 108.

36 Lamson, 186.

37 Rachel Treisman, "Liz Cheney Offers a Stark Message to the GOP Members Who Continue to Support Trump," NPR website, Jun. 9, 2022, retrieved from https://www.npr.org/2022/06/09/1104083111/liz-cheney-stark-message-gop-trump-supporters on Feb. 28, 2025; Eric Cortellessa, "Republican Congressman Adam Kinzinger on Where the Jan. 6 Committee Goes Next," *Time* website, July 25, 2022, retrieved from https://time.com/6200347/adam-kinzinger-interview-jan-6-committee/ on Feb. 28, 2025; Kipp Jones, "Liz Cheney Says Conservatives Might Have to Form New Party Because GOP Has 'Been So Corrupted' by Trump," *Mediaite* website, Sept. 21, 2024, retrieved from https://www.mediaite

.com/trump/liz-cheney-says-conservatives-might-have-to-form-new-party
-because-gop-has-been-so-corrupted-by-trump/ on Feb. 28, 2025; Arthur Delaney,
"Republican Adam Kinzinger Addresses DNC: 'I'm Putting Our Country First,'"
Huffington Post website, Aug. 22, 2024, retrieved from https://www.huffpost.com
/entry/adam-kinzinger-dnc-speech_n_66c7e8cae4b0b9c7b360bf11 on Feb. 28,
2025.

38 Thomas Holt, *Black over White: Negro Political Leadership in South Carolina During
Reconstruction* (Urbana: University of Illinois Press, 1977), 178–79.

39 Lamson, 205.

40 Christopher, 31–32.

41 Office of the Historian, *Black Americans in Congress, 1870–2022*, 80.

42 Christopher, 102; Office of the Historian, *Black Americans in Congress, 1870–2022*, 89.

43 "Speeches of African-American Representatives Addressing the Civil Rights Bill
of 1875," *Neglected Voices* website, undated, retrieved from https://www.law.nyu
.edu/sites/default/files/RaineyFeb031875.pdf on Feb. 27, 2025.

7: POLITICAL POLARIZATION (1875–1877)

1 "The Beginnings of Parris Island," U.S. Marine Corps website, 2024, retrieved
from https://www.mcrdpi.marines.mil/Centennial-Celebration/Historical
-information/1-The-Beginnings-of-Parris-Island/ on Dec. 4, 2024.

2 Maurine Christopher, *America's Black Congressmen* (New York: Thomas Y. Crowell
Company, 1971), 44.

3 Isabel Wilkerson, *Caste: The Origins of Our Discontent* (New York: Random House,
2020), 227.

4 Michael Powell, "Making Light of a Dixiecrat's Dark Past," *Washington Post*, July
12, 2000, retrieved from https://www.washingtonpost.com/archive/lifestyle
/2000/07/13/making-light-of-a-dixiecrats-dark-past/8e728225-bfc1-4845-ad02
-09f055833bc6.

5 Walter Edgar, *South Carolina: A History* (Columbia: University of South Carolina
Press, 1998), 521.

6 Powell, "Making Light of a Dixiecrat's Dark Past."

7 Powell, "Making Light of a Dixiecrat's Dark Past."

8 Peggy Lamson, *The Glorious Failure: Black Congressman Robert Brown Elliott and the
Reconstruction in South Carolina* (New York: W.W. Norton, 1973), 184.

9 Hyman S. Reuben III, "Taxpayers' Convention," in *South Carolina Encyclopedia*, ed.
Walter Edgar (Columbia: University of South Carolina Press, 2006), 949; Edgar,
South Carolina: A History, 402.

10 Philip Dray, *Capitol Men: The Epic Story of Reconstruction Through the Lives of the
First Black Congressmen* (Boston, Mariner Books, 2008), 250.

11 Ethan J. Kytle and Blain Roberts, *Denmark Vesey's Garden: Slavery and Memory in the
Cradle of the Confederacy* (New York: New Press, 2018), 87; Robert K. Ackerman,
Wade Hampton III (Columbia: University of South Carolina Press, 2007), 152;
Richard Zuczek, *State of Rebellion: Reconstruction in South Carolina* (Columbia:
University of South Carolina Press, 1996), 167.

12 From the papers of Martin Witherspoon Gary, the South Caroliniana Library,
Columbia, South Carolina.

13 Joel Williamson, *After Slavery: The Negro in South Carolina During Reconstruction, 1861–1877* (New York: Norton Library, 1975), 266–67.

14 Zuczek, 171.

15 Lamson, 235.

16 Lamson, 236; Zuczek, 163–64.

17 Ackerman, 163–64.

18 Ackerman, 185.

19 Sidney Blumenthal, "Deny, Attack, Reverse — Trump Has Perfected the Art of Inverted Victimhood," *Guardian*, Feb. 1, 2024, retrieved from https://theguardian.com/commentisfree/2024/feb/01/trump-victim-political-strategy-manipulation on Dec. 5, 2024.

20 Office of the Historian, *"We Are in Earnest for Our Rights": Representative Joseph H. Rainey and the Struggle for Reconstruction* (Washington, D.C.: Government Publishing Office, 2020), 28.

21 Douglas R. Egerton, *The Wars of Reconstruction: The Brief, Violent History of America's Most Progressive Era* (New York: Bloomsbury Press, 2014), 313; Andrew Billingsley, *Yearning to Breathe Free: Robert Smalls of South Carolina and His Family* (Columbia: University of South Carolina Press, 2007), 128.

22 Billingsley, 128.

23 Damon L. Fordham, *Voices of Black South Carolinians: Legend and Legacy* (Charleston, SC: History Press, 2009), 60.

24 Dray, 239–40; Lamson, 237.

25 Lamson, 237–38; Dray, 240.

26 Ulysses S. Grant. "Letter from Ulysses S. Grant to D. H. Chamberlain (1876)," July 26, 1876, *Teaching American History* website, retrieved from https://teachingamericanhistory.org/document/letter-to-d-h-chamberlain-governor-of-south-carolina/ on Mar. 5, 2025.

27 Lamson, 246.

28 Okon Edet Uya, *From Slavery to Public Service: Robert Smalls 1839–1915* (New York: Oxford University Press, 1971), 100–101; Edward A. Miller Jr., *Gullah Statesman: Robert Smalls from Slavery to Congress, 1839–1915* (Columbia: University of South Carolina Press, 1995), 103; Christopher, 45–46; Dray, 256–57; Ackerman, 167.

29 Kristin Haltinner and Dishani Sarathchandra, "Tea Party Health Narratives and Belief Polarization: The Journey to Killing Grandma," AIMS Public Health, Nov. 27, 2017, 557–78, retrieved from https://doi.org/10.3934/publichealth.2017.6.557 on Dec. 9, 2024.

30 Robert Pear, "Spitting and Slurs Directed at Lawmakers," *New York Times*, Mar. 20, 2010, retrieved from https://archive.nytimes.com/prescriptions.blogs.nytimes.com/2010/03/20/spitting-and-slurs-directed-at-lawmakers/?hp on Dec. 8, 2024.

31 Egerton, *The Wars of Reconstruction*, 313; Office of the Historian, *"We Are in Earnest for Our Rights,"* 28–29.

32 Zuczek, 178; Edgar, *South Carolina: A History*, 403.

33 Ackerman, 185.

34 Ackerman, 166.

35 Ackerman, 179–80.

36 Thomas Holt, *Black over White: Negro Political Leadership in South Carolina During*

Reconstruction (Urbana: University of Illinois Press, 1977), 185–87; Lamson, 222–24.

37 Lamson, 231; Ackerman, 155; Louise Pettus, "6th Circuit Judge Was Colorful Character," *York County Roots and Recall* website, Jan. 17, 1998, retrieved from https://www.rootsandrecall.com/york-county-sc/files/2012/12/Judge-Mackey -Part-II.pdf on Dec. 3, 2024.

38 George Brown Tindall, *South Carolina Negroes 1877–1900* (Columbia: University of South Carolina Press, 1952), 14; Lamson, 241–43; Zuczek, 151, 166.

39 Office of the Historian, U.S. House of Representatives, *Black Americans in Congress, 1870–2007* (Washington, DC: Government Publishing Office, 2008), 97.

40 Kytle and Roberts, 87.

41 Lamson, 251–52.

42 Office of the Historian, *Black Americans in Congress, 1870–2007*, 140; Uya, 102.

43 Suzy Khimm, "Tea Partiers Allegedly Harass Black Student Voters in SC," *Mother Jones Daily* website, Nov. 2, 2010, retrieved from https://www.motherjones.com /politics/2010/11/tea-party-black-voter-intimidation-south-carolina/ on Dec. 6, 2024.

44 Office of the Historian, *"We Are in Earnest for Our Rights,"* 29.

45 Office of the Historian, *Black Americans in Congress, 1870–2007*, 65.

46 Christopher, 95; Office of the Historian, *Black Americans in Congress, 1870–2022*, 81.

47 Ackerman, 187–90; Lamson, 255.

48 Ackerman, 192.

49 Edgar, *South Carolina: A History*, 404–5.

50 Zuczek, 199–200.

8: REDEMPTION TAKES HOLD (1877–1879)

1 Walter Edgar, *South Carolina: A History* (Columbia: University of South Carolina Press, 1998), 413.

2 Philip Dray, *Capitol Men: The Epic Story of Reconstruction Through the Lives of the First Black Congressmen* (Boston: Mariner Books, 2008), 271.

3 Thomas Holt, *Black over White: Negro Political Leadership in South Carolina During Reconstruction* (Urbana: University of Illinois Press, 1977), 208.

4 Dray, 271–72; Robert K. Ackerman, *Wade Hampton III* (Columbia: University of South Carolina Press, 2007), 202.

5 Dray, 272.

6 Damon L. Fordham, *Voices of Black South Carolina: Legend and Legacy* (Charleston: History Press, 2009), 45.

7 Office of the Historian, U.S. House of Representatives, *Black Americans in Congress, 1870–2007* (Washington, DC: Government Publishing Office, 2008), 108.

8 Office of the Historian, U.S. House of Representatives, *"We Are in Earnest for Our Rights": Representative Joseph H. Rainey and the Struggle for Reconstruction* (Washington, D.C.: Government Publishing Office, 2020), 29.

9 Federal Writers' Project, 1936, WPA Federal Writers' Project Papers (the South Caroliniana Library, University of South Carolina, Columbia), 5, retrieved from https://digital.library.sc.edu/collections/wpa-federal-writers-project-materials

-on-african-american-life-in-south-carolina on Jan. 6, 2024; Maurine Christopher, *America's Black Congressmen* (New York: Thomas Y. Croswell Company, 1971), 113; Eric Foner, *Freedom's Lawmakers: A Directory of Black Officeholders During Reconstruction*, rev. ed. (Baton Rouge: Louisiana State University Press, 1993), 149–50; Stephen Middleton, ed., *Black Congressmen During Reconstruction: A Documentary Sourcebook* (Westport, CT: Praeger, 2002), 227–28.

10 Federal Writers' Project, 2–3.

11 Holt, 54.

12 James E. Clyburn, *Blessed Experiences: Genuinely Southern, Proudly Black* (Columbia: University of South Carolina Press, 2014), 53.

13 Holt, 209; George Brown Tindall, *South Carolina Negroes 1877–1900* (Columbia: University of South Carolina Press, 1952), 16; Ackerman, 208.

14 Tindall, 23–25; Okon Edet Uya, *From Slavery to Public Service: Robert Smalls 1839–1915* (New York: Oxford University Press, 1971), 115.

15 Holt, 209–10; Tindall, 18; John F. Marszalek, *A Black Congressman in the Age of Jim Crow: South Carolina's George Washington Murray* (Gainesville: University Press of Florida, 2006), 7–8.

16 Derek W. Black, "Kids Will Suffer Because Court Refused to Do Its Duty," *State* (South Carolina), Nov. 26, 2017, retrieved from https://www.thestate.com /opinion/op-ed/article186489863.html on Jan. 5, 2025.

17 Joel Williamson, *After Slavery: The Negro in South Carolina During Reconstruction, 1861–1877* (New York: W.W. Norton, 1965), 414–15.

18 Tindall, 17–18.

19 Andrew Billingsley, *Yearning to Breathe Free: Robert Smalls of South Carolina and His Family* (Columbia: University of South Carolina Press, 2007), 145–46; Uya, 83–84.

20 Billingsley, 147.

21 Billingsley, 151–52.

22 Christopher, 47–48; Billingsley, 149; Tindall, 19.

23 Clyburn, 68–69.

24 Holt, 214.

25 Williamson, 408.

26 Ackerman, 228; Tindall, 25; Billingsley, 152.

27 Edward A. Miller, *Gullah Statesman: Robert Smalls from Slavery to Congress, 1839–1915* (Columbia: University of South Carolina Press, 1995), 15.

28 *The Letters and Diary of Laura M. Towne: Reconstruction Era Edition*, ed. Rupert Sargent Holland (North Charleston: Palmetto Publishing Group, 2019), 308–10.

29 Tom Gjelten, "Peaceful Protesters Tear-Gassed to Clear Way for Trump Church Photo-Op," NPR website, June 1, 2020, retrieved from https://www.npr.org /2020/06/01/867532070/trumps-unannounced-church-visit-angers-church -officials on Jan. 7, 2025.

30 Uya, 111.

31 Office of the Historian, National Park Service, *The Life and Legacy of Robert Smalls of South Carolina's Sea Islands* (Fort Washington, PA: Eastern National, 2020), 41.

32 Uya, 110.

33 Office of the Historian, U.S. House of Representatives, *Black Americans in Congress, 1870–2022* (Washington, DC: Government Publishing Office, 2023), 82; Neal D. Thigpen, "Edmund William McGregor Mackey" in *South Carolina*

Encyclopedia, ed. Walter Edgar (Columbia: University of South Carolina Press, 2006), 582; Christopher, 96.

34 Peggy Lamson, *The Glorious Failure: Black Congressman Robert Brown Elliott and the Reconstruction in South Carolina* (New York: Norton Library, 1973), 272.

35 Office of the Historian, *"We Are in Earnest for Our Rights,"* 30.

36 Joseph H. Rainey, "The Destruction of a Free Ballot" (Mar. 3, 1879) from *Reconstruction, Voices from America's First Great Struggle for Racial Equality,* (Library of America, 2018), 659–60, retrieved from https://loa-shared.s3.us-west-2.amazonaws.com/static/pdf/Rainey_Free_Ballot.pdf on Dec. 17, 2024.

37 Office of the Historian, *"We Are in Earnest for Our Rights,"* 31, 34.

38 Office of the Historian, *Black Americans in Congress, 1870–2022,* 29; Office of the Historian, *Black Americans in Congress, 1870–2007,* 66.

39 Bobby J. Donaldson, "Meet Joseph Rainey, the First Black Congressman," *Smithsonian,* January 2021, retrieved from https://www.smithsonianmag.com/history/joseph-rainey-first-black-congressman-180976502/ on Dec. 17, 2024.

40 "Joseph H. Rainey, the South Carolina Colored Congressman, Dead," *Chicago Tribune,* August 4, 1887, 5.

9: THE ASSAULT FROM WITHOUT AND WITHIN (1880–1884)

1 Peggy Lamson, *The Glorious Failure: Black Congressman Robert Brown Elliott and the Reconstruction in South Carolina* (New York: Norton Library, 1973), 273.

2 George Brown Tindall, *South Carolina Negroes 1877–1900* (Columbia: University of South Carolina Press, 1952), 48.

3 Thomas Holt, *Black over White: Negro Political Leadership in South Carolina during Reconstruction* (Urbana, IL: University of Illinois Press, 1977), 209.

4 John F. Marszalek, *A Black Congressman in the Age of Jim Crow: South Carolina's George Washington Murray* (Gainesville: University Press of Florida, 2006), 10.

5 Holt, 216–18.

6 James E. Clyburn, *Blessed Exoeriences: Genuinely Southern, Proudly Black* (Columbia: University of South Carolina Press, 2014), 27–28.

7 Okon Edet Uya, *From Slavery to Public Service: Robert Smalls 1839–1915* (New York: Oxford University Press, 1971), 112–13; Office of the Historian, U.S. House of Representatives, *Black Americans in Congress, 1870–2007* (Washington, DC: Government Publishing Office, 2008), 141.

8 Philip Dray, *Capitol Men: The Epic Story of Reconstruction Through the Lives of the First Black Congressmen* (Boston: Mariner Books, 2008), 310–11.

9 Office of the Historian, U.S. House of Representatives, *Black Americans in Congress, 1870–2022* (Washington, DC: Government Publishing Office, 2023), 116.

10 Lamson, 280–83.

11 Office of the Historian, *Black Americans in Congress, 1870–2007,* 81; Lamson, 288–89.

12 W.E.B. Du Bois, "The Talented Tenth," in *The Negro Problem: A Series of Articles by Representative American Negroes of Today,* ed. Booker T. Washington (New York: J. Pott, 1903), 33–75, retrieved from https://teachingamericanhistory.org/document/the-talented-tenth on Dec. 18, 2024.

13 Marszalek, 63–64.

14 Marszalek, 6, 9.

15 Tindall, 171–73.

16 Tindall, 238–39.

17 Tindall, 182; Uya, 134.

18 Uya, 133.

19 Walter Edgar, *South Carolina: A History* (Columbia: University of South Carolina Press, 1998), 413.

20 Aaron W. Marrs, "'Black' Seventh District" in *South Carolina Encyclopedia*, ed. Walter Edgar (Columbia: University of South Carolina Press, 2006), 75; Office of the Historian, *Black Americans in Congress, 1870–2007*, 141, 220.

21 Edgar, *South Carolina: A History*, 421.

22 Edgar, *South Carolina: A History*, 414.

23 Hyman S. Rubin III, "Eight Box Law" in *South Carolina Encyclopedia*, 292; Tindall, 69.

24 Tindall, 70.

25 Edgar, *South Carolina: A History*, 415.

26 Marszalek, 10–11; Holt, 220.

27 Holt, 221; Marszalek, 10–11; Neal E. Thigpen, "Edmund William McGregor Mackey" in *South Carolina Encyclopedia*, 582–83; Uya, 117–18.

28 Indianapolis Journal, September 26, 1883, page 4. (accessed online: https://news papers.library.in.gov/?a=d&d=IJ18830926.1.4&e=—en-20—1—txt-txIN—.)

29 "Lest We Forget…Frederick Douglass: The Color Line in America (1883)," *New Pittsburgh Courier*, Oct. 31, 2012, retrieved from https://newpittsburghcourier.com/2012/10/31/lest-we-forgetfrederick-douglass-the-color-line-in-america-1883/ on May 22, 2023.

30 "The Civil Rights Cases (1883)," National Constitution Center website, undated, retrieved from https://constitutioncenter.org/the-constitution/supreme-court-case-library/the-civil-rights-cases on Dec. 24, 2024; Eric Foner, *The Second Founding: How the Civil War and Reconstruction Remade the Constitution* (New York: W.W. Norton, 2009), 151, 154.

31 Bernard E. Powers Jr., *Black Charlestonians: A Social History, 1822–1885* (Fayetteville: University of Arkansas Press, 1994), 216.

32 Lamson, 273.

33 Tindall, 43.

34 Marszalek, 11–12.

35 Uya, 120–25.

36 Office of the Historian, *Black Americans in Congress, 1870–2022*, 39; Edward A. Miller, *Gullah Statesman: Robert Smalls from Slavery to Congress 1839–1915* (Columbia: University of South Carolina Press, 1995), 153.

10: TILLMANITES TAKE CONTROL (1885–1894)

1 Walter Edgar, *South Carolina: A History* (Columbia: University of South Carolina Press, 1998), 430.

2 John F. Marszalek, *A Black Congressman in the Age of Jim Crow: South Carolina's George Washington Murray* (Gainesville: University Press of Florida, 2006), 121.

3 Marszalek, 11–12.

4 Okon Edet Uya, *From Slavery to Public Service: Robert Smalls 1839–1915* (New York: Oxford University Press, 1971), 126–29.

5 Office of the Historian, U.S. House of Representatives, *Black Americans in Congress 1870–22* (Washington, D.C.: Government Printing Office, 2023), 39.

6 Office of the Historian, National Park Service, *The Life and Legacy of Robert Smalls of South Carolina's Sea Islands* (Fort Washington, PA: Eastern National, 2020), 41.

7 Edgar, 432–38.

8 "Title VII of the Civil Rights Act of 1964" (U.S. Equal Employment Opportunity Commission website, undated). Retrieved from https://www.eeoc.gov/statutes/title-vii-civil-rights-act-1964—:~:text=Title%20VII%20prohibits%20employment%20discrimination,Pay%20Act%20of%202009%20(Pub. on Jan. 13, 2025.

9 Paul Dans and Steven Groves, eds., *2025 Mandate for Leadership: The Conservative Promise* (Project 2025 website, Heritage Foundation, 2023–24), 342, retrieved from https://www.project2025.org/policy/ on Jan. 13, 2025.

10 Marszalek, 13–14.

11 Marszalek, 14–17.

12 Marszalek, 22.

13 Edward A Miller Jr., *Gullah Statesman: Robert Smalls from Slavery to Congress, 1839–1915* (Columbia: University of South Carolina Press, 1995), 162–63.

14 Office of the Historian, U.S. House of Representatives, *Black Americans in Congress, 1870–2007* (Washington, DC: Government Publishing Office, 2008), 216.

15 Maurine Christopher, *America's Black Congressmen* (New York: Thomas Y. Crowell, 1971), 114; Richard Zuczek, *State of Rebellion: Reconstruction in South Carolina* (Columbia: University of South Carolina Press, 1996), 207.

16 Office of the Historian, *Black Americans in Congress 1870–2007*, 216.

17 Edgar, 436–37.

18 Marszalek, 31–32.

19 Miller, 192.

20 Marszalek, 27–28, 33; Office of the Historian, *Black Americans in Congress 1870–2007*, 216.

21 Speech of Hon. Thos. E. Miller of South Carolina, in the House of Representatives, February 14, 1891, Schomburg Center for Research in Black Culture, Jean Blackwell Hutson Research and Reference Division, New York Public Library, retrieved from https://digitalcollections.nypl.org/items/92fa31ba-3384-cfef-e040-e00a18061f0d on Jan. 13, 2025.

22 Office of the Historian, *Black Americans in Congress 1870–2007*, 217.

23 *Congressional Record*, House, 51st Cong., 2nd sess. (Feb. 14, 1891), 2694.

24 Office of the Historian, *Black Americans in Congress 1870–2007*, 217.

25 Edgar, 438; Miller, 195.

26 Miller, 196–97.

27 Miller, 197–98; Edgar, 439.

28 Marszalek, 42–43; Miller, 198.

29 George Brown Tindall, *South Carolina Negroes 1877–1900* (Columbia: University of South Carolina Press, 1953), 56–57; Marszalek, 44.

30 Marszalek, 46.

31 Marszalek, 56.

32 Marszalek, 59; Andrew Billingsley, *Yearning to Breathe Free: Robert Smalls of South Carolina and His Family* (Columbia: University of South Carolina Press, 2007), 110; Thomas C. Barnwell Jr., Carolyn Grant, and Emory Campbell, *Gullah Days: Hilton Head Islanders Before the Bridge 1861–1956* (self-published, 2020), 102–4.

33 William J. Gaboury, "George Washington Murray and the Fight for Political Democracy in South Carolina," *Journal of Negro History* 62 (July 1977): 261.

34 Office of the Historian, *Black Americans in Congress 1870–2007*, 222.

35 Marszalek, 69.

36 Marszalek, 68–71; Tindall, 58.

37 Marszalek, 77.

38 Office of the Historian, *Black Americans in Congress 1870–2007*, 158.

39 Office of the Historian, *Black Americans in Congress 1870–2007*, 223; Christopher, 121.

40 Tindall, 75.

41 Marszalek, 88, 85.

11: THE FIRST EIGHT ERA ENDS (1895–1935)

1 George Brown Tindall, *South Carolina Negroes 1877–1900* (Columbia: University of South Carolina Press, 1952), 76.

2 John F. Marszalek, *A Black Congressman in the Age of Jim Crow: South Carolina's George Washington Murray* (Gainsville: University Press of Florida, 2004), 88–89.

3 Marszalek, 89.

4 Marszalek, 86–87; William J. Gaboury, "George Washington Murray and the Fight for Political Democracy in South Carolina," *Journal of Negro History* 62 (July 1977): 262–63.

5 Gaboury, 264.

6 Marszalek, 86–92.

7 Damon L. Fordham, *The 1895 Segregation Fight in South Carolina* (Charleston: History Press, 2022), 22–27.

8 Tindall, 79.

9 Tindall, 80.

10 Okon Edet Uya, *From Slavery to Public Service: Robert Smalls 1839–1915* (New York: Oxford University Press, 1971), 138–39.

11 Journal of South Carolina Constitutional Convention of 1895 (Library of Congress), 464, retrieved from https://archive.org/stream/journalofconstit00sout_0/journalofconstit00sout_0_djvu.txt on Jan. 3, 2025.

12 Tindall, 82.

13 Uya, 143.

14 Uya, 144; Philip Dray, *Capitol Men: The Epic Story of Reconstruction Through the Lives of the First Black Congressmen* (Boston: Mariner Books, 2008), 342.

15 Fordham, *The 1895 Segregation Fight in South Carolina*, 53.

16 Andrew Billingsley, *Yearning to Breathe Free: Robert Smalls of South Carolina and His Families* (Columbia: University of South Carolina Press, 2007), 169.

17 Tindall, 87–88.

18 Maurine Christopher, *America's Black Congressmen* (New York: Thomas Y. Crowell, 1971), 53.

19 Dray, 342–44.

20 Kevin Fellner, "Voting Rights Act (1965)" in *South Carolina Encyclopedia,* ed. Walter Edgar (Columbia: University of South Carolina Press, 2006), 1000.

21 William C. Hine, "Miller, Thomas Ezekiel," *American National Biography* 15 (New York: Oxford University Press, 1999): 518–20, retrieved from https://doi.org/10.1093/anb/9780198606697.article.0500527.

22 Tindall, 230; "Fast Facts," South Carolina State University website, undated, retrieved from https://scsu.edu/sc_state_about/fast-facts.php on Jan. 14, 2025.

23 Tindall, 230–31.

24 Janet G. Hudson, *Entangled by White Supremacy: Reform in World War I–era South Carolina* (Lexington: University of Kentucky Press, 2009), 19.

25 Claudia Sanchez, "Trump, and Most Black College Presidents, Absent from Meeting" (NPR website, Sept. 19, 2017), retrieved from https://www.npr.org/sections/ed/2017/09/19/552121259/trump-and-most-black-college-presidents-absent-from-annual-meeting on Jan. 14, 2025.

26 Sara Chernikoff, "HBCUs Get Historic Funding from Biden Administration. How Has $16 Billion Been Spent?" *USA Today,* May 21, 2024, retrieved from https://www.usatoday.com/story/news/education/2024/05/21/hbcus-funding-biden-administration-16-billion/73774449007 on Jan. 17, 2025.

27 "Fact Sheet: Biden-Harris Administration Highlights a Record of Championing Historically Black Colleges and Universities (HBCUs)," U.S. Department of Education website, Sept. 29, 2023, retrieved from https://www.ed.gov/about/news/press-release/fact-sheet-biden-harris-administration-highlights-record-of-championing on Jan. 14, 2025.

28 Derek W. Black, "Kids Will Suffer Because Court Refused to Do Its Duty," *State* (South Carolina), Nov. 26, 2017, retrieved from https://www.thestate.com/opinion/op-ed/article186489863.html on Jan. 5, 2025.

29 Ashley Elliott, "Leading Change: Congressman James E. Clyburn's Journey from Civil Rights Activist to Congress Leader," *HBCU Times,* Summer 2019, 27, retrieved from https://issuu.com/hbcutimes/docs/final_summer_issue2__1_ on Jan. 14, 2025.

30 Marszalek, 102–7; Tindall, 89–90; Christopher, 121.

31 Gaboury, 266–67.

32 Marszalek, 108.

33 Marszalek, 109.

34 Marszalek, 112–13.

35 Gaboury, 266–67.

36 Marszalek, 117.

37 Marszalek, 118.

38 Marszalek, xv.

39 Marszalek, 158.

40 Marszalek, 122.

41 Marszalek, 151–53; 159.

42 Marszalek, 159–60; Office of the Historian, U.S. House of Representatives, *Black Americans in Congress 1870–2022* (Washington, D.C.: Government Printing Office, 2023), 141.

43 Cate Lineberry, *Be Free or Die: The Amazing Story of Robert Smalls' Escape from Slavery to Union Hero* (New York: Picador, 2017), 87.

44 Christopher, 51; Edward A. Miller Jr., *Gullah Statesman: Robert Smalls from Slavery to Congress, 1839–1915* (Columbia: University of South Carolina Press, 1995), 250.

45 Fordham, *The 1895 Segregation Fight in South Carolina*, 84.

46 Uya, 162.

47 Office of the Historian, *Black Americans in Congress 1870–2007*, 217.

48 "Ex-Congressman Thomas Ezekiel Miller," Federal Writers' Project 1936, WPA Federal Writers' Project Papers, the South Caroliniana Library, University of South Carolina, 4, retrieved from https://digital.library.sc.edu/collections/wpa-federal-writers-project-materials-on-african-american-life-in-south-carolina/ on Jan. 16, 2025.

49 "Ex-Congressman Thomas Ezekiel Miller," 5.

50 Uya, 143.

INDEX

Note: Italic page numbers refer to illustrations.

INDEX

INDEX

INDEX

INDEX

ABOUT THE AUTHOR

James E. Clyburn is the Congressman representing South Carolina's Sixth Congressional District in the U.S. House of Representatives, where he previously served as majority whip. A more than thirty-year congressional veteran, he has been an influential and effective legislative leader and an unwavering voice for civil rights. Born in Sumter, South Carolina, during the Jim Crow era, he has been awarded the NAACP's highest honor—the Spingarn Medal—the Lyndon Baines Johnson Foundation's Liberty and Justice for All Award, and the Harry S. Truman Foundation's Good Neighbor Award, and he holds honorary degrees from forty colleges and universities. In 2024, he was bestowed the Presidential Medal of Freedom, the highest civilian honor in the United States.